U.S. INTERVENTION
in
BRITISH GUIANA

THE NEW COLD WAR HISTORY

John Lewis Gaddis, editor

U.S. Intervention
in British Guiana
A Cold War Story

Stephen G. Rabe

THE UNIVERSITY *of*

NORTH CAROLINA PRESS

CHAPEL HILL

Designed by Kimberly Bryant
Set in Filosofia by Keystone Typesetting, Inc.

Frontispiece: Cheddi Jagan in Georgetown on
23 August 1961 following his party's victory in
British Guiana's general elections. (AP/Wide
World Photos)

The paper in this book meets the guidelines for
permanence and durability of the Committee on
Production Guidelines for Book Longevity of the
Council on Library Resources.

Library of Congress Cataloging-in-Publication Data
Rabe, Stephen G.
U.S. intervention in British Guiana : a Cold War
story / Stephen G. Rabe.
p. cm. — (The new Cold War history)
Includes bibliographical references and index.
ISBN 0-8078-2979-x (cloth : alk. paper)
ISBN 0-8078-5639-8 (pbk. : alk. paper)
1. Guyana—Politics and government—1803–1966.
2. Guyana—Politics and government—1966– .
3. Subversive activities—Guyana—History—20th
century. 4. United States. Central Intelligence
Agency—History—20th century. 5. Guyana—
Relations—United States. 6. United States—
Relations—Guyana. 7. Cold War. I. Title. II. Series.
F2384.R33   2005
988.103—dc22   2005008004

cloth   09 08 07 06 05   5 4 3 2 1
paper   09 08 07 06 05   5 4 3 2 1

FOR THE PEOPLE OF GUYANA,
who have endured slavery, servitude,
colonialism, and imperialism

contents

map & illustrations

acknowledgments

In investigating and writing this book, I incurred many scholarly debts. I thank the archivists at the U.S. National Archives, the U.K. National Archives, and the Eisenhower, Kennedy, and Johnson presidential libraries for their assistance. I am also grateful for the help I received from staffs who guided me through manuscript collections at the George Meany Memorial Labor Archives, the Kheel Center at Cornell University, and the Thomas J. Dodd Research Center at the University of Connecticut.

I am especially grateful to Nadira Jagan-Brancier for providing me with photographs for this book. Suzanne Wasserman of City College of New York kindly offered me several excellent insights about the political milieu of British Guiana/Guyana. Professor John Lewis Gaddis of Yale University and an anonymous referee read the manuscript twice and gave me innumerable constructive criticisms and suggestions.

This study represents my third book with the University of North Carolina Press. I salute editor Charles Grench and Amanda McMillan for supporting this project. I also thank Paula Wald for managing the production process.

I was able to devote a full year to writing with a Special Faculty Development Grant from the University of Texas at Dallas. I thank Dean Dennis Kratz of the School of Arts and Humanities and especially Provost B. Hobson Wildenthal for supporting my research and writing.

Stephen G. Rabe
Dallas, Texas
19 February 2005

aßßreviations

U.S. Intervention
in
British Guiana

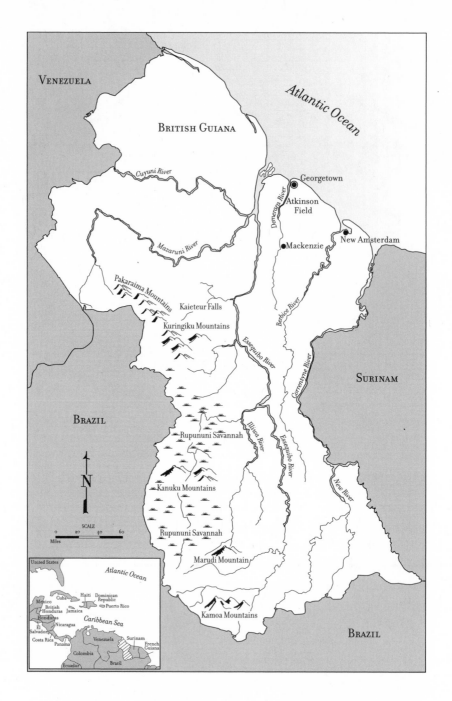

VENEZUELA

Atlantic Ocean

BRITISH GUIANA

Cuyuni River

Georgetown

Atkinson
Field

Mazaruni River

Mackenzie

New Amsterdam

Pakaraima Mountains

Kaieteur Falls

Kuringiku Mountains

Essequibo River

Berbice River

Corentyne River

SURINAM

BRAZIL

Rupununi Savannah

Iisua River

Essequibo River

N

Kanuku Mountains

New River

SCALE
0   20   40   60
Miles

Rupununi Savannah

Marudi Mountain

Kamoa Mountains

BRAZIL

United States

Atlantic Ocean

Haiti Dominican
Cuba   Republic
Mexico   Puerto Rico
British   Jamaica
Honduras
El   Caribbean Sea
Salvador Nicaragua
Costa Rica Panama
Venezuela Surinam
Colombia   French
                          Guiana
Ecuador   Brazil

British Guiana in the 1950s

INTRODUCTION

Guyana is a unique but troubled land. Offi-
cially known as the "Co-Operative Republic of
Guyana," the nation is situated on the northeastern coast of the South American continent, bordered on the west by Venezuela, by
Surinam to the east, and by Brazil to the south.
It is one of the smallest nations on the continent, about the size of the U.S. state of Idaho.
Guyana is the only English-speaking nation in
South America. It is also the only nation in the
Western Hemisphere where the majority of
the population is South Asian in origin, prin-
cipally from India.

At the beginning of the twenty-first century, political, socioeconomic, and epidemio-
logical problems bedevil the people of Guyana.
With a per capita income of $824, it is one of
the poorest nations in the Western Hemisphere, ranking just below Paraguay and
somewhat above Haiti. Guyana is significantly
poorer than Trinidad and Tobago, the other
Western Hemisphere nation with a sizeable

South Asian population. Guyana's infant mortality rate of 49 per 1,000 live births is about 700 percent higher than in the United States. With an average life expectancy of about 62 years, Guyanese can expect to enjoy 15 years less of life than do U.S. citizens. Guyana can boast of a literate population, with 97 percent of adults having attended school. But the nation is struggling to maintain its educational standards because of its deep poverty. Along with Haiti, Guyana is the Western Hemisphere nation that suffers most from the contemporary plague of AIDS. Over 3 percent of Guyana's adult population is infected with HIV/AIDS.

In the past four decades, the populations of Western Hemisphere nations have boomed, with big countries like Brazil and Mexico and small ones like Costa Rica more than doubling their populations. The United States has added over 80 million people to its population since 1960. Guyana's population has barely grown from 560,000 in 1960 to about 700,000 in 2000. In the recent past, Guyana's population has actually declined because of high mortality rates and emigration. In both 1998 and 1999, Guyana lost more than 1 percent of its population through emigration.[1] Many Guyanese now reside in the cosmopolitan city of Toronto.

Under the happiest of circumstances, Guyana would struggle to achieve high rates of economic growth. Less than 4 percent of its territory, a narrow belt of land on the coastal plain, is arable. For a depth of five to eight miles, the coastal plain is below sea level at high tides. Guyanese have been forced to construct seawalls, canals, and dikes in a constant struggle to keep the land dry. Sugar and rice have been the traditional cash crops of Guyana. Neither crop has commanded a strong price on global markets in the past few decades. Guyana does mine a valuable natural resource, bauxite, from which aluminum is extracted. Unlike neighboring Venezuela or Trinidad and Tobago, Guyana does not, however, produce petroleum. Guyana also offers no haven for tourists. Its beaches are a muddy mess, when the tides recede. With its dense rain forests, Guyana could perhaps appeal to ecotourists.

Although not naturally blessed, Guyana has not always been one of the most desperate places in the hemisphere. In 1960, it seemed to have a future. A colonial possession of the United Kingdom, British Guiana antici- pated its independence within two to three years. Its population was growing steadily through natural increase. With a per capita income of $384, British Guiana was better off than the smaller Central American nations and ahead of South American nations like Bolivia and Paraguay. It had substantial foreign investments, principally from Great Britain and Canada. International economic teams that surveyed British Guiana in the 1950s issued optimistic reports about the country's future. Colonial officials and domestic political leaders further believed that the United States, United Kingdom, and Canada would generously provide foreign aid to assist the newly independent, English-speaking nation.

Why Guyana failed to achieve its visions is not a complex mystery. Both the U.S. Department of State and the Central Intelligence Agency (CIA) provide persuasive explanations. Both agencies annually compile useful fact books and background notes on individual countries complete with thumbnail sketches on a country's history, politics, and economy. These studies are readily available on the agencies' websites.[2] Both the State Department and the CIA note that, after achieving independence in 1966, Guyana suffered misrule until 1992, principally under the autocratic Forbes Burnham (1964–1985). Burnham developed a personality cult, pillaged the national economy, and trampled on civil liberties and human rights. Burnham and his henchmen also discriminated against Indians, denying Guyana's majority population political and economic opportunities. Since 1992, Guyana has conducted free and fair national elections. The redoubtable Jimmy Carter, the former U.S. president, assisted Guyana's transition to democracy. But as the State Department points out, voting and life in Guyana are racially polarized. Indians, about 50 percent of the population in 2000, vote for the People's Progressive Party (PPP), whereas Guyanese of African heritage, about 35 percent of the population, vote for the People's National Congress (PNC), the party founded by Forbes Burnham. The palpable tension that exists between Indians and Afro-Guyanese hampers national progress. The State Department properly concludes that Guyana's racial and ethnic tensions can be traced back to the "politically inspired racial disturbances" that erupted between Indo-Guyanese and Afro-Guyanese in the pre-independence years, especially between 1962 and 1964. Political agitators murdered or injured over a thousand Guyanese, and arsonists burned the central part of the capital city, Georgetown, to the ground.[3]

The irony inherent in the State Department's and CIA's concise accounts of Guyana's history would probably not be lost on politically informed Guyanese who perused the agencies' websites. Forbes Burnham would not have had the opportunity to perpetrate his crimes against the Guyanese people had it not been for the political machinations of the John F. Kennedy and

Lyndon B. Johnson administrations. Both administrations demanded that the British devise a shameless electoral scheme that would guarantee Burnham's election and deprive the PPP and its leader, Cheddi Jagan, of power. The Johnson administration subsequently aided and abetted Burnham's manipulation of the electoral machinery to ensure that he stayed in office. Knowledgeable Guyanese also understand that the CIA, using the good offices of U.S. labor unions, encouraged and funded the marches, demonstrations, and strikes that degenerated into arson, murder, and terrorism between 1962 and 1964. During the time of the civil rights movement in the United States, U.S. officials backed Afro-Guyanese in their campaign to deprive the majority Indo-Guyanese of their basic political rights.

The State Department and CIA's omission of the critical U.S. role in Guyana's brief history can perhaps be passed off as a need to be diplomatic and forward looking. In any case, institutional memories are short, and few people who made policy in the 1960s are alive in the early twenty-first century. Historical consciousness is also not a strong U.S. national trait. But this lack of historical awareness can have tragicomic consequences. President Bill Clinton conducted excellent relations with President Cheddi Jagan (1992–1997), who finally gained power when Guyana had its first free and fair election. In 1994, Clinton blundered, however, when he nominated a U.S. trade union official, who had worked against Jagan in the 1960s, to be the U.S. ambassador to Guyana. Jagan protested, wryly observing that "maybe President Clinton doesn't know our history, but the people who advise him should at least know their own history."[4]

If Clinton's staff had consulted the published literature on U.S. relations with British Guiana/Guyana, they would have found little to guide them. Scholars, like Thomas J. Spinner and Chaitram Singh, who wrote fine analyses of Guyana's domestic political milieu, learned from their Guyanese sources of the extensive U.S. role in the 1960s. But neither scholar had access to U.S. archival sources.[5] Following sensational revelations in the late 1960s by muckraking journalists like Drew Pearson, a flurry of books appeared that highlighted the relationship between the CIA and the U.S. labor movement. These books usually touched on the U.S. intervention in British Guiana.[6] Former CIA agents Philip Agee and Joseph Burkholder Smith indicated in their memoirs that the CIA conducted extensive covert operations in the British colony.[7] Their assertions were, however, based on hearsay evidence. In 1967, both the *New York Times* and the *Sunday Times* of London published exposés of the CIA intervention in British Guiana.[8] Little public discussion ensued, however, perhaps because the newspapers' readers had more immediate issues to ponder, like the ongoing U.S. war in Vietnam. Indeed, Neil Sheehan, who wrote the article for the *New York Times*, would subsequently devote his career to analyzing the Vietnam debacle.

In 1994, historian Cary Fraser explored the U.S. role in British Guiana in his outstanding monograph on the U.S. response to decolonization in the British West Indies from 1940 to 1964. Fraser devoted two chapters of his study to British Guiana as a way of amplifying his theme of "ambivalent anticolonialism." Fraser found that, although U.S. officials employed the rhetoric of anticolonialism and national self-determination, they subordinated ideals to Cold War imperatives. In preparing his chapters, Fraser gained access to Department of State records for the 1950s and a few documents from the Kennedy and Johnson presidential libraries.[9] A research breakthrough occurred in the mid-1990s, when the Historical Office of the State Department published two volumes on Cuba and one on the other American Republics for 1961–63 in its magnificent *Foreign Relations of the United States* (*FRUS*) series. The volume on the American Republics contained a section on British Guiana. The Historical Office reported that the CIA and State Department initially resisted declassifying major portions of the compilation on British Guiana. Appeals from the Historical Office and the Advisory Committee on Historical Diplomatic Documentation, which were considered "at the highest levels" within the State Department, led to the declassification of most but not all vital documents.[10] Nonetheless, the documents in the *FRUS* volume served as the basis for a chapter on British Guiana in *The Most Dangerous Area in the World*, my study of John Kennedy's Latin America policy.[11] Two doctoral dissertations also drew on the new documentary evidence. Gordon Oliver Daniels used the *FRUS* documents in his doctoral dissertation on the U.S. intervention in British Guiana. A native Guyanese, Daniels recalled, as a young man, seeing U.S. labor union officials allotting food to strikers opposed to Cheddi Jagan. Jane L. Sillery combined her research in U.S. and British archives with interviews with Guyanese officials. Sillery discovered, however, that there are no publicly available records on the major political parties in Guyana. Both Daniels and Sillery limited their studies to the period from 1961 to 1964.[12]

Scholarship on the U.S. intervention in British Guiana is remarkably thin, especially as compared to the voluminous literature that exists on the

U.S. interventions in Guatemala (1954), Brazil (1962–64), Chile (1970–73), Central America (1980s) and Panama (1989) and the seemingly perpetual U.S. efforts, beginning in 1959, to undermine the Cuban Revolution. Historian Thomas Leonard noted, for example, that over 900 books had appeared from 1979 to 1992 purporting to explain the Central American crisis.[13] These studies are substantiated by strong documentary evidence. In 2003, the Historical Office released a special volume devoted to the U.S. covert intervention in Guatemala in 1954. In part, the Historical Office wanted to rectify a mistake of the past, when in 1983 it published a volume, *American Republics, 1952–1954*, that gave scant attention to the intervention.[14] Numerous documents are available for even a relatively recent intervention, such as the Reagan administration's war against the Sandinistas of Nicaragua. Government officials who opposed U.S. policy "leaked" documents to journalists, and public-interest groups, such as the National Security Archive, persistently pursued documents.[15]

Scholarly neglect of British Guiana may indicate that the U.S. intervention does not rank as a significant Cold War event. But the actions of policymakers, past and present, seem to belie that judgment. In 2003, the CIA declined to declassify CIA Director Allen Dulles's briefing to President Eisenhower and the NSC about the British decision to suspend the constitution of British Guiana and to send troops to the colony. (Dulles delivered his comments in October 1953, fifty years before my declassification request![16]) Although it has acknowledged conducting eleven covert operations, including ones in Guatemala, Cuba, and the Dominican Republic, the CIA declines to confirm or deny an operation in British Guiana. In 1997, Nick Cullather of Indiana University, who had worked as a historian at the CIA, reported that in the 1960s the CIA had burned records of its covert operation in British Guiana.[17] Not all significant documents, however, ended up in the CIA's furnaces. The Historical Office has had to delay its volume on South America for the 1964–68 period because of disputes over twenty-four documents pertaining to British Guiana.[18] A well-informed archivist at the Kennedy library related to me that he never understood why the library held so many records on such a small, obscure colony. In fact, President Kennedy seemingly thought that his presidency depended on keeping Cheddi Jagan from leading an independent Guyana. In March 1962, for example, presidential aide Arthur M. Schlesinger Jr. wrote to the president that the U.S. government was "spending more man-hours per capita on British Guiana than any other current problem!"[19] President Johnson did not display the same intense interest in British Guiana, but he assigned his national security advisers, McGeorge Bundy and Walt W. Rostow, to monitor developments in the British possession. Secretary of State Dean Rusk relentlessly pursued an anti-Jagan policy in both administrations.

Although governmental agencies, such as the CIA, tenaciously hold on to records of an operation that may or may not exist, multiarchival work can help locate the pieces of a historical puzzle. Decisions to open or close records are often arbitrary and capricious. Copies of important memorandums also turn up in the private papers of former officials. For example, Kennedy and Prime Minister Harold Macmillan exchanged several letters on British Guiana. One exchange is classified in the United States but is available in the prime minister's correspondence at the Public Record Office in London.[20] The FRUS volume includes a "Special National Intelligence Estimate" on British Guiana, which was submitted by the director of the CIA in April 1962. Four and one-half lines of the paragraph on Forbes Burnham remain classified. The unabridged version of the intelligence paper, which can be found at the Johnson library, states that the U.S. intelligence community considered Burnham an opportunist, a thief, and a racist and predicted that Guyana would undergo conflict and instability if Burnham gained power.[21] Perhaps because the United States supported Burnham in the 1960s, a government agency decided in the mid-1990s to censor a critical statement about an autocrat who had been dead since 1985. Fortunately, government censors normally do not comb through private archives. Labor union records, particularly the records of the AFL-CIO on deposit at the George Meany Center in Silver Spring, Maryland, proved a rich source for this study on U.S. policy toward British Guiana. The AFL-CIO worked intimately with U.S. intelligence agents in British Guiana and boldly advised the president, the State Department, and the CIA on how to conduct policies in the colony. Indeed, the correspondence of President George Meany demonstrates that labor union officers developed techniques to transfer substantial sums of U.S. money to Cheddi Jagan's political enemies.[22] In the parlance usually associated with nefarious activities, the AFL-CIO "laundered" CIA money.

Beyond being an important story with ample evidence, an analysis of the U.S. intervention in British Guiana opens several modes of inquiry that have become important to historians of U.S. foreign relations. Diplomatic historians customarily address the political, economic, and military manifestations of power. They enjoy writing about a dramatic "crisis-event." They are also relentlessly empirical, basing their interpretations on archival evidence from official sources. And they employ traditional narrative techniques to present their findings.[23] This study of the U.S. intervention in British Guiana from 1953 to 1969 easily fits within those conventions. It analyzes why U.S. presidential administrations tried to control British Guiana's political development and details the ways the United States exercised its awesome power against a small, weak colony. Reflecting concerns voiced by historians over the past three decades, this study tries, however, to steer clear of potholes in the traditional path. U.S. historians have been properly criticized for relying too much on U.S. sources for their ideas and interpretations and writing international history solely from the perspective of the White House and Department of State. Incorporating the perspectives of British and Guyanese actors helps avoid what is disparagingly dubbed the "view from Washington" syndrome.[24] This study further accepts the argument that nations and governments are never of one mind and that what serves as policy is often a complex interplay of competing bureaucratic interests.[25] The "bureaucratic politics" paradigm helps explain the inconsistent policies of London toward British Guiana. Harold Macmillan (1957–63) and Harold Wilson (1964–70) led different political parties. Nonetheless, both prime ministers found themselves caught in the middle of a rivalry between their Foreign and Colonial Offices.

In addition to urging historians to take an inclusive, nuanced approach to international history, scholars have also called on students of U.S. foreign relations to appreciate the roles played by corporations, universities, foundations, and missions in the export of U.S. values, ideas, and lifestyles.[26] U.S. and British labor unions were obvious "nonstate actors" that played a major role in determining British Guiana's fate. Domestic interest groups also influenced policy. African American politicians hosted Afro-Guyanese in the United States and suggested that Forbes Burnham and his followers be viewed within the context of the U.S. civil rights movement. Democrats, like Presidents Kennedy and Johnson, were eager to display their civil rights credentials and to court favor with African American leaders. Both Democrats also closely monitored domestic politics, wishing to deflect any charges of being "soft on communism" either from Republican opponents or conservative Democratic supporters.

A study of the U.S. covert intervention in British Guiana also opens up issues of race and gender, which are of increasing significance to historians of U.S. foreign relations. Scholars, many of whom engage in colonial discourse analysis and posit postcolonial theory, have argued that powerful nations and their elite leaders employ the language of race and gender to create and reinforce their hegemony over others.[27] In choosing to back Afro-Guyanese over Indo-Guyanese, U.S. officials displayed complex, contradictory views in their representations of the two groups. They accepted a "hierarchy of race," suggesting in their language that Indians lacked the essential qualities requisite for self-governance. Among the alleged deficiencies of Indians was that their men lacked the masculine properties of people of African heritage. This concern for gender extended to Cheddi Jagan's partnership with his wife, Janet Rosenberg Jagan, a native of Chicago and ostensible political radical. U.S. and British officials constantly spoke of Cheddi Jagan being "dominated" by a willful wife. Diplomats even took to speculating in official dispatches about Janet Jagan's alleged sexual promiscuity with nonwhite males.

Although responding to contemporary scholarly concerns is important, the central purpose of this study is analyzing what happened to British Guiana/Guyana in the 1950s and 1960s. Guyanese deserve a complete and accurate historical record of their nation's fate during the Cold War. An account of the U.S. destruction of British Guiana's popular democracy might also help bring some balance to the history of the Cold War. Scholars and pundits appropriately celebrate the demise of the Soviet Union and its cruel tyrannies and the liberation of Eastern Europeans.[28] But this "triumphalist" attitude should not be permitted to conceal the stories of the victims of the West.

CHAPTER ONE

BrITISH GuIana,
1831–1953

British Guiana/Guyana's modern political history began in April 1953, when the People's
Progressive Party (PPP) led by Cheddi Jagan
and Forbes Burnham achieved an overwhelming victory in the colony's first national election. The PPP's triumph seemingly heralded
the beginning of British Guiana's evolution
into an independent nation with a multiracial,
parliamentary democracy. Within five months
after the election, however, imperial Great
Britain, citing fears of communism, sent
troops to British Guiana and suspended the
new constitution. The tumultuous events of
1953 would force the United States to consider
what it envisioned for British Guiana, a foreign colony within its traditional Western
Hemisphere sphere of influence. Over the
next two decades, U.S. policies would bear out
Prime Minister Winston Churchill's smug
prediction that, when it came to British Guiana, their "anti-Colonialism will be more than
balanced by their anti-Communism."[1]

NEITHER GEOGRAPHY NOR HISTORY has been especially kind to the people of Guyana. Guyana is part of the general region of the Guiana Highlands on the northeastern coast of South America, bounded by the Amazon, Negro, and Orinoco rivers. The Guianas today include the nations of Guyana, Surinam, a former Dutch colony, and French Guiana. The Guianas all border Brazil, with Guyana sharing to its west a disputed border with Venezuela. The visual beauty of the region is spectacular, serving as locale for romantic fables, including Sir Walter Raleigh's mythic El Dorado and Sir Arthur Conan Doyle's *Lost World*. England's great poets, William Shakespeare and John Milton, refer to Guiana's "good and bounty" and its "unspoiled" nature. Making a living in this fabled land has proved, however, challenging.

The word "Guiana" is a word of Amerindian origin, signifying "land of many waters." Three major rivers, the Essequibo, Demerara, and Berbice, drain Guyana, originating in a system of mountain ranges in the interior and descending northward into the Atlantic Ocean. The rivers flow through largely uninhabitable land. More than 80 percent of Guyana is tropical rain forest. The rain forests do produce some commercially valuable trees, but the timber industry has never been a leading sector of Guyana's economy. Prospectors have not found significant quantities of precious minerals, like gold and diamonds, in the forested mountains. Two other interior regions—the savanna and the hilly sand and clay belt—also provide poor prospects for agricultural development. For cattle ranching, for example, one animal requires approximately seventy acres of savanna for grazing. The three regions comprise 96 percent of Guyana's territory.

Guyana's human history has played out along Guyana's fertile coastal plain, which stretches along the Atlantic shoreline and varies in depth from ten to forty miles. The rich land is capable of producing cash crops like coffee, cotton, rice, and sugar. Heavy rain and high humidity make the region's climate difficult but tolerable. The major city, Georgetown, situated at the mouth of the Demerara River, has a mean temperature of 80 degrees Fahrenheit, but with cooling sea breezes at night. Tidal flooding and river flooding caused by torrential downpours bar easy cultivation of Guyana's coastal plain. For a depth of five to eight miles, the coastal plain is below sea level at high tide. Guyanese have had to construct and constantly maintain an intricate network of seawalls and dikes to hold back the sea and canals, dams, and sluices to improve drainage and pump water back into the Atlantic at low tide. A typical sugar plantation would have 250 miles of waterways for irrigation and transport of sugar cane and 80 miles of drainage canals. Agricultural production in the coastal plain has consequently required abundant sources of labor and constant work.[2]

The first European explorers found the Guianas thinly settled by Amerindian people, who lacked the great wealth and resources of urban societies like those of the Aztecs and Incas. The Amerindians either succumbed to European diseases or fled to the interior, resisting European attempts to enslave them; by the mid-twentieth century, Amerindians comprised only about 4 percent of Guyana's population. The Dutch became the first permanent European occupier of Guyana. Under the aegis of the West India Company of the Netherlands, they founded a colony on the Berbice River in 1620s. They subsequently established the colonies of Essequibo and Demerara. Until the mid-eighteenth century, the three colonies were small and economically insignificant. In 1701, only sixty-seven Europeans resided in the Essequibo colony. But in the mid-eighteenth century, the governor general of the West India Company opened the colonies to British settlement, and the colonies, especially Demerara and Essequibo, began to grow and prosper. British planters migrated from agriculturally depleted, overpopulated areas such as Barbados. Settlers also gradually mastered the techniques of draining the coastal plain.[3]

During the period between the Seven Years' War (1756–63) and the end of the Napoleonic Wars (1815), Europeans fought among themselves for control of the South American continent and domination of the world. The colony of Demerara changed colonial hands a bewildering six times during this period. Despite its loss of its thirteen North American colonies, Great Britain emerged triumphant in this global struggle. In 1803 Great Britain assumed effective control over the Dutch colonies and in 1814–15, at the Congress of Vienna, the Dutch formally ceded Berbice, Demerara, and Essequibo to the British. In 1831, the imperial British united the colonies to form the colony of British Guiana, with Georgetown as its administrative center. Georgetown had previously carried the Dutch name of Stabroek. The British ruled British Guiana until 1966, when the colony secured its independence and took the name of Guyana.

Although the colonial masters of the region changed hands, the socioeconomic structure of colonial life—plantation agriculture based on imported coerced labor—remained constant. On the river banks and coastal plain, Dutch planters oversaw the cultivation of coffee, cotton, and especially sugar for sale on the international market. Slaves stolen from Africa nurtured these cash crops. Africans quickly became the largest group in the three Dutch colonies. Although only 67 Europeans resided in Essequibo in 1701, thirty of them owned 800 slaves. Slavery grew rapidly from the mid-eighteenth century on, when British planters from the West Indian islands migrated to the Dutch colonies and quickly came to dominate plantation life. By 1800 perhaps 100,000 slaves toiled in the three colonies. By 1820, about 80,000 people lived in Demerara and Essequibo, with 75,000 of them being slaves. The other 5,000 consisted of approximately 2,500 whites and 2,500 free blacks. Some plantations became like giant factories with over 300 slaves harvesting the sugarcane and processing it in the sugar mills. Slavery lasted until 1838 in British Guiana. In 1807, the House of Commons made it illegal for any British ship to be involved in the international slave trade after 1 January 1808. British legislators followed this with a gradual, compensated emancipation law in 1834. In 1838, approximately 85,000 slaves gained their freedom in British Guiana.[4]

Twentieth-century Afro-Guyanese had the right to bitter historical memories of the viciousness and cruelty that their ancestors endured under slavery and the disappointments and injustices they experienced after emancipation. Sugar planters customarily worked slaves to death and, before 1808, imported new ones. Slaves were supposed to work twelve hours a day but their work days often stretched over twenty hours. Pregnant women and nursing mothers often did not receive the reduced work loads that the slave codes promised. In 1824, a British doctor reported that twenty-nine of the sixty-seven children born on one estate died within two years. Disease, inadequate medical care, overwork, unhealthy working conditions, and poor diet all contributed to high slave mortality rates. Between 1808 and 1821 in Demerara, the slave population declined by almost 20 percent. Little wonder that slaves resisted their oppression in every conceivable way from physical aggression to insubordination. In 1828, colonial officers recorded over 20,000 "Offences Committed by Slaves." A dramatic challenge came in 1823 when perhaps 12,000 slaves in Demerara rebelled in one of the most massive slave rebellions in the history of the Western Hemisphere. British troops forcibly suppressed the rebellion, killing over 200 slaves and executing many others thereafter following summary trials. British authorities placed the heads of the executed on poles, hoping to terrorize the slaves.[5]

Emancipation brought neither progress nor prosperity to British Guiana's oppressed black majority. Slave owners received an average rate of fifty-one pounds sterling per slave or a total of over £4 million in compensation for losing control over 85,000 people. But as one historian of nineteenth-century British Guiana ironically remarked, "It occurred to no one to compensate the slaves for their previous bondage."[6] Freed people also had no opportunity to exercise their numbers to bring about meaningful change in the colony. Voting rights were tied to high property requirements, ensuring continued planter control under British rule through the nineteenth century. Despite their poverty and powerlessness, former slaves made heroic efforts to improve their lives. Groups bought abandoned sugar plantations and tried establishing rural cooperative ventures. These enterprises failed because of a lack of capital and the unending difficulty and cost in British Guiana of draining the land. Blacks further thought that they might bargain collectively with planters at the critical harvesting times for the sugar cane. Planters successfully resisted these efforts by finding alternative labor sources. In any case, many blacks associated plantation labor with their former degradation. They drifted toward the coastal towns and especially toward Georgetown, becoming wage laborers. As the colonial bureaucracy grew, a few blacks gained lower-level civil service positions and entered the lower ranks of the police force. In the twentieth-century, the blacks of British Guiana also became miners and workers in the bauxite industry. Former slaves, many of whom were born in Africa, and their descendants gradually became acculturated to British colonial life, learning English and converting to Protestant Christianity. They also gradually gained literacy. In the mid-nineteenth century, the colonial government began to support financially a system of schools owned and operated by Christian churches.[7]

The end of slavery did not abolish British Guiana's system of plantation agriculture based on imported coerced labor. Colonial authorities and planters responded to the end of slavery and demands by freed people for good wages by returning to a labor system used in the seventeenth century in the North American colonies—indentured servitude. Antislavery groups in Britain actually encouraged the practice, believing the resuscitation of plantation agriculture in the British West Indies and British Guiana would demonstrate to slaveholders in the United States that they need not fear abolition. British authorities were also meeting imperial labor demands, shifting impoverished people from one part of the empire to another. In the period from 1838 to 1860, Portuguese from the Madeira Islands and Chinese from Hong Kong were the predominant groups to arrive as indentured servants in British Guiana. Both groups, about 25,000 people in total, detested plantation work and either returned home or moved to villages and towns after completing their contracts. Portuguese and Chinese came to dominate British Guiana's retail trade, becoming shopkeepers, peddlers, and merchants. Colonial India, however, provided the bulk of British Guiana's new labor force. Between 1838 and 1917, when indentured servitude was abolished in the empire, approximately 240,000 "East Indians" arrived in British Guiana as indentured servants.[8] (British colonial authorities used the misleading term "East Indians" to characterize their colonial subjects in India and to distinguish them from their subjects in the Caribbean, the "West Indians".) With this influx of Portuguese, Chinese, and Indians, combined with Amerindians, blacks, and English, British Guiana became in the nineteenth century one of the most ethnically, racially, and religiously diverse places in the Western Hemisphere.

The hungry and poor Indians who were persuaded to risk their lives in British Guiana generally belonged to lower agricultural and laboring castes, and a few were outcastes or "pariahs." The vast majority were illiterate. Most Indians were Hindus but a substantial proportion, perhaps 18 percent, were Muslims. India insisted that at least 25 percent of the recruits be female. Most Indians came from Bengal, Bihar, and the Northwest Provinces, agricultural regions located in contemporary India. These regions experienced periodic famines in the nineteenth century. The indentured servants embarked from the ports of Calcutta and Madras. The voyage to British Guiana lasted about ninety days, with ships going around the Cape of Good Hope. Voyagers were subjected to cold, poor diet, and seasickness. Mortality rates on the overcrowded ships averaged 2 percent for each month aboard in the 1860s and could soar if a catastrophic disease broke out.[9] Helpless Indians got a taste of what West Africans had suffered during the infamous "middle passage."

Upon arriving in British Guiana, Indians entered what contemporary observers denounced as "slavery." The immigrants signed a five-year contract to work on sugar plantations, but actually had to serve ten years in order to win passage back to India. Colonial ordinances mandated seemingly reasonable work and living conditions for indentured servants. Planters, with the silent acquiescence of most colonial officers, ignored those ordinances.

British Guiana's survival depended on the sale of sugar in a globally competitive market. As a British governor reported to London in 1871, sugar was "the one great staple export, upon the prosperity of which the general welfare of the Colony may be said almost wholly to depend."[10] After the mid-1850s, Great Britain, which was embracing free trade principles, no longer granted a preference to sugar from its West Indian colonies. British Guiana's sugar also competed with Brazilian and Cuban sugar produced by slave labor. These economic imperatives, when fused with racism and planter control, made, in one historian's view, "for an oppressive society which allowed no serious opposition."[11]

Indian workers, referred to as "coolies" by planters and colonial officers, lived in the former slave quarters, dubbed "nigger yards." They worked endlessly, cultivating the fields, maintaining drainage systems, and boiling the sugarcane. They had to meet roll call every morning at 6:00 A.M., and they needed a pass to leave the plantation. Mortality rates were ghastly, averaging 4–6 percent a year, with some plantations having a 10 percent mortality rate. In 1863, for example, 1,718 indentured servants out of 32,001 died in the colony. Indians were also subjected to legal abuse. In 1872, 9,045 out of 38,918 indentured immigrants on plantations, a full 23 percent, were charged with breaching their contracts.[12] They stood no chance in the colonial judicial system, for, as one appalled colonial magistrate charged in a report to the Colonial Office in late 1869, "the manager can always produce a number of overseers, drivers, and others dependent upon him to make an overwhelming weight of testimony in his favor." Without legal protections, the immigrants "are thus often reduced to a position which in some respects is not far removed from slavery."[13] Such dispatches prompted London to send an inquiry commission in 1870 to investigate life in British Guiana. The commissioners confirmed the horror that was life on a sugar plantation in British Guiana, but the Colonial Office predictably ended up supporting the planters.

As had the black slaves of British Guiana, Indians resisted their abusers, frequently rioting on the plantations. But most servants concentrated on living and building a community. Of Indians who survived indenture, perhaps two out of three stayed in British Guiana. They recreated Indian village life, with a strong emphasis on family life, and celebrated their religion, building temples and mosques. Groups of immigrants combined their meager earnings to buy a cow to be shared by the group. Hindus and Moslems lived peacefully together. Indians also gradually submerged the communal and caste differences of Mother India. Most Indians continued working on sugar plantations, often as wage laborers. Some Indians purchased tracts of British Guiana's inexpensive wetland and remarkably became independent rice farmers, creating a small property-owning class. Rice production did not require the massive capital investments associated with sugar production. By the early twentieth century, British Guiana began to export rice. Indian life remained largely rural, and most Indians lacked literacy skills. Colonial authorities declined to fund schools operated by non-Christians. Indians were reluctant to send their children to Georgetown for education in Christian denominational schools. As Joseph A. Luckhoo, an Indian barrister whose family had converted to Christianity, noted in 1919, for an Indian "to send his boy to a denominational school to be taught English is to denationalize him and jeopardize his religious faith, and so the Indian maintains a calm indifference towards it."[14] As British Guiana moved into the twentieth century, the colony's largest groups—the peoples of West Africa and India and their descendants—remained physically and culturally separated.

Whereas sugar remained the basis of British Guiana's political economy, significant change rocked the industry in the late nineteenth and early twentieth centuries. The planters prospered in the 1870s as British Guiana, along with Trinidad, became leading producers of sugar in the empire. In the 1880s, however, cane producers faced tough competition in the British market from beet sugar produced in Germany. British Guiana's sugar also lost its place in the U.S. market. After the United States occupied Cuba in 1898, it negotiated the Reciprocity Treaty of 1903, which gave Cuban cane sugar preferential treatment in the U.S. market. With prices collapsing, economic consolidation quickly followed. In 1870, British Guiana had 136 sugar estates, with 123 of them having indentured servants. By 1900, the number of plantations had fallen to fifty and would further fall to nineteen by 1950. Ownership of the plantations also changed hands from individual planters to shipping and transport companies. In 1900, the two leading sugar operators—Booker Brothers and John McConnell and Company—combined to form Booker Brothers McConnell and Company Limited, a London-based, limited liability company. Booker Brothers had a virtual monopoly in sugar production, controlling eighteen of the surviving nineteen plantations. Booker Brothers also owned a host of retail, manufacturing, and transport services in British Guiana. In the twentieth century, Guyanese jested that British Guiana should be called "Booker's Guiana."[15] The company had the same overwhelming presence in the colony as did United Fruit Company of Boston in Honduras and Guatemala.

Political and economic change came slowly to British Guiana during the first forty years of the twentieth century. Colonial authorities allowed a modicum of political freedom. Workers gained the right to join unions, with sugar workers forming in the Manpower Citizen's Association in the 1930s. The colony also permitted ethnic organizations, like the League of Coloured Peoples and the British Guiana East Indian Association, to articulate their respective group's concerns. Property requirements for voting were also slightly relaxed, giving a few thousand colonists the right to vote for advisers to the colonial governor. The Colonial Office in London actually strengthened its hold on the colony, making British Guiana a "crown colony" with a royal governor in 1929, whereas in the nineteenth century, the governor had shared power with the sugar barons. The colony's economy made minimal progress. The prices for sugar and rice soared during World War I but collapsed during the global depression of the 1930s. Mining for bauxite began in 1914, centering about seventy miles up the Demerara River near Linden. Canadian metals companies began to invest in the colony. The colony's population grew throughout the period, reaching 375,701 at the end of World War II. Efforts to control malaria had helped reduce mortality rates for rural people. Indians had become the largest group in the colony with 163,343 people. British Guiana's blacks numbered 143,385.[16]

By the end of the 1930s, the economic hardships engendered by the global depression had fueled discontent in the British possessions in the Western Hemisphere. Violent strikes and demonstrations erupted in Barbados, Jamaica, Trinidad, and British Guiana. Between 1935 and 1938, workers repeatedly protested their life and work in British Guiana's sugar plantations. The Colonial Office dispatched in 1938 a study team, the Moyne Commission, to investigate and make recommendations. The commission's report, which was withheld until after World War II, documented the deep poverty in the British West Indies and lack of educational and employment opportunities. It also noted that the populations of the colonies were growing rapidly. British Guiana's population would grow at the rate of 3.3 percent a year from 1946 to 1960. The Moyne Commission wanted London to expand suffrage, invest in the colonies, and enact far-reaching socioeconomic reforms.[17]

Change in British Guiana and throughout the British West Indies would ensue less, however, from internal reforms and more from external pressures. British Guiana was one of the most isolated parts of the empire, with Indians being especially cut off. But the aspirations and grievances of the outside world gradually intruded into British Guiana. Literate colonists learned of the promises of national self-determination made in Woodrow Wilson's Fourteen Points (1918) and the Atlantic Charter (1941). Guyanese also followed the struggles for independence launched by Mahatma Gandhi in India and Kwame Nkrumah in the African Gold Coast (Ghana). Great Britain emerged from World War II badly weakened and in little position to make the financial commitments called for by the Moyne Commission. Furthermore, during the war, the United States developed a significant presence in British possessions in the Western Hemisphere. As part of the "destroyers for bases" deal of 1940, the United States developed military bases throughout the region, including an airfield, Atkinson Field, in British Guiana. The U.S. military assumed the defense of Great Britain's hemispheric possessions during the war. U.S. advice inevitably followed U.S. military aid. The Franklin D. Roosevelt administration dispatched a team of experts, the Taussig Commission, to study conditions in Jamaica. U.S. diplomats pressed the British to initiate economic reforms and to sponsor economic diversification projects. Domestic civil rights groups, like the National Association for the Advancement of Colored People (NAACP), questioned the treatment of blacks in the British possessions.[18] As reflected in the Fourteen Points and the Atlantic Charter, the United States opposed colonialism in principle. President Roosevelt also had a strong aversion to European colonial empires and was determined to use the war as an opportunity to dismantle them. Decolonization would also benefit the postwar U.S. economy, opening British colonial possessions in the Caribbean region to U.S. trade and investment.

Gaining experience in the outside world proved critical to the personal development of British Guiana's anticolonial leaders, Forbes Burnham and Cheddi Jagan. Both men, who studied abroad, would bring a global outlook to a largely impoverished, unaware population. Linden Forbes Sampson Burnham (1923–85) was born in Kitty, a suburb of Georgetown, into the small black professional class. He was the second of five children. His father served as headmaster of a Methodist primary school. An outstanding student, in 1942 Burnham won the Guiana Scholarship, the colonial government's yearly award to the top student in British Guiana for study in Great

Britain. At the conclusion of the war, Burnham entered the University of London where he earned a law degree in 1947 and subsequent admission to the bar at Gray's Inn. Burnham won academic awards from the law faculty for his public-speaking abilities. Observers always commented on Burnham's dignified personal style and remarkable communication skills. A handsome man, the young Burnham dressed neatly in a suit with a bow tie. He conversed in a calm, unhurried, thoughtful manner, befitting a lawyer. V. S. Naipaul, the Nobel laureate in literature, who heard Burnham speak both at Oxford University and in British Guiana, wrote that Burnham was "the finest public speaker I have ever heard."[19] Burnham also became politically active in student politics, serving as an officer in the West Indies Student Association and as a delegate to the World Youth Festival in Czechoslovakia. Burnham developed relationships with left-wing members of the British Labour Party and with members of the British Communist Party. Burnham usually referred to himself as a socialist. As did other West Indian and African members of the empire who came to Great Britain, Burnham encountered racial discrimination in the mother country. Working with the League of Coloured Peoples, he helped organize demonstrations in London to protest racism. Burnham, who returned to British Guiana in 1949, emerged from his experiences in London with a strong sense of racial pride and an understandable distrust of white people.[20]

When Burnham returned to British Guiana, he found a colony that had awakened politically. Cheddi Jagan had begun to organize a mass political party. Like Burnham, Jagan achieved much outside of his homeland. Indeed, within a U.S. context, Jagan's life might have been interpreted within the Horatio Alger "rags to respectability" motif. Cheddi Jagan (1918–97) was born on a sugar plantation, Port Mourant, in the eastern coastal region of Berbice. Jagan's grandparents arrived from India as indentured servants at the beginning of the twentieth century. His grandparents, reflecting village customs, arranged his parents' marriage when they were ten years of age. Jagan's parents worked in the cane fields as small children, with his father eventually achieving the position of gang leader or "driver" on the Port Mourant plantation. Cheddi was the couple's eldest surviving child in a family that grew to eleven children. His parents were determined that their offspring break out of the intense poverty that had characterized their families' lives in both India and British Guiana. Jagan's parents sent him to study at a government secondary school in Georgetown after he received a primary education at a Christian school. In 1936, carrying with him the family's life savings of $500, Jagan sailed for the United States and Howard University, the famous university established for freedpeople after the Civil War. During the next seven years, Jagan won scholarships at Howard and then transferred to prestigious Northwestern University, where he achieved a degree in dentistry. Jagan supported himself by working at a series of low-wage jobs—patent medicine salesman, pawnbroker, ice cream vendor, elevator operator—in Washington, D.C., New York City, and Chicago.[21]

Jagan became politically aware during his stay in the United States. In Washington and nearby Virginia, he witnessed the problems Howard University students encountered in the segregated South. He also saw the deep poverty of U.S. blacks when he worked in the neighborhood of Harlem in New York. As an Asian, Jagan was not permitted to work day shifts when he operated elevators in Chicago. These experiences, combined with the collapse of the world order in the late 1930s, led Jagan to enroll in history and political science classes at the YMCA College of Chicago, even as he pursued his dentistry classes. He became impressed with left-wing U.S. scholars, like Charles Beard and Matthew Josephson, and with the Communists, Marx and Lenin. He also admired Roosevelt's New Deal and became acquainted with the anticolonial ideas of the Indian National Congress. In effect, Jagan engaged in the political ferment that characterized urban life in the United States during the economic depression and the period leading to World War II. Although his political philosophy stemmed from eclectic sources, Cheddi Jagan would later readily accept being called a "Communist." He once testified: "I am a Communist in accordance with my own views on communism." Jagan regularly added, however, that he embraced parliamentary democracy and that he equated communism with democratic socialism and the ideals of early Christian communities. Jagan further identified himself as a "Marxist and left-wing Socialist." Such responses, which often came from Jagan's lifelong habit of speaking "off the cuff," regularly baffled both his friends and enemies.[22]

Jagan's wife became his political partner. In 1943, Jagan married Janet Rosenberg (b. 1920), who came from a middle-class family and lived in a Jewish neighborhood in the South Side of Chicago. Janet Jagan's parents were conservative but largely apolitical. The family encountered anti-Semitism, with the father changing his last name to "Roberts" to aid his career as a salesman. Janet Jagan would later claim that her experiences with anti-Semitism fueled her desire to aid the poor and downtrodden. Although she came from a "typical" urban, Jewish family, Janet Rosenberg hardly acted like her female contemporaries of the late 1930s and early 1940s. Independent, self-confident, and perhaps rebellious, she rode horses and became an outstanding competitive swimmer. She frightened her parents, taking flying lessons without their permission. She attended Wayne State University and became involved in left-wing student politics. Labor agitation in the Detroit area and the famous "sit-down" strikes of the 1930s by auto workers had influenced students on the Wayne State campus. Back in Chicago, Janet studied nursing at Cook County Hospital and became a member of the Young Communist League of Chicago. She met Cheddi at political gatherings of international students. Her parents initially opposed the interracial marriage, with her father threatening to shoot Cheddi on sight. They despised his skin-color, religion, nationality, and politics. In fact, Janet's father, who died in the 1950s, never met Cheddi Jagan. The family predicted that the marriage would not last a year if Cheddi brought his bride to British Guiana. The couple would stay married, however, for over fifty years and have two accomplished children. The Jagans' wedding photographs depict a gorgeous young couple.[23]

Cheddi Jagan underwent a personal crisis during World War II. In light of the ensuing U.S. confrontation with Jagan, the crisis is laden with irony. Jagan contemplated living permanently in the United States. He probably also would have served in the U.S. military as an officer and doctor of dentistry. He later admitted that he was philosophically torn between Roosevelt's internationalism and the studied neutrality of the Indian National Congress. But Jagan was not permitted to take Illinois's examination to become a licensed dentist, because he was not a citizen. The immigration authorities classified Jagan as an "oriental," even though he was born in South America. Under prevailing immigration laws, Asians could not readily become citizens. The U.S. Selective Service issued a draft notice in 1943 to the "oriental" Jagan, giving him six months to achieve his dental license. With the only alternative becoming a private in the U.S. military, Jagan returned alone to British Guiana in 1943. Jagan needed time to persuade his family to accept a white, Jewish woman into the family. Janet Jagan dramatically arrived in British Guiana at the end of 1943, landing on the Demerara River on a Pan American seaplane.[24]

Cheddi and Janet Jagan brought the ideas of the outside world to British

Cheddi Jagan and Janet Rosenberg Jagan in
the United States in 1943. Courtesy of Nadira
Jagan-Brancier.

Guiana. They joined with Burnham and other Afro-Guyanese, such as trade unionist Ashton Chase who had studied at Ruskin College in England, to transform the colony's political life. The couple joined a political discussion group that met at the Carnegie Library in Georgetown. In 1946, the Jagans, Chase, and H. J. M. Hubbard, a white Marxist, founded the Political Action Committee, using as a model the Political Affairs Committee of the U.S. union organization, the Congress of Industrial Organizations (CIO). The founders intended for the new political group, based on the principles of "scientific socialism," to foster labor and progressive movements in British Guiana. The Political Action Committee quickly attracted Guyanese who called for self-government. In late 1947, Cheddi and Janet Jagan and Hubbard targeted the elections for the colony's Legislative Council. The Colonial Office had further relaxed the voting requirements, creating an electorate of 60,000. With the help of Sidney King, a black school teacher, Cheddi Jagan appealed to both blacks and Indians and won a seat on the Legislative Council.[25]

National support for the Political Action Committee broadened in 1948 following a confrontation later celebrated as a momentous event in Guyanese history. Colonial police fired on a crowd of 600 sugar workers protesting changes in work rules on the Enmore Sugar Estate. Five workers died and another fourteen were wounded. Some had been shot in the back. The Jagans led a mass funeral march from the estate to Georgetown. Guyanese would thereafter commemorate the tragedy, making annual pilgrimages to the graves of the "martyrs." In the aftermath of the Enmore incident, the leaders of the Political Action Committee moved to form a political party. Borrowing ideas from Henry Wallace's Progressive Party in the United States and Norman Manley's People's National Party in Jamaica, they established the People's Progressive Party (PPP) in 1950. The PPP's platform called for an independent nation built on socialist principles. The party's leadership reflected the multiracial nature of colonial society. Blacks and Indians shared the top posts. Janet Jagan edited the party organ, *Thunder*. Clinton Wong, a Guyanese of Chinese background, became a vice chairman. The party tapped Forbes Burnham as chairman; after leaving London in 1949, Burnham had stopped in Jamaica to study the organization of the People's National Party. With Burnham as chairman, the PPP had a prestigious leader with, in Jagan's words, "an impressive scholastic record."[26]

The PPP's founders undoubtedly hoped that nationalist aspirations, a shared sense of historical injustice, and class consciousness would over-whelm whatever ethnic, racial, and religious tensions existed in the colony's diverse society. At midcentury, British Guiana had a complex socioeconomic structure that defied facile characterization. Physical, residential, and em-ployment barriers limited communication and interaction among the col-ony's now 400,000 people, consisting of Indians, blacks, "mixed" groups, whites, Chinese, and Amerindians. Except for Amerindians, who lived deep in the interior of the country, Guyanese resided in a curious "linear struc-ture," strung out on a long line along the coast. There was probably less communication between the settlements and distinct cultural groups than there would have been if they had occupied a compact circular or rectangular area. The colonists were mainly rural folk, with about 70 percent living on sugar plantations and nearby villages. Most Indians, who were approaching 50 percent of the population, continued to live a rural life. Georgetown and its surrounding suburbs and New Amsterdam, near the mouth of the Berbice River, constituted British Guiana's major urban areas. New Amsterdam had just over 10,000 people. Georgetown dominated with about 125,000 people. Like the rest of the country, urban areas were growing because of the colony's postwar population boom. Blacks, about 40 percent of the colony's popu-lation, mixed groups, whites, and Chinese lived in Georgetown and New Amsterdam.

Employment generally indicated ethnic and racial identity in British Gui-ana. Sugar production, rice farming, mining, civil service, and education offered work for the colonists. Indians worked as paid laborers on the sugar plantations and owned and farmed the rice-producing lands. Blacks mined the bauxite in regions sixty to seventy miles from the coast near the towns of Mackenzie and Kwakwani, respectively along the Demerara and Berbice Rivers. Blacks and mixed groups dominated the civil service and educational sectors. Most police officers, for example, were Afro-Guyanese. Guyanese of Chinese and Portuguese descent were prominent in the urban merchant trade. Except for Indian rice farmers, few Guyanese owned anything of con-sequence in the colony. Booker Brothers controlled the sugar plantations, and Canadian and U.S. aluminum companies owned the bauxite industry.

Guyanese were not as separated, however, as raw residential and employ-ment statistics might suggest. Blacks also worked on the sugar plantations and enjoyed a peaceful coexistence with Indians in rural villages. Indians constituted about 20 percent of urban residents. Upwardly mobile Indians, who had learned English and had some education and money, had begun to try to enter the civil service and merchant trade. Although British Guiana's distinct communities assuredly did not always interact on a daily basis, they nonetheless drew similar conclusions about colonial life. Indians on sugar plantations and blacks in mining camps resented meager wages, endemic poverty, colonial rule, and foreign control of the economy. They pointed to the colony's persistently high unemployment and underemployment rates. Young men and women found it especially hard to find work in Georgetown. Guyanese were not divided along class lines, because most engaged in the daily struggle to survive. Indians and blacks favored nationalist politicians who promised independence and thoroughgoing, even radical, economic change. At midcentury, Guyanese believed they had compelling reasons to reject imperialism and to disdain the international capitalist system.[27]

Some scholars, dubbed "cultural pluralists," have suggested that British Guiana's politicians could never have constructed a cohesive nation out of this diverse immigrant society. Primarily employing anthropological per-spectives, the cultural pluralists argue that under British colonialism blacks and Indians "lived side by side without much mingling." The two groups developed "very different systems of compulsory or basic institutions." Na-tionalism could be a disruptive force, when disparate groups are forced to work together. The "forces of nationalism" would expose cultural differ-ences and "pose a threat to cultural autonomy."[28] Contemporary observers could have found evidence to support such abstract theories. Afro-Guyanese intellectuals posited that blacks had suffered more under slavery than had Indians under indentured servitude and thereby merited special consider-ations in the postcolonial era. Moreover, because Afro-Guyanese controlled the lower-level civil service positions in the colony, they naturally assumed they would control real political power when independence came. They also worried about the demographic shifts in the colony, for Indians had a higher birth rate than blacks did. On the other hand, Indian thinkers focused on the horrors of indentured servitude and objected to colonial discrimination. Indians deeply resented the Christian control of schools and the lack of educational opportunity, particularly since illiterates were not permitted to vote. Indians were also uneasy about blacks dominating the police force. Indians further favored government spending that would bring electricity, potable water, and indoor plumbing to rural areas. The urban blacks of Georgetown objected that spending on rural development meant less money for industrial projects and jobs for blacks. Economic development issues seemingly involved matters of race, ethnicity, and religion.[29]

Other scholars have rejected the racial pessimism of the cultural pluralists. Raymond T. Smith, who wrote one of the first historical studies of British Guiana, noted that "the really interesting thing about British Guiana is not the extent of ethnic differences but the degree to which a common culture already exists." Smith, who conducted research in the colony in the 1950s, pointed to the triumph of the English language, the common experience of plantation labor, and the agreement among blacks and Indians to end the traditional prerogatives of whites. Both groups were now divorced from their ancestors' homelands and were committed to creating a distinctly Guyanese identity. Indians took pride in both India's and Ghana's independence. Both communities also shared a common passion for the sport of cricket. Smith conceded that Indians rejected denominational schools but also noted that they still admired the English educational system. The historian predicted that economic development and independence would resolve lingering racial tensions. A team of economists seconded Smith's prediction. In 1952, the International Bank for Reconstruction and Development sent a mission to British Guiana to survey the colony's economic needs. The mission commented on the colony's lack of rigid social and economic barriers and hoped that the onset of political activity would not impair the "present racial harmony." The mission conceded that British Guiana had obvious economic challenges, with its "rapidly increasing population confined to a narrow ribbon of the coast, preserved from the encroachments of the sea with great difficulty." Nonetheless, the mission believed "the problems of the colony can be resolved and its continued progress assured."[30]

Whether Guyanese could have built an efficient, harmonious, multiracial community remains a moot issue. As indicated by the formation of the PPP, the colony's young political leaders envisioned such a country. Such an undertaking would have required great wisdom, forbearance, and love. The European colonial powers had bequeathed a difficult legacy to the Guyanese. Nonetheless, as late as 1962, a multiracial, multiethnic investigative commission dispatched to British Guiana by the Colonial Office reported "little evidence of any racial segregation in the social life of the country and in Georgetown." The commission added that "East Indians and Africans seemed to mix and associate with one another on terms of the greatest cordiality." The commission noted, however, that "unprincipled and self-seeking" politicians had already appealed to racial passions and that "there is, of course, always present the danger that hostile and anti-racial sentiments may be aroused by a clash of the hopes and ambitions of rival politicians."[31] The commission's forecast of potential danger became a reality. Unscrupulous domestic politicians and a meddling foreign power incited Guyanese to hate one another.

AS GUYANESE ORGANIZED FOR INDEPENDENCE, imperial Great Britain was reassessing its role in British Guiana, and the United States was contemplating its future relations with the colony. Shortly after the defeat of Nazi Germany, the Labour Party led by Clement Attlee defeated Prime Minister Winston Churchill's Conservatives and retained power until late 1951. Prime Minister Attlee's government believed that the United Kingdom's strategic and economic interests would be enhanced by supporting the United States internationally, improving the United Kingdom's war-ravaged economy, and cutting costs. It judged that initiating the process of decolonization would facilitate reaching those goals. In any case, after two bloody global conflicts and the economic depression of the 1930s, the British had neither the power nor money to hold on to the far-flung and increasingly restive empire. The Attlee government managed to transfer power to India, Pakistan, Ceylon, and Burma. It also transferred its League of Nations mandate over Palestine to the new United Nations. But it did not fix a timetable for independence for its other forty possessions and 70 million colonial subjects, most of whom lived in Africa. It held that economic development must precede independence. In the words of George Hall, the Colonial Office secretary, the mother country would help develop the colonies "so as to enable their peoples speedily and substantially to improve their economic and social conditions, and, as soon as practicable, to attain responsible self-government." This limited pledge disappointed many colonists.[32]

The Attlee government's policy of guided decolonization was readily apparent in British Guiana. In 1950, the government dispatched a study team to British Guiana headed by Dr. E. J. Waddington, a veteran colonial officer who had served in the colony, and Dr. Rita Hinden, a South African economist. The decision to send the Waddington Commission reflected not only the new imperial policy but also London's concerns about the violence of 1948 and the unresolved socioeconomic problems highlighted by the Moyne Commission of 1938. The Commission recommended a new constitution for the colony. All adults over twenty-one who spoke English would have the right to vote. Property and income tests for voting would be abolished. A bicameral legislature would be established with Guyanese having the right to elect members of the lower House of Assembly. An Executive Council, presided over by the royal governor, would govern the country but the majority of its members would come from the House of Assembly. The governor retained, however, absolute veto powers and the right to certify elections. In presenting the constitution, which the Colonial Office accepted on 6 October 1951, the Waddington Commission noted racial separation existed in British Guiana but predicted integration when Indians became involved in self-government.[33] PPP leaders objected that the Waddington Constitution did not grant independence but conceded that it was "one of the most advanced colonial constitutions for that period."[34] The vast majority of Guyanese would have their first opportunity to vote in April 1953.

Until April 1953, imperial officials gave scant attention to British Guiana. Although its population had grown to 450,000 in 1953, Guyanese constituted less than 1 percent of colonial subjects. The colony was poor, and London did not consider British Guiana's sugar, rice, and bauxite to be vital to the health and security of the United Kingdom. In early 1953, the Colonial Office transferred Sir Alfred Savage, who had been the royal governor in Barbados for four years, to British Guiana. In the Colonial Office, midlevel officers supervised the colony. They estimated that the PPP's political strength was growing and that it might emerge as the strongest party in the 1953 elections. Officials worried about the Jagans' contacts with international Communists. Cheddi Jagan had attended a world youth festival in Berlin and had come back impressed with East Germany. Janet Jagan had traveled to Copenhagen to attend a conference of the Women's International Democratic Federation. While touring British Guiana in 1952, N. L. Mayle of the Colonial Office told Cheddi Jagan "that he acted very much like a Communist." On the other hand, Mayle had previously reported to his superiors that "the Jagans were checked with Security recently and reported not to be Communist." They allegedly had, however, received Communist Party literature through the mail.[35]

As British Guiana prepared for its first national election, the colony's future was again altered by elections in Great Britain. The Conservatives, led again by Winston Churchill, regained power in October 1951. Churchill and his colonial secretary, Oliver Lyttleton, took pride in the British Empire. Colonialism to Churchill meant "bringing forward backward races and opening up the jungles." Decolonization, if it came, needed to be measured, and change had to be kept within bounds.[36] As Lyttleton wrote, "the dominant theme of colonial policy had to be the careful and if possible gradual and orderly progress of the colonies towards self-government within the Commonwealth." His words reflected a marked shift of emphasis on the speed and possibilities of decolonization from even the limited pledges offered by Labour. In his memoirs, Lyttleton suggested that the pace of progress depended on how many whites resided in a particular colony. He complained that he could find few wise leaders in Africa. Lyttleton and Churchill forcibly suppressed rebellions in Malaya and Kenya.[37] As for British Guiana, Churchill lamented, as the colonial subjects voted in 1953, that his government was "committed to this new Constitution by our predecessors."[38]

The elections of 1953 and the political leanings of Guyanese politicians also began to spark some concern in the United States about British Guiana. Prior to 1953, the United States had virtually no interest in the British possession. U.S. officials had taken notice of the colony at the end of the nineteenth century, when the Grover Cleveland administration, led by Secretary of State Richard Olney, confronted Great Britain over the issue of the proper boundary between British Guiana and Venezuela. But the Venezuelan Boundary Crisis of 1895 had little to do with the British possession. It was about the United States establishing its dominance in the Western Hemisphere, forcing the British to concede, in Olney's colorful language, that the United States was "practically sovereign" in the region and that "its infinite resources combined with its isolated position" rendered it "master of the situation." After World War II, the U.S. deactivated the military base Atkinson airfield. U.S. trade with the colony was minuscule and, as late as 1960, U.S. investments in British Guiana amounted to only $30 million. U.S. strategic planners considered bauxite a critical wartime natural resource, and British Guiana produced about 25 percent of the world's output. Planners concluded, however, that U.S. and Canadian aluminum companies had several sources of supply, including Jamaica and Surinam.[39]

The U.S. Department of State oversaw reporting on British Guiana but, reflecting U.S. neglect of the colony, actually closed the U.S. consulate in Georgetown in early 1953 in order to save money. Between 1953 and 1957, consular officers reported on British Guiana from the vantage point of Trinidad and Tobago, several hundred miles from Georgetown. Prior to 1953, consular reporting mirrored Colonial Office analyses. Consular officers noted the growing strength of the PPP and reported on the travels of the Jagans. They also forwarded to Washington, without comment, documents like the Waddington Commission's report and the political platform of the PPP. American Cyanamid's decision in 1952 to close its operation in British Guiana and release its 500 employees sharply reduced the U.S. presence in British Guiana. The company determined that Jamaica produced a higher quality of bauxite than the metal mined in British Guiana.[40]

The new U.S. president, Dwight D. Eisenhower (1953–61), initiated a colloquy with Winston Churchill that indirectly touched on British Guiana. Eisenhower found fault with the prime minister's decision to slow the decolonization process. In a private letter, the president urged his wartime comrade to give a speech on the right of self-government. The Western nations needed to embrace the spirit of nationalism in the world. Eisenhower noted that he longed "to find a theme which is dynamic and gripping and which our two countries can espouse together." Churchill should tell the world that within a space of twenty-five years every one of the British possessions will have been "*offered a right to self government and determination*." Eisenhower predicted that Churchill would "electrify the world" with his speech. Prime Minister Churchill declined Eisenhower's challenge. Colonialism was a positive good, rescuing India from its "ancient forms of despotic rule." Reflecting the racism that underlay the imperial mind, Churchill further noted, "I am a bit skeptical about universal suffrage for the Hottentots even if refined by proportional representation." Great Britain would maintain its graduated policy of decolonization even though Churchill despised the dismantling of the empire. Instead of an electrifying speech on self-government, the aging Englishman wanted his "swan song" to be about "the unity of the English-speaking peoples" and their special ability to resolve the world's problems.[41]

President Eisenhower reminded Churchill that nationalism could be channeled against the power of the Soviet Union. U.S. and United Kingdom support for the principle of national self-determination could be contrasted favorably with the Soviet domination of Eastern Europe. Eisenhower admitted, however, that Communists could take advantage of areas not ready for self-rule. Churchill confidently told aides that the president's anticommunism would triumph over his anticolonialism. Eisenhower accepted the fundamental finding of National Security Council Memorandum No. 68

(NSC 68), which the Harry S. Truman administration secretly adopted in 1950: the Soviet Union directed the international Communist movement and was bent on world domination. Indeed, according to NSC 68, an apocalyptic struggle loomed, with the Soviet Union intending to subvert or destroy the "integrity and vitality" of the United States.[42] Eisenhower worried, however, that NSC 68, which called on the United States to confront the Soviet Union globally with massive military power, might bankrupt the U.S. economy. President Eisenhower replaced NSC 68 in 1953 with his own national security paper, NSC 162/2, which summoned the United States to strengthen its nuclear forces. Eisenhower further proved ready to authorize the Central Intelligence Agency (CIA) to carry out covert interventions. He ordered the CIA to attack nationalist leaders in Iran in 1953 and Guatemala in 1954. Eisenhower and his advisers feared that Iranian and Guatemalan nationalists were either Communists, friendly to Communists, or blind to the international Communist conspiracy.[43] Such thinking repeatedly characterized U.S. analyses of British Guiana after 1953.

Although neither the United Kingdom nor the United States would think hard about British Guiana until after April 1953, one nongovernmental organization, the U.S. trade union movement, had already begun to make up its mind about the Jagans and the PPP. By the end of the 1940s, both major labor organizations in the United States, the American Federation of Labor (AFL) and the Congress of Industrial Organizations (CIO), had enlisted in the Cold War. Since the late nineteenth century, the AFL had favored "business unionism," meaning AFL unions would negotiate higher wages and better work conditions for its members but would not challenge the basic capitalist system. The AFL rejected political radicalism at home and always displayed implacable hostility toward the Soviet Union. In 1944, for example, George Meany, the secretary-treasurer of the AFL, voted for Republican Thomas Dewey over Franklin Roosevelt, because he judged Dewey more capable of handling the Soviet Union in the postwar world. This was a remarkable vote, because union leaders heartily approved of Roosevelt's New Deal domestic programs. In 1944, Meany, along with veteran unionists like David Dubinsky and Matthew Woll, established the Free Trade Union Committee to promote the AFL's ideas abroad. Meany named Jay Lovestone the secretary-treasurer of the new organization. Lovestone had been a prominent member of the American Communist Party in the 1920s and 1930s, but he soured on the Soviet Union and its leader, Joseph Stalin, and broke with the party in the late 1930s. Lovestone, who controlled the union's international activities from 1944 to 1974, became a ferocious anticommunist and inveterate cold warrior. Although largely unknown to the public, Lovestone played a critical role in the making of U.S. foreign policy. Lovestone acted with the full knowledge and support of Meany, who served as president of the AFL from 1952 to 1979. Both men had direct access to presidents, secretaries of state, and CIA directors, especially when Democrats controlled the White House.[44]

The CIO eventually followed the lead of the AFL in international affairs. Famous for their "sit-down" strikes in automobile plants in the 1930s, the CIO initially accepted Communists in its movement. By the end of the 1940s, the CIO had purged Communists from its ranks. CIO leaders, led by Walter Reuther, concluded that American Communists were more loyal to the Soviet Union than the United States and that Communist ideology and practices were incompatible with independent trade unionism and a progressive, free society. Many unionists were also members of the traditionally anticommunist Roman Catholic Church and were of Eastern European heritage and naturally resented the Soviet domination of Eastern Europe. Internationally, the CIO at first worked with Communist unions. In 1945, the CIO, along with its British counterpart the Trade Unions Council (TUC), established the World Federation of Trade Unions. The AFL denounced the new organization because it included unions from the Soviet Union. Both the CIO and TUC left the World Federation of Trade Unions when the organization, under Soviet pressure, refused to support the Marshall Plan. For the TUC, the Marshall Plan meant rebuilding the battered economy of the United Kingdom and seeing British unionists back on the job. The CIO, which closely identified with the Democratic Party, felt obligated to support President Truman's Cold War policies. By 1950, the CIO had adopted the same Cold War positions as the AFL. The two unions merged in 1955, with George Meany serving as president.[45]

The AFL-CIO went from supporting U.S. foreign policy to implementing it. Lovestone organized the union's International Affairs Department to mirror the bureaucratic structure of the State Department. Lovestone dispatched agents around the world and advised the State Department on who should be assigned the position of labor attaché in U.S. embassies. Unknown to rank and file members or U.S. taxpayers, Lovestone's operation was principally funded by public money. Beginning in 1948, both the AFL and CIO accepted CIA funds and joined the fight against Communist unions in France and Italy. CIA agents worked undercover as union organizers. The AFL-CIO also served as conduit for the dispersal of CIA funds abroad. The CIA, which paid Lovestone's salary, gave him direct access to the legendary spy, James Jesus Angleton. There is no reliable accounting of how much CIA money the unions handled from 1948 to 1967, when the connection was first publicly exposed. In British Guiana alone, the AFL-CIO probably spent millions of CIA dollars. Labor historians who have studied the issue believe that Meany, Lovestone, and others cooperated with the CIA because historical evidence proved to them that workers always lost their basic political rights under communism, whether in the Soviet Union or in Soviet-dominated Eastern Europe. U.S. labor leaders also probably enjoyed being near the seat of power and having presidents, generals, and foreign leaders asking for their covert assistance.[46]

U.S. unions first began denouncing Cheddi and Janet Jagan and the PPP in January 1951, calling the PPP "the Communist party of the colony." Serafino Romualdi, a protégé of Lovestone and president of Inter-American Regional Organization (ORIT) headquartered in Mexico City, made the first allegation against the PPP. Both the AFL and the CIA backed ORIT. British Guiana came to Romualdi's attention because the Jagans had challenged the Manpower Citizen's Association's representation of the sugar workers. In fact, many Guyanese had concluded that the sugar workers union was little more than a "company union," unwilling to bargain hard with the sugar producers led by Booker. The leaders of the sugar workers union, such as Lionel Luckhoo, had ties to U.S. and British union officials and warned them that the Manpower Citizen's Association was being threatened by Communists. They further averred that Cheddi Jagan associated with the now Communist-dominated World Federation of Trade Unions. Romualdi accepted their arguments and became a dedicated foe of the Jagans.[47]

After receiving alarming reports from Romualdi, Lovestone launched his own investigation in 1953, dispatching Dr. Robert J. Alexander of Rutgers University to investigate British Guiana. Alexander was a prominent political scientist and student of Latin American politics who frequently conducted fact-finding missions in Latin America for Lovestone. Alexander, a prolific scholar, published a study on communism in Latin America. Alexander became a good friend of the Venezuelan democratic, anticommunist leader, Rómulo Betancourt, and he helped design President Kennedy's Alliance for Progress economic development program for Latin America. In a six-page, single-spaced typewritten report to Lovestone, Alexander repeated Romauldi's assertion that the Jagans were Communists, although he conceded that the PPP was "not a disciplined Stalinist party." He pointed out that Janet Jagan had been a member of the Young Communist League, and he guessed that she was the "brains behind the organization." Alexander thought Forbes Burnham not to be a Communist. The political scientist offered no hard evidence to substantiate his opinions. His method of inquiry was to talk to Guyanese. Alexander referred to the Manpower Citizen's Association as "our people" and wrote that the organization had helped the workers. He conceded, however, that the sugar workers still lived in huts used by black slaves in the nineteenth century. He further noted that the sugar union opposed Cheddi Jagan's proposed legislation modeled on the Wagner Act of the United States. The Wagner Act of 1935, which established the National Labor Relations Board, empowered workers to choose their own bargaining representatives. The legislation had, for example, given a great boost to the CIO. Nonetheless, Alexander advised Lovestone to contact the State Department about the Jagans, which Lovestone apparently did.[48] Probably unbeknownst to the Jagans, Romualdi and Lovestone had decided by 1953 to become their lifelong enemies.

ALTHOUGH THE COLONIAL OFFICE and the State Department had misgivings about the PPP, and U.S union officials had grave fears about the party and the Jagans, the voters of British Guiana showed no anxieties about handing power to the multiracial party led by Cheddi Jagan. On 27 April 1953, the PPP astonished even itself by winning eighteen of the twenty-four seats in the House of Assembly. The party also celebrated the multiracial nature of its triumph. One of its Afro-Guyanese candidates won the seat in a majority Indian district. Janet Jagan also won a seat. The party badly defeated the National Democratic Party, a multiracial party composed of British Guiana's small, conservative middle class. The National Democrats won only two seats. The victorious party chose its six members—three blacks and three Indians—for Governor Savage's Executive Council. Both Cheddi Jagan and Forbes Burnham were among the six who joined the Executive Council. In April 1953, the PPP established a precedent that has held throughout the colony and nation's political history: whenever a free and fair election has been held, the PPP has garnered the most votes.

The PPP shocked the colonial establishment with the speed and manner in which it moved to enact its electoral promises. PPP representatives were young, brash, and perhaps impolitic. They violated British protocol, not bowing at the proper times during legislative functions. They further offended colonial sensibilities by declining to spend money to send representatives to Jamaica to greet the new queen, Elizabeth II. The party organ, *Thunder*, engaged in political hyperbole. The PPP also took on the world, passing a resolution urging President Eisenhower to grant clemency to Ethel and Julius Rosenberg, the convicted atomic spies. As Cheddi Jagan wryly noted afterwards, Pope Pius XII made a similar plea to Eisenhower.[49] Although PPP representatives may have behaved immaturely, what they proposed in 1953 for British Guiana easily fit within the traditions of the Democratic Party of the United States, the Labour Party of Great Britain, and the Indian National Congress. The PPP's platform had promised measures to improve the working and living conditions of the colony's downtrodden majority. The proposals included support for low-cost housing, workmen's compensation, schemes to increase land ownership, new taxes on the wealthy, and public education. Such measures implied the transfer of some power to the poor and predictably evoked, as it had against Roosevelt's New Deal, cries of "communism." Outrage among the political opposition mounted when the PPP voted to repeal the Undesirable Publications Act, a ban on "subversive" literature. With sugar workers on strike, political warfare broke out in September 1953 over British Guiana's version of the Wagner Act, which would give workers the right to choose their bargaining agent. The PPP actually modified the bill, requiring a 65 percent vote of workers, instead of 51 percent, if workers wanted to decertify an existing union, like the Manpower Citizen's Association.[50]

British imperial authorities in London assumed that the PPP would carry out a Communist revolution in British Guiana. Like most Guyanese, the Colonial Office predicted that the 1953 election would reveal a divided electorate. Prime Minister Churchill was shocked to hear of the PPP's victory and on 5 May 1953 asked Colonial Secretary Oliver Lyttleton whether he had to accept the result. Churchill added that "we ought surely to get American support in doing all we can to break the Communist teeth in British Guiana." Churchill also joked that "perhaps they could even send Senator [Joseph] McCarthy down there," referring to the reckless anticommunist extremist from Wisconsin. Lyttleton responded that Governor Savage was unworried, because the PPP's platform was moderate or, as the Colonial Secretary put it, "no more extreme than that of the Opposition here." The major concern was that some PPP leaders had visited Communist countries. Lyttleton reminded Churchill, however, that the governor retained extensive veto powers. Lyttleton added that the Colonial Office adamantly rejected the suggestion of seeking U.S. assistance on British Guiana. The colonial secretary assured the prime minister that he would monitor the colony's politics.[51]

Despite Governor Savage's optimism, anti-PPP diatribes quickly arrived at the Colonial Office. J. M. "Jock" Campbell, the director of Booker Brothers, called on the Colonial Office in June 1953 and pointedly asked if the government would act if his sugar business was disrupted by the PPP. Campbell implied that Governor Savage was not tough enough with the PPP. The Demerara Company of Liverpool passed on a report that alleged that "communism is openly on the rampage" and that British Guiana was run by a "body of unscrupulous Communist gangsters."[52] Less colorful but no less dangerous to the PPP were the analyses prepared by officers within the Colonial Office. By mid-July 1953, less than three months after the election, officers were speaking of banning the PPP. As James N. Vernon of the Colonial Office saw it, "Communism is an international faith and with Communists or near-Communists in the Government the international repercussions of their actions cannot be ignored." British Guiana could become a "center" of the Communist organization. The Colonial Office objected to PPP's civil liberties campaign. The PPP had overturned the subversive literature ban and then lifted the ban on suspect West Indian leaders visiting British Guiana. "Secret sources" informed the Colonial Office that Janet Jagan had once met Harry Pollitt, the leader of the British Communist Party, and that Cheddi Jagan had asked for literature from the World Federation of Trade Unions. In a radio interview, Jagan had also said he admired the Soviet Union and the People's Republic of China. The Colonial Office especially worried about Janet Jagan, for she was "an exceptionally able, ruthless, and energetic woman" who was "the dominating influence in the party." As for Forbes Burnham, the Colonial Office considered him "violently anti-British, anti-white, and lacking in balance and judgment." For good measure, officers added that Burnham was "lazy, flippant, and sarcastic." By August 1953, the Colonial Office had concluded that the government needed to revoke British Guiana's constitution and remove the PPP from power.[53]

Governor Savage did not encourage such extreme measures. In his reporting to London, the governor set another pattern in the saga of British Guiana that would persist through the 1950s and 1960s. Diplomats who actually served in the colony argued that political life in British Guiana was complex and did not easily fit into the structures of the Cold War. British Guiana had its own troubled history separate and apart from the East-West confrontation. Savage pointed to the PPP's surprising ability to maintain a biracial coalition, although he acknowledged that racial tension persisted in the colony. PPP leaders were inexperienced and also bitter about the colony's treatment by past governments and big business. Savage thought that moderates and constitutional processes could ultimately triumph. He did not accuse anyone of being a Communist. He dubbed Janet Jagan and Sidney King, a member of the Executive Council, as "acknowledged Communists," meaning "generally acknowledged to be Communists by others." Governor Savage never recommended military intervention in British Guiana, and it "came as a great shock to us" when it happened.[54] The Colonial Office would later criticize Savage for not being forceful enough and for being dedicated to the common man. Savage confessed to having "sympathy for coloured people."[55]

Governor Savage received backing in his analysis of the PPP from another British official stationed in British Guiana, D. J. G. Rose, chief of the colonial intelligence services known as the "Special Branch." Rose flatly discounted any plot or conspiracy in British Guiana, noting that Cheddi Jagan had shown no sign of subordinating his ambition to be a successful leader of the colony to any "International design by International communism for creating chaos." Jagan's only experience with communism came when he visited East Germany. Rose opined that Jagan was a hero to Indians, because they were intensely anticolonial based on their dire poverty and history of suffering in the sugarcane fields. The black urban laborers held Burnham in similar esteem. Like Savage, Rose noted that the biracial leadership of the PPP had helped relax racial tensions. Rose principally worried about Janet Jagan, an "orthodox Communist." Her husband was "a misguided colonial intellectual" who leaned on her during times of stress. Rose alleged that Cheddi Jagan had learned about communism from his wife and wondered whether Janet Jagan could "dominate her husband's plans." Rose vowed to be watchful to insure that Janet Jagan did not "dominate her husband."[56]

Savage and Rose's reports made no impression on the Churchill government. By late September, the prime minister, after checking with his cabinet, ordered Lyttleton to stop what the Colonial Office called a brewing "Communist conspiracy."[57] On 9 October 1953, upon instruction from London, Governor Savage suspended the constitution and took full control of the colony. British troops, who were stationed on warships, had already landed in British Guiana. The PPP had held power for a mere 133 days. Colonial Secretary Lyttleton explained that he acted because he had received reports from intelligence services of plots to burn down Georgetown, which consisted largely of wooden buildings. Guyanese who did not own automobiles were purportedly obtaining petrol and kerosene. Lyttleton's allegations would have had no standing in a British court of law. As Governor Savage later explained, the information that colonial police obtained on arson and sabotage plots came from paid informers who had second- and third-hand sources.[58] Churchill's government had reoccupied British Guiana because it wanted to demonstrate to nationalist movements throughout the empire that it would control the pace and direction of decolonization.[59]

The Labour opposition initially issued a sharp public challenge to the intervention, prompting the government to issue a "White Paper." British officials privately conceded that it would be "convenient" to say that the intervention forestalled a Communist plot. Because such an allegation was not "tenable," the White Paper emphasized maladministration, disorder, and the potential for violence and bloodshed. It further pointed to the Communist associations of PPP leaders and suggested that their legislative initiatives represented a blueprint for Communist domination. Party officials were "zealots in the cause of communism."[60] The Colonial Office provided, however, no evidence proving that PPP leaders worked with or accepted support from international Communists based in the Soviet bloc. It also did not prosecute PPP leaders, although Lyttleton reportedly personally threatened Jagan and Burnham with imprisonment.[61] Labour Party spokesmen had observed that if the government knew that Jagan, Burnham, and others were potential arsonists then they should present that evidence in a legal setting. Cheddi and Janet Jagan each served five hard months in prison in 1954 but that was for engaging in proscribed political activity and travel after the suspension of the constitution.

Although Labour members pointed to inconsistencies in the government's arguments, the Labour Party proved a disappointment to the PPP. After the military occupation, Jagan and Burnham journeyed to London and met with Clement Attlee. The interview went badly with Attlee objecting to both past associations of PPP leaders and their inflammatory rhetoric. Labour felt more comfortable with Caribbean leaders, such as Grantley Adams of Barbados and Norman Manley of Jamaica, who were nationalists and vocal anticommunists. Rita Hinden, who had served on the Waddington Commission, further hurt the PPP cause when she accused the PPP leadership of not accepting democratic values and of attempting to create a one-party state in British Guiana. Hinden had helped establish the Fabian Colonial Society, an association which lobbied for colonial self-rule and the orderly move toward independence.[62] In fact, the PPP had not bothered to consult with its small, scattered opposition. Jagan would later acknowledge that "we allowed our zeal to run away with us, we became swollen-headed, pompous, bombastic."[63] In the House of Commons, Labour tried to have it both ways, "condemning methods toward the establishment of a totalitarian regime" but noting that it was "not satisfied that the situation in British Guiana was of such a character as to justify the extreme step of suspending the constitution." The Conservatives handily defeated the resolution. Oliver Lyttleton laughed at Labour's meek and mealy effort. He taunted that "the amendment was nearly all soda water; only a drop of whiskey could be risked."[64]

In parliamentary debates, Lyttleton denied Labour suggestions that the United States had pressured the government to send troops to British Guiana. On that issue, Lyttleton spoke truthfully. Contemporary observers and foreign nations assumed that the United States urged the British to remove Jagan. Indeed, when a U.S. diplomat called in Georgetown after the suspension of the constitution, wealthy Guyanese thanked the diplomat, persistently asserting "that the United States deserved all the credit."[65] Scholars have also implied that the United States played some role.[66] Although Churchill and the Colonial Office perceived a U.S. interest in British Guiana, they did not receive meaningful advice or guidance from the Eisenhower administration. Colonial officers frequently expressed the view that "in the case of British Guiana there were external considerations such as our position in the Caribbean and our relations with South America and the United States which must inevitably be taken into account in determining our policy." Such external considerations mattered less, however, to the Colonial Office than their conviction that the PPP was misruling a British colony. At a meeting of Churchill's cabinet on 2 October 1953, cabinet members agreed that the

United States should be informed of the invasion plan only twelve hours before it went into effect.[67] Prime Minister Churchill was always keen, of course, on preserving imperial prerogatives.

Without a diplomatic presence in British Guiana, the United States could not readily shape events in the colony. Consul Thomas P. Maddox reported on British Guiana from Port of Spain, Trinidad. Maddox read Guyanese newspapers, most of which were violently anti-PPP, and interviewed those who had been in British Guiana. The other source of hearsay information for the State Department was its embassy in London. One officer, Second Secretary Margaret Joy Tibbetts, read British newspapers and conversed with officers in the Colonial Office. In mid-1953, the State Department received a firsthand account of the colony's politics when it ordered Consul Maddox to visit British Guiana. In part, department officials were reacting to an article in the conservative news magazine, *Time*, that declared that the election of 1953 "returned the first group of Communist leaders ever to rule in the British Empire." *Time* further observed that, at the inaugural ceremonies, male PPP legislators had worn white suits and red ties and the three female legislators had worn white dresses with red rosettes. The magazine warned that this might be "a new sort of Communist uniform for the tropics."[68] Once in Georgetown, Maddox found that choices in the color of ties and rosettes may have been more about fashion than about politics. He met with PPP leaders, including Jagan, and found that they were interested in hastening the process of independence, escaping the economic domination of British interests, and developing economic ties with U.S. firms. Maddox doubted that the PPP intended to nationalize the economy. He further reported that Janet Jagan had not received economic instructions from Communists when she traveled to Europe. Maddox concluded that he did not have enough experience with the PPP to predict which policies the party would pursue.[69] His lack of experience in British Guiana did not, however, prevent Maddox from speculating on the Jagans' home life. He thought Janet Jagan was the "dynamic" person in the relationship and that she had an extramarital relationship that had been "hushed up," although the alleged affair "nearly broke up the Jagan household." Maddox also thought it his duty to inform Washington that an alleged lover of Janet Jagan's had returned to British Guiana.[70]

Consul Maddox's reporting on the PPP became more critical, albeit less titillating, in the late summer and fall of 1953, but he was back to relying on secondhand sources. For example, Robert F. Cardwell, the general manager of ESSO Standard in Trinidad, told Maddox that "he had seen few instances of political movements more ominous to the western democratic interest than that represented by the PPP in British Guiana." As a showdown loomed between the PPP and the Churchill government, Maddox confessed he could not report accurately on the crisis and suggested that his bosses rely on reports from the embassy in London.[71] On 5 October 1953, an officer in the State Department's Bureau of North American Affairs put in a hurried telephone call to the embassy in London to find out what the British intended to do in British Guiana.[72]

As Churchill had predicted, the Eisenhower administration welcomed the overthrow of the Jagan government. The British had won a small victory in the Cold War. On 8 October 1953, CIA Director Allen Dulles gave an oral briefing to President Eisenhower and his National Security Council about the British operation. Dulles reminded the president and the NSC that British Guiana was a major source of the world's supply of bauxite. Communist influence in the colony had grown rapidly after the April 1953 elections. The CIA apparently considered Janet Rosenberg Jagan to be the organizer of the communist conspiracy. In Dulles's words, "The leader of the dominant party in the new government of British Guiana was an American-born Communist whose East Indian husband was the head of the People's Progressive Party."[73] Thereafter, Secretary of State John Foster Dulles instructed his ambassadors throughout Latin America to justify the British action and assure Latin Americans that the issue was communism in the Western Hemisphere and not British colonialism. Latin Americans were told that the United States took "genuine satisfaction" in the firm British action. The State Department found, however, that Latin Americans remained "unsatisfied" with the U.S. defense of the overthrow of Jagan, believing that communism was peripheral to the central question of colonialism.[74] The State Department further assured India, the ancestral homeland of the majority of Guyanese, that the United States had not pressured the British to send troops. Nonetheless, the United States was gratified by the British decision, because, as Under Secretary of State Walter Bedell Smith telegraphed New Delhi, "total evidence leads us to conclude definite plan existed establish Commie bridgehead in Colony with implications idea make of Colony a Commie center at least for Caribbean and possibly more general Western Hemisphere operations."[75] Although he did not use the term popularized in the later 1950s, Smith implied that the United States believed that British Guiana, with a population of less than 500,000, had become a "domino."

In deciding that British Guiana under PPP leadership had become a threat to U.S. national security interests, the Eisenhower administration unthinkingly accepted the arguments of the Churchill government. The administration had not developed its own evidence. It was unaware that Governor Savage offered nuanced arguments about the political intentions of the PPP. And it apparently forgot that when Consul Maddox had actually conferred with Cheddi Jagan that the session had been productive. It was enough to know, in Under Secretary Smith's words, that "PPP statements closely parallel the Moscow line" or that, as one State Department officer noted, the PPP used Communist slogans like "capitalist imperialism" and "colonialism."[76] In essence, Cheddi and Janet Jagan and the PPP had passed the "duck test." As developed in 1950 by U.S. Ambassador to Guatemala Richard Patterson Jr., neither ducks nor Communists wore labels identifying themselves. But if a bird looked, swam, and quacked like a duck, it was a duck. This was the way, Patterson advised, to detect Communists.[77] Indeed, in 1953–54, the Eisenhower administration would use the duck test in deciding to destroy the popularly elected government of Jacobo Arbenz Guzmán of Guatemala.

U.S. OFFICIALS UNDOUBTEDLY HOPED that British Guiana would never again pose a mortal threat to the Western world. The U.S. consulate in Georgetown remained closed until 1957. But problems persisted. The United States, Canada, and Latin American nations opposed colonialism. No matter how loudly Prime Minister Churchill trumpeted the virtues of colonialism, the British would one day have to leave its colony in South America. The majority of Guyanese resented the suspension of their constitution. They knew that they had not been rescued by the British from some awful, impending crisis. U.S. and British analysts agreed that, if given the chance, the Guyanese would put the PPP back in power. After 1953, the United States would wrestle with this dilemma. It preferred a free and independent Guyana, but it did not want the Guyanese to hold a free and fair election. The U.S. search for a solution would lead to disturbing consequences for the people of British Guiana.

imperial adjustments, 1953–1960

Between 1953 and 1960, critical developments took place in the political life of British Guiana and in the colony's relationship to the United Kingdom and the United States. After suspending British Guiana's constitution, the ruling Conservative Party embarked on a concerted campaign to destroy the People's Progressive Party. The Conservatives' tactics included stimulating racial politics in the colony, pitting blacks against Indians. The U.S. government and the U.S. trade union movement quietly backed the British. But the effects of two momentous international events—the Suez Crisis and the Cuban Revolution—shattered the Anglo-American alliance on British Guiana. In the aftermath of the Suez debacle, Britain's new leaders concluded that they should dismantle the empire. The British decision to allow Cheddi Jagan and his supporters back into government dismayed U.S. policymakers. Their dismay grew into alarm as they persuaded themselves that an independent Guyana led by Jagan would be a facsimile of Fidel Castro's Cuba. By the end of the decade, British Guiana had become a Cold War battleground and the scene of an Anglo-American diplomatic confrontation. The colony had also been transformed into a divisive society, with its politics marred by deep ethnic and racial divisions.

AFTER SENDING TROOPS to British Guiana and suspending the colony's constitution in October 1953, the Conservatives, led first by Prime Minister Winston Churchill and then by Prime Minister Anthony Eden (1955–57), set out to mold British Guiana's political future. The PPP would not be permitted to govern the colony again. As the Colonial Office resolved in February 1955 in a major paper on the crisis in British Guiana, "While the extremist leaders of the PPP dominate the policy of the party and the party itself maintains its present influence among the people, there can be no return to representative government, and no full confidence in the security forces in the Colony to maintain order without U.K. troops." The PPP used classical Communist methods, exploiting popular demand for self-government and reform. Among the PPP's many sins was that it even organized youth organizations "on the communist pattern" and attempted "to undermine the position and influence of the Boy Scouts and Girl Guides."[1] The Conservative governments pursued a classic policy of intimidation and incentive to destroy the PPP and convince Guyanese to join new political parties.

The United Kingdom continued to occupy British Guiana militarily long after the alleged conspiracy to burn Georgetown had passed. In September 1954, Churchill overruled cabinet objections and ordered that the battalion of British troops in British Guiana would stay. The prime minister was loath to accept the wisdom of Treasury officers who persistently argued through the 1950s that the country could no longer afford the empire. The Treasury worried that it cost £170,000 to maintain a battalion and that it would cost another £70,000 to rotate out the battalion that had occupied British Guiana over the past year.[2] Churchill's decision to maintain a military presence was not based on a direct security threat, for the colony remained calm after the suspension of the constitution. Churchill primarily intended to overawe the colonial subjects with British power. To be sure, a malcontent had attacked a symbol of imperial pride in May 1954 by dynamiting and partially damaging a statue of Queen Victoria in front of the Laws Court building in Georgetown.[3]

The Conservatives fortified the military with a new governor in George-town, Sir Patrick Renison, a veteran colonial officer who had recently served in British Honduras. In June 1955, Alan Lennox-Boyd, the new colonial secretary, told Prime Minister Anthony Eden, who had recently replaced the eighty-year-old Churchill, that "British Guiana has undoubtedly become one of the more difficult Colonies." The government needed a forceful hand in Georgetown, and Lennox-Boyd had become "uneasy" about Savage. He also pointed out to the prime minister that Great Britain's rule in British Guiana was "ever under the keen and critical eye of the American states, especially the United States, and I feel that we cannot afford to take any un-necessary risks."[4] The Colonial Office decided to take the extraordinary step of giving Renison formal guidance before he journeyed to South America. Renison would be instructed to make unpopular decisions, and he needed to know that he would have the complete backing of the colonial secretary.[5] Despite the Colonial Office's desire to control him, Renison would demon-strate independent judgment. As had Governor Savage, Governor Renison would eventually conclude, based on firsthand knowledge, that the character of political life in British Guiana was not necessarily what officials in London or Washington believed it to be.

Governor Savage undoubtedly did not endear himself to the Conserva-tives with his reporting in the period after the suspension of the constitu-tion. Colonial Secretary Lyttleton had told Churchill that he wanted to arrest without charges the leadership of the PPP. Churchill had demurred on that extreme step, noting that the full cabinet would have to approve.[6] In Decem-ber 1953, Governor Savage informed the Colonial Office that his government could not prosecute PPP leaders because the charges enumerated in the White Paper were political and could not be easily translated into criminal prosecutions. After a year of investigation, Savage further told London that no credible evidence could be found to sustain charges that Cheddi and Janet Jagan and other PPP leaders planned to commit acts of arson and sabotage. The case of the "Arson Plot" was closed.[7]

British authorities did find a way to put the Jagans in prison. After meet-ing in October and November 1953 in London with Labour Party officials and then being threatened with imprisonment by Lyttleton, Cheddi Jagan and Forbes Burnham journeyed to India seeking support from Prime Minister Jawaharlal Nehru. India declined to intercede or raise the issue at the United Nations. Jagan did, however, take advantage of the trip to learn about the tactics of passive resistance and civil disobedience. He and Burnham returned to British Guiana in February 1954. The government prohibited political activities and confined PPP leaders to the vicinity of Georgetown. Jagan quickly challenged the travel ban and found himself in a colonial jail. While in jail, Jagan engaged in Gandhi-like gestures, organizing hunger strikes, protests, and political discussion groups. After her husband's release, Janet Jagan was sent to prison for violating the ban on political activities. Her experience in prison proved harder for her than for her husband. Cheddi Jagan served his time with fellow political prisoners. Janet Jagan was thrown into jail with common criminals, especially prostitutes. She also suffered in prison, because she could not digest the miserable prison food. She survived for five months on bread and water. Janet Jagan endured another injustice. Because of the ban on travel imposed by British colonial authorities, she could not return to Chicago to visit her dying father.[8] To the Indians of British Guiana, it probably appeared that the Jagans were reliving the experiences of Gandhi and Nehru in colonial India. Such a comparison could only redound to the political benefit of the Jagans and the PPP.

Colonial officials recognized that repression had not weaned the Guyanese from the PPP. They privately conceded that the post-1953 government that they had established had no measure of popular support and that it was "thoroughly authoritarian." They also understood that, if the Colonial Office restored representative, democratic government, Cheddi Jagan and the PPP would win power. Colonial officials spoke about exiling Janet Jagan, assuming that she was "the brain behind" her husband. They regretfully concluded that they had no legal justification for such a harsh measure. One action British officials took to diminish Jagan's appeal was to plant unfavorable stories in the colony's newspapers. The U.S. Information Agency assisted the propaganda campaign, supplying British Guiana's newspapers with anti-communist material.[9]

Beyond burnishing the image of the West, another way to counter the appeal of communism was to foster social and economic development. Colonial officers reasoned that Guyanese had voted for the PPP in 1953 because they were poor and had horrific memories of the past abuses of slavery and indentured servitude. Indeed, a study conducted in the mid-1950s by the International Labor Organization confirmed British Guiana's economic problems. A full 30 percent of the colony's labor force was unemployed or underemployed, working less than thirty hours a week.[10] Governors Savage and Renison lobbied for a massive British investment in the colony both to address labor issues and to enhance "our political and public relations position." In 1954, Savage asked the Colonial Office to increase expenditures by 300 percent in British Guiana by spending $10 million immediately in the colony and by establishing a $36 million line of credit. Pleading poverty, the Colonial Office could only provide about $5 million a year in economic aid for 1954–55. At the end of 1955, Governor Renison presented an ambitious five-year economic development program that would cost $96 million. Renison noted that the United States generously dispensed aid and that the Soviet Union had begun to promise aid to developing nations. The Colonial Office accepted Renison's point that it provided too little aid to British Guiana, but it lamented that the United Kingdom had balance of payments problems. A frustrated Renison sent a series of angry letters to London, pointing out the lack of progress in housing, roads, land, and local government. In his public addresses, the governor promised progress to the colonial subjects. In his dispatches, Renison warned that "in the eyes of this country it is the Colonial Office as well as the interim government which is on trial."[11]

Although the Conservative governments proved unsuccessful either in suppressing political activity or in persuading Guyanese to love colonialism, they did partially succeed in their campaign to weaken the PPP. This success portended grave consequences for British Guiana's political future. Emulating the collaboration between the CIA and U.S. trade unions, colonial officers worked with officials in the British Trade Union Council (TUC) to train anticommunist union leaders in British Guiana and to support them with covert funds. In particular, the British wanted to strengthen the Manpower Citizen's Association, which opposed the PPP, and break the relationship between British Guiana's TUC and the PPP. The Manpower Citizen's Association, which represented Indian sugar workers, was a timid union led by Richard Ishmael, who was widely disparaged as a disorganized opportunist. So dubious was Ishmael's reputation that the Colonial Office accepted for a time a suggestive rumor that Ishmael had "fallen under the spell of Janet Jagan and is working closely with her." By comparison, Afro-Guyanese made up the bulk of the membership of the TUC, which was led by the lethargic Rupert Tello. The British wanted the TUC to stay out of the colony's politics and focus solely on its relationship with employers. After close consultation with the Colonial Office, British TUC official George Woodcock sent representatives, such as Andrew Dalgleish, to British Guiana to work with Ishmael, Tello, and their unions. The plan was for Dalgleish to portray himself as having no relationship with the governor and other colonial authorities. There also would be no public disclosure of the funds, dubbed "a quiet subvention," that union people from Great Britain distributed in the colony. Compared to the amount of money U.S. unions would funnel into British Guiana, the quiet subventions were small. Dalgleish gave, for example, about $15,000 to the Manpower Citizen's Association over the first six months of 1955.[12] British trade union officials were not consciously encouraging racial division in the colony. But by encouraging British Guiana's black members of the TUC to oppose a PPP led by Cheddi Jagan, the Colonial Office and union people were creating the preconditions for racial confrontation.

Another Conservative effort to fracture the PPP directly intensified racial tensions in the colony. In 1954, London dispatched a study team, the Robertson Commission, to review the constitutional crisis of 1953 and make recommendations for British Guiana's future. Reporting in November 1954, the commission predictably echoed the White Paper, blaming an irresponsible, radical PPP for the suspension of the constitution. As for the future, it could not predict when self-government could be restored. But it took a morose tone, repudiating the optimistic predictions about racial harmony in British Guiana made in 1951 by the Waddington Commission. The Robertson Commission foresaw the growing Indian majority of the colony asserting itself, awakening "the fears of the African section of the population." The commission accepted the charge made by some blacks that Indians did not want independence within the British Commonwealth but rather that they desired to join an empire led by India. "Suspicion and distrust" characterized relations between the two groups, with little hope of "any coalescing process," such as intermarriage. The Robertson Commission therefore affirmed that "we do not altogether share the confidence of the Waddington Commission that a comprehensive loyalty to British Guiana can be stimulated among peoples of such diverse origins."[13]

The Robertson Commission drew distinctions about political leaders in British Guiana. It branded the Jagans and some of their black colleagues, like Sydney King and Brindley Benn, as international Communists. Great Britain could never allow them and their ilk to have power again. British Guiana's

Communists were the "sole barriers" to progress, self-government, and independence. The commission judged, however, that Forbes Burnham was the leader of moderate, democratic socialists who had been overwhelmed by PPP extremists. The commission quoted Guyanese who believed that Burnham should have stood up to the Jagans.[14] Colonial officials underscored the points made by the Robertson Commission by relaxing the political proscriptions on Burnham and maintaining them on the Jagans. They also encouraged Lionel Luckhoo, an Indian lawyer, to form a political party. But the prosperous Luckhoo, who admired Western culture and whose family had converted to Catholicism, had little appeal to poor Hindus and Muslims who worked in the sugar fields and rice paddies.[15]

Forbes Burnham had seemingly received an invitation from the Robertson Commission either to take control of the PPP or to leave it. In February 1955 at a party meeting, Burnham challenged Cheddi Jagan for the leadership and split the party into two factions. Between 1955 and 1958, the Burnham and Jagan factions contested each other for power, with each side using the PPP label. In 1958, Burnham founded his own party, the People's National Congress (PNC). Although some blacks stayed with Jagan and a handful of Indians followed Burnham, British Guiana had by the end of the decade a political party system based on the colony's racial divide. Several radical black politicians, like Sydney King, Martin Carter, and Rory Westmaas, quit the PPP, because they judged Jagan too moderate and eclectic in his political views. British Guiana's mainly black trade unionists aligned with Burnham and the PNC, whereas Indian sugar workers stayed with the PPP.

Burnham may have had many reasons for breaking the PPP apart. As a fervent nationalist, he may have taken seriously the Robertson Commission's threat that British Guiana would never gain its independence with Jagan leading the PPP, although Burnham denied that he was responding to the Robertson Commission. Publicly, he stated that he broke with Jagan because he opposed communism and because he thought Jagan placed too much emphasis on international events. These explanations are belied by his subsequent actions. By the 1980s, after twenty years of Burnham's dictatorship, Guyana reminded observers of Communist North Korea under Kim Il Sung, with Guyanese addressing one another as "comrade." Burnham also loved acting on a global stage. He certainly coveted power and had a strong sense of his historical importance. He judged himself the better man, over Jagan, to lead his country to independence. In April 1953, after the PPP's great electoral triumph, Burnham briefly unsettled the party by demanding that he should be the lead figure in the new government. He further knew that Jagan opposed joining a West Indies Federation. Burnham envisioned British Guiana associating with Jamaica, Barbados, British Honduras, and Trinidad and Tobago and creating a federation in which blacks had an over-whelming numerical superiority. Burnham may also have decided that it would be politically advantageous to pander to racial fears and tensions. Burnham initially blamed British colonialists for stoking racism between blacks and Indians as a part of a divide and conquer strategy. But by 1961, Burnham was issuing explicit racial appeals, warning blacks that Indians wanted to take their jobs and businesses.[16] Contemporary observers of British Guiana's political scene agreed that, as Canadian scholar Elisabeth Wallace put it, Burnham, as compared to Cheddi Jagan, was "more willing to make capital out of racial passions and far less willing to consider possible compromises."[17]

As British authorities struggled between 1953 and 1956 to shape British Guiana's political future, U.S. officials stood on the side, occasionally speculating on what should be done with the colony. President Eisenhower and his national security advisers essentially forgot about the British colony after the suspension of British Guiana's constitution. The administration applauded the British for their "firm action" and lamented that Latin Americans saw the intervention as "unjustified," for Latin Americans continued to perceive communism as peripheral to the question of European colonialism in the Western Hemisphere. To counter this dissatisfaction, the administration instructed the U.S. Information Agency to coordinate its activities with British information services.[18] Despite the president's philosophical commitment to decolonization, the administration made no effort in the mid-1950s to support independence movements in the Caribbean. Having just witnessed the defeat of what it perceived to be communism in British Guiana and Guatemala, the administration now favored a cautious approach toward political change in the Western Hemisphere. It contented itself with calling for the acceptance "of the principle that dependent and colonial peoples in this hemisphere should progress by orderly processes toward a self-governing status." To assist those processes, the administration authorized the U.S. International Cooperation Agency to provide technical assistance to the colonies. But the amount of money allocated was minuscule. For fiscal year 1957, the United States authorized spending a total of only $1.25 million in British Guiana, British Honduras, Jamaica, and Surinam. Between 1954 and 1957, the United States allocated about $1 million to British Guiana for technical assistance in the fields of agriculture, housing, and community development.[19]

British efforts to master British Guiana's political life prompted only limited discussion within the State Department. Without diplomatic representation in Georgetown, the State Department continued not to receive regular analyses about the colony. Based on their reading of newspapers, interviews, and brief visits to Georgetown, U.S. consuls in Trinidad reported the obvious facts of political life in British Guiana. They noted that the PPP remained widely popular and would win any election the colonial authorities permitted. The Guyanese were intensely nationalistic, and the ban on political activities and Cheddi Jagan's imprisonment had provoked "fanatical hero-worship of the Jagans, Burnham, and their ilk." In mid-1955, Consul Thomas Maddox interviewed J. M. Campbell of Booker Brothers and John Gutch, an aide to Governor Savage. They emphasized that a political vacuum existed in British Guiana that was "very unsatisfactory." Colonial authorities could not indefinitely impose a government backed by troops upon the people of British Guiana. Cheddi Jagan also had not been intimidated by the repression. In April 1956, Consul Douglas Jenkins Jr. advised Washington that Jagan "gave no sign that he is less recalcitrant in his points of view or that the Emergency Regulations have had any chastening effect upon him."[20]

State Department officers in Washington, London, and Port of Spain talked among themselves about the colony's future. As did the British, they wanted to see the PPP break apart. In 1954, an officer in Washington spoke of Forbes Burnham as the "leader of the African Christians," and Maddox suggested "discreetly playing up the Burnhamites and other non-Communists to produce a split in the PPP." Maddox tempered his own idea a year later, however, by pointing to Burnham's demagogic statements and expressing doubts that Burnham could become a "sane and responsible leader." In 1956, Consul A. John Cope reported that Governor Renison hoped that Burnham would lead democratic forces in the colony. But Renison added that Burnham was "opportunistic and untrustworthy." As the U.S. embassy in London had earlier bemoaned, after discussing British Guiana with the Colonial Office, all were "baffled" as to what to do constitutionally in the colony.[21]

Although the Eisenhower administration mainly talked about British Guiana, it did deploy technical assistance money to influence one area of the colony's life—labor relations. The administration cooperated with the British in assisting anti-PPP trade unions. The administration paid for labor leaders, like Richard Ishmael and Rupert Tello, to travel to Maryland to attend labor leadership seminars sponsored by the AFL-CIO. The State Department cleared the assistance with the Colonial Office and British unions to ensure that British unions did "not regard this as an intrusion on its functions by the U.S. Government."[22] In the mid-1950s, the United States still trusted British officials to pursue the proper course in the colony. The Colonial Office reluctantly accepted the offer, noting that "we remain extremely apprehensive about the risk of possible influence of American lecturers in the trade union field in British Guiana." Colonial officers reasoned that it would be "embarrassing" to reject the offer, because the Colonial Office welcomed U.S. technical assistance in areas such as housing and community development.[23]

Whereas the Eisenhower administration acted circumspectly, the U.S. labor movement actively intervened in British Guiana. During the Eisenhower years, U.S. labor officials did not have the ready access to the White House and the State Department that they enjoyed during the Truman, Kennedy, and Johnson presidencies. Nonetheless, they continued to use covert government funds to support their international activities. Labor people, like Jay Lovestone, Serafino Romualdi, and Robert Alexander, seemingly worried more about British Guiana's future than did the Eisenhower administration. After the 1953 overthrow of Jagan and the PPP, Lovestone chastised J. M. Campbell of Booker Brothers for creating the inequities and misery in which Communists flourished. In personal letters to Campbell, Lovestone accused the company of having "a nineteenth-century concept of social justice," paying sugar workers a miserly wage. Campbell responded by claiming that Booker Brothers made little money because of the expenses of reclaiming British Guiana's land from the sea. He further reminded Lovestone that the company opposed the PPP. Lovestone concluded the exchange by affirming the anticommunist, progressive faith of the U.S. trade union movement. The "first duty" was "to prevent the Communists from grabbing British Guiana." Defeating the PPP was "the first prerequisite before we can even attempt any sound progressive basic social reforms and full national freedom for the people of British Guiana."[24]

Lovestone kept himself informed about the colony by sending Robert Alexander in 1954 and 1956 to interview the colony's politicians and union leaders. Alexander found that the Manpower Citizen's Association was disorganized and "unwilling or unable to take a militant position with regard to the victimization of the workers." Its past leaders had allegedly accepted bribes from Booker Brothers. Alexander recommended that Romualdi and his inter-American labor organization, ORIT, provide the sugar worker's union with money and anticommunist material. Booker Brothers now seemed ready to cooperate with the Manpower Association in order to counter the appeal of the PPP. Alexander further advised Lovestone that U.S. unions should work with Forbes Burnham. Alexander labeled Burnham an impressive figure who was a nationalist with socialistic leanings. Burnham assured Alexander that he would never reconcile with Cheddi Jagan. Like officials in the Colonial Office and State Department, Alexander also found that Janet Jagan was the most dangerous person in the colony. Based on interviews with Richard Ishmael and his wife, Alexander recounted that Janet Jagan "dominated" her husband and transformed him into a Communist. Moreover, she "used her sex effectively for political purposes," making herself attractive to Guyanese men. Richard Ishmael opined that Janet Jagan consciously used her fair complexion to attract Guyanese males of dark-colored skin.[25]

Lovestone and Romualdi carried out Alexander's recommendations. In the post-1953 period, the AFL-CIO developed a working relationship with labor groups in British Guiana, supplying them with equipment such as loud speakers and printing presses. The AFL-CIO's international affiliates, like ORIT and the International Confederation of Free Trade Unions, began to make cash contributions of up to $1,000 to British Guiana's unions. The U.S. union also brought Ishmael and Rupert Tello to the United States to meet with affiliates like the United Steelworkers. Romualdi worked with representatives of the British Trade Union Council to strengthen anti-PPP groups. The inter-American representative of the AFL-CIO, Harry Pollak, toured British Guiana and called on international labor groups to save British Guiana from the "Stalinist Jagan." The AFL-CIO would also decide to back Forbes Burnham. U.S. labor leaders never wavered from the conviction, as expressed by Romualdi, that "the Jagans and others of their collaborators are confirmed, 100 percent Communists who have never deviated one iota from the Stalinist line, either in their writings or their utterances."[26] Such fervor infused the AFL-CIO's war against Jagan in the early 1960s.

PRIOR TO THE LATE 1950S, the United States was content to lend it support and approval to the United Kingdom's efforts to control its troublesome South American colony. London apparently shared Washington's view of the dangers of communism. The CIA had carried out a covert intervention in Guatemala, and the British had reoccupied British Guiana. In both cases, the Western powers had overthrown popularly elected governments that they considered in sympathy with the international Communist movement. The two allies would develop sharply contrasting views on British Guiana, however, in the aftermath of two critical international events—the Suez Crisis of 1956 and the Cuban Revolution of 1959. The United States would come to believe that the United Kingdom no longer sufficiently appreciated the dangers of communism in the Western Hemisphere.

Students of the British Empire believe that the rash attempt by Prime Minister Anthony Eden's government in the fall of 1956 to restore British control over the Suez Canal marked a turning point in British imperial history. The British military strike on Gamal Abdul Nasser's Egypt outraged nationalists throughout Asia, Africa, and the Middle East and infuriated President Eisenhower. The United Kingdom, which acted in concert with France and Israel, had foolishly directed the world's attention away from the reprehensible invasion of Hungary by the Soviet Union in October 1956. Eisenhower publicly denounced the attack on Egypt, introduced a resolution in the United Nations demanding withdrawal, refused oil shipments to the British, and declined to intercede on international financial markets to support the price of the collapsing British currency. In the face of this diplomatic pressure, Eden was forced to abandon his imperial venture. The prime minister's colossal diplomatic blunder had achieved the impossible; it had created a tacit alliance between the United States and the Soviet Union over Suez. Eden had also exposed the military and economic weakness of his country. The colonial subjects in Asia, Africa, the Caribbean, and South America took note of those facts.

The Suez debacle hastened Prime Minister Eden's decision to step down as prime minister. The Conservatives replaced Eden with Harold Macmillan (1957–63). Prime Minister Macmillan proved notably successful in reorienting his nation's domestic, international, and imperial policies. Having served as Chancellor of the Exchequer in Eden's government, Macmillan concluded that the United Kingdom could no longer afford its colonies. His country's rate of domestic economic growth had fallen behind other Western European nations. The country needed money to modernize its nuclear forces. Macmillan further believed that his country must maintain close relations with the United States. The Anglo-American rapprochement, which had emerged out of the Venezuelan-British Guiana Boundary Crisis of 1895, had served the British well throughout the first half of the twentieth century. The prime minister developed good relationships with President Eisenhower and especially with President John Kennedy. As Macmillan and his advisers saw it, decolonization would strengthen the kingdom both at home and abroad. Macmillan moved boldly after October 1959, when he scored a resounding electoral triumph. He put in the Colonial Office advisers, like Iain N. MacLeod and Reginald Maulding, who shared his goal of dismantling the empire. He also garnered international praise when he delivered in February 1960 his "Winds of Change" speech to the South African Parliament. He pointed to the growth of political consciousness among Africa's repressed people and rejected "the idea of any inherent superiority of one race over another." Macmillan did not fully embrace the cause of freedom and independence, wanting always to maintain control of the process. In December 1960, he instructed his delegation at the United Nations to abstain on a resolution that called for the "necessity of bringing to a speedy and unconditional end . . . to colonialism in all its forms and manifestations." Nonetheless, during Macmillan's tenure, key colonial possessions—Ghana (1957), Malaya (1957), Nigeria (1960), and Kenya (1963)—secured their independence.[27]

In the aftermath of the Suez Crisis, the Macmillan government began to test new policies in British Guiana. To be sure, even as the British were attacking Egypt, colonial officers were reassessing past approaches. By the end of 1956, they were privately admitting they had failed to tame the colony. With inadequate imperial funding, progress on roads, land, housing, and local government was judged unsatisfactory. The Jagans and the PPP retained a loyal following. Governor Renison persistently told the Colonial Office that the political restrictions on the Jagans had to be lifted. Renison argued that Guyanese who opposed the PPP needed to learn to face and counter the party in open political debate. In February 1957, the Colonial Office authorized the governor to lift the restrictions on the Jagans and simultaneously to announce a "partial return to elected government."[28] The British would permit a legislative election in August 1957, with the governor having a strong veto power and the power to appoint members to the legislature and the executive council. Colonial Secretary Alan Lennox-Boyd also mandated a monthly intelligence report on the Jagans and the PPP.[29] The Colonial Office further made the "distasteful" decision to permit Cheddi Jagan to attend Ghana's independence ceremony. Kwame Nkrumah, the first prime minister of Ghana, had shocked the Colonial Office by inviting both Jagan and Forbes Burnham to the ceremony and offering to pay for the trip.[30] Nkrumah's invitation pointed to the growing international concern about the military occupation of British Guiana.

As Guyanese politicians campaigned for the August 1957 election, the new British government tried to prepare the United States for change. Anglo-American lines of communication had improved, because the State Department reopened its consulate in Georgetown in early 1957. Governor Renison informed Consul John Cope that the Conservative Party now recognized that the 1953 intervention had been a mistake. The PPP remained popular. The government had conferred the status of martyrdom on the Jagans. The governor theorized that the colonial subjects needed more time to learn that the PPP would inevitably disrupt the colony's political and economic life. Renison noted that Forbes Burnham had been told that his past errors had been forgiven and that he had been encouraged to maintain his break with Jagan. He added, however, that the Colonial Office had not forgotten about Burnham's shortcomings.[31] Just prior to the elections, Renison journeyed to London for two months of consultation with his superiors. Before returning to Georgetown, he stopped in Washington in late July 1957 to brief State Department officers in the Division of European Affairs. Renison stunned the State Department with his news. Washington operated on the premise that the Jagans were "openly Communist." Renison now declared that members of the PPP were not Communists and left the question of the Jagans' political allegiance open. He implied that the PPP would win the election because of its political skills, with Janet Jagan being the party's "organizational wheel horse." Renison promised to balance the power of Cheddi Jagan and the PPP in a new government but was uncertain how he would do it. He predicted that Jagan "would be either tamed or hung" by the responsibility of power. Economic development would be the best way to combat "Jagan and/or Communist influence" and suggested that the United States should assist the colony. State Department officers gave no response to Renison's presentation.[32]

The extent of Cheddi Jagan's victory in the mid-August 1957 elections surprised the governor. Both Jagan and Burnham sponsored a slate of candidates under the PPP label. While in Ghana, Jagan had unsuccessfully tried to convince Burnham to reunite the party. Jagan's wing of the PPP won nine of the fourteen seats available in the new legislature. Governor Renison had sharply reduced the number of legislators from the twenty-four permitted in the 1953 constitution. Burnham's wing of the PPP won only three seats. After this poor showing, Burnham announced his new party, the PNC. Governor Renison invited five members of Jagan's PPP, including Cheddi and Janet Jagan, to join his executive council. Cheddi Jagan became the chief minister. Governor Renison demonstrated good faith, declining to stack the legislature and the council with his appointees. The governor informed London that negotiations for the new government had been productive and that "Jagan was throughout entirely reasonable and friendly and gave a great impression of sincerity in desiring to take the responsibility of government, avoid crises, and to show to British Guiana and the world that he is not the ogre that some think him to be." Indeed, Jagan had given "statesmanlike" public statements.[33]

Over the next three years, the Macmillan government found Cheddi Jagan's leadership satisfactory. PPP ministers focused on improving the living and working conditions of the population. They sponsored drainage and irrigation schemes, built houses for sugar workers, extended workmen's compensation laws, and mandated paid annual vacations for workers. As the Colonial Office saw it, the resumption of limited self-rule was a "testing time" for the colony. "Only by providing an opportunity for political life" would there be "a chance of reasonable political leadership emerging." If the PPP proved unreliable, the governor could call on a "beefed up" police force of 1,500, the Special Branch intelligence unit, and a company of United Kingdom troops. The Colonial Office understood, however, that racial relations now constituted the key issue for British Guiana. The continued division between Jagan and Burnham would likely stimulate racial animosity in the colony.[34]

The Eisenhower administration did not share the Macmillan government's optimism about British Guiana. As it went forward with its new policy, the prime minister had instructed the Colonial Office to keep Washington "in close touch with what is going on." As Macmillan wrote in a personal minute, the United States had been "quite good when the last troubles occurred and if it should be necessary for the Governor to suspend the Constitution again we shall certainly need their help in keeping the other Latin Americans quiet."[35] The Eisenhower administration did not want, however, to hear that the PPP had another substantial electoral victory and that Cheddi and Janet Jagan were ministers in the new government. Immediately after the election, the State Department summoned Ambassador Sir Harold A. Caccia to hear of "our deep concern over a Communist victory." The administration wondered why the $1 million in technical assistance that the United States had provided had not counteracted Communist influence. Speaking for the administration, Deputy Under Secretary of State Robert D. Murphy pointed out to Caccia that "with its vital hemispheric and Caribbean interests the United States could not ignore what had happened in British Guiana." Murphy added that "he felt certain that Communists would build up Jagan" and turn British Guiana into a base for the expansion of international communism.[36] Such doomsday predictions led one historian to conclude that they "reflected the ideologically driven perceptions of American policymakers" and their "uninformed appreciation of the nuances of politics in British Guiana."[37]

The State Department went beyond expressing its Cold War fears to the British. Acting Secretary of State Christian Herter ordered diplomatic officers stationed in Georgetown and London to report on the United Kingdom's concrete plans to cope with the Communist threat. Murphy had also suggested to Ambassador Caccia that British Guiana could not be viewed as an internal matter of the British Empire. Murphy called on the British to consider joint measures "we can take to improve the political situation in British Guiana."[38] British intelligence services began to send reports about the colony to the United States. CIA agents may also have begun to operate in British Guiana. The State Department decided to maintain its small technical assistance programs and to open a U.S. Information Services office in Georgetown. U.S. officials further began to develop ties with Forbes Burnham. State Department officers noted that Burnham openly pleaded for financial assistance for his new political party. They also met with Adam Clayton Powell Jr. of New York, an African American member of the House of Representatives, who had become Burnham's patron in the United States.[39]

To their surprise, U.S. officials found themselves negotiating with Cheddi Jagan. British Guiana needed to develop a viable economy to sustain its independence. Because the colony did not produce enough goods and services to generate income for development, the process of diversifying the plantation-based economy would require foreign aid and direct private investments for a sustained period. Although British Guiana's economy was growing in the late 1950s, it was barely keeping pace with the annual population growth of 3.2 percent. Unemployment and underemployment remained over 25 percent. British Guiana also had poor health conditions, with its infant mortality rate approaching an appalling 7 percent. If he could attract outside funds and spur economic development, Cheddi Jagan calculated that he could build a solid political future for the PPP.[40]

Sponsored by Governor Renison, Jagan journeyed to London in 1958 seeking money. He proposed that the British pledge approximately $120 million to a five-year development plan. As it had in the mid-1950s, the Colonial Office rejected the development request, noting it might find funds for about half of the request. The Colonial Office took the unusual step of introducing Jagan to Japanese and West German diplomats stationed in London, suggesting nations wealthier than the United Kingdom might help. It also pointed him toward Washington, where he went in August 1959. Jagan submitted requests for development assistance that amounted to $34 million. In particular, Jagan wanted money to finance a ten-year road building program that would tie mineral, agricultural, and coastal areas together.[41]

As it reviewed Jagan's request, officials in Washington received advice from several sources about British Guiana and its chief minister. British officials assured the State Department that Jagan was a new man, "becoming less aggressive, more moderate, and mature in presenting his arguments." The Special Branch found no cause for alarm, although it once noted that PPP members had several "Communist and left-wing contacts," including Carey McWilliams, the editor of the U.S. news and opinion weekly, the *Nation*. The Special Branch's monitoring of the mails turned up that Janet Jagan and the PPP received several pieces of Communist literature from Czechoslovakia and the United Kingdom.[42] Also available in Washington was Senator George Aiken's 1958 report on his study tour of the Caribbean for the Senate Committee on Foreign Relations. The Vermont Republican, known for his independent streak and forthright manner, condemned British rule in British Guiana and highlighted the colony's dismal living conditions.

Aiken left little doubt that the British should leave immediately and that the United States should help an independent nation with economic development assistance.[43]

Jagan's loan application also received the endorsement of the new U.S. consul in Georgetown, Carroll H. Woods. Woods belittled the idea that British Guiana was ripe for Communist takeover. The PPP was not a Communist party, although a few members of the inner circle were "card-carrying Communists." Cheddi Jagan was attracted to communism for idealistic reasons. In any case, no PPP member had a direct link to Moscow. The PPP was financially dependent on Indian merchants and small landowners who were anticommunist. The colony also had a strong opposition press, a civil service, and a second political party, the PNC. "In this milieu," Woods reasoned, "it is difficult to visualize a handful of leaders having appreciable success in exploiting the country for Communist ends." Woods also observed that conservative sectors of British Guiana had concluded that the PPP was honest and tried to govern efficiently. Booker Brothers now cooperated with the PPP. On the other hand, businessmen had doubts about Burnham and the PNC. In Woods's judgment, a U.S. loan would represent "an inexpensive insurance policy against communism" and would have a "psychological impact" by encouraging private investors. The United States should take up the Colonial Office's policy of tying British Guiana to the West. Woods conceded a loan would boost the PPP but that this was preferable to allowing economic stagnation and "waiting for radicalism to proliferate."[44]

U.S. officials neither accepted nor rejected these recommendations. The State Department did not formally invite Jagan to Washington, although it listened politely to his overtures when he showed up in the capital. Economic aid officers suggested they would give "sympathetic" consideration to a "reasonable" loan. They rejected the idea of $34 million without actually saying so, finding inadequate preparation and technical faults with British Guiana's loan application. By the end of 1959, officials in the U.S. Development Loan Fund were speaking favorably of a $3.5 million package for an irrigation project, although they did not receive authorization from the Eisenhower administration to make a commitment.[45] From 1957 to 1959, the State Department took a self-described "wait and see" attitude toward Jagan and the PPP. In a special U.S. National Intelligence Estimate, the intelligence community deemed British Guiana's political future as "uncertain." U.S. officials did not yet perceive British Guiana as a critical Cold War battleground.

Between 1957 and 1960, President Eisenhower met with Prime Minister Macmillan four times to discuss global issues. The issue of the future of British Guiana did not appear on the Anglo-American agenda.[46]

In his campaign to raise money for British Guiana, Cheddi Jagan tried a ploy that highlighted the sharply different perceptions that he and U.S. officials had about the proper role of small South American nations. Frustrated by Western parsimony, Jagan openly spoke about being forced to ask the Soviet Union for a loan. Jagan knew, of course, that neutral nations like Egypt and India had received money from both capitalist and Communist sides during the Cold War. Consul Woods quickly dismissed Jagan's talk as a "bluff" and "leverage for accelerating or increasing the Western ante."[47] Jagan wanted U.S. and British private and public money, and he understood the Colonial Office would never sanction a loan from the Soviet Union. But Jagan's gambit perhaps also revealed how he viewed British Guiana's place in the international system. Colonial officers reported that Jagan, after returning from India in 1954, often referred to "the Indian system."[48] By his own definition, his trip had been unsuccessful. India had not denounced the suspension of the 1953 constitution, and Jagan thought that he embarrassed himself there, because he could not speak Hindi or Urdu or identify the village of his forebears.[49] Nonetheless, Jagan saw that the United States abided an India that preached the virtues of national planning, built a mixed economy, conducted warm relations with the Soviet Union, and regularly criticized the United States. India had also sponsored the 1955 Asian-African Conference at Bandung, Indonesia, where the twenty-nine nations participating declared their nonaligned status in the East-West confrontation. Jagan often seemed surprised when the United States reacted negatively to actions that he took that they tolerated from an Indian leader. Jagan similarly seemed dumbfounded that U.S. officials could not appreciate the communist ideal he admired in the kibbutz system of Israel, a U.S. ally. Jagan did not always grasp that the United States put British Guiana, its ethnic composition notwithstanding, within the concept of the U.S. sphere of influence in Latin America. The United States opposed Latin American nations having diplomatic or economic relationships with the Soviet Union. During the early Cold War, only larger nations like Mexico tried to resist that extreme pressure.

Chief Minister Jagan's talk of a flirtation with the Soviet Union did not dissuade the Macmillan government from pushing forward with political liberalization in British Guiana. In late 1959, the Colonial Office sent Governor Renison to Kenya and replaced him with Sir Ralph Grey, a New Zealander and an experienced colonial officer who had served in Nigeria. In a 1956 radio address, Renison had denounced Jagan as a Communist who would attempt to install one-party rule. By the end of the decade, colonial officials perceived Jagan and the PPP as responsible political actors.[50] As the new colonial secretary, Iain Macleod, explained to Macmillan, the PPP had learned the lessons of 1953 and that "there has been for some time a feeling that British Guiana has largely purged its offence."[51] Such assessments proceeded on the debatable proposition that the PPP had pursued a radical, undemocratic agenda in 1953. Perhaps Macleod could have added that the nostalgic imperialists—Churchill, Eden, Lyttleton—no longer judged the political culture of British Guiana.

In March 1960, Colonial Secretary Macleod presided over a constitutional convention in London to determine British Guiana's future. Both Forbes Burnham and Cheddi Jagan attended. After three weeks of wrangling, Macleod ruled that British Guiana would have new elections in 1961. He divided the country into thirty-five single-member districts for election to the Legislative Assembly. The leader of the victorious party would form a government, become prime minister in a cabinet system, and have authority over the colony's internal affairs. The governor would retain control over defense and foreign affairs. All parties understood that the new government would bring British Guiana to independence, although Macleod declined to set a specific date. Macleod handed Jagan and the PPP a big victory by rejecting Burnham's bid to have the election based on proportional representation. Victory in a legislative district would be based on the traditional "first across the post" British electoral system. If voting broke down on racial lines, the PPP had a bright future. Indo-Guyanese, with their high birth rates, constituted almost 50 percent of the population at the end of 1959, although many had not reached voting age. Jagan unsuccessfully lobbied Macleod to lower the voting age from twenty-one to eighteen. Patterns of residency also favored the PPP, which could count on being competitive in most districts. Afro-Guyanese, who made up 34 percent of the population, were concentrated in urban districts, whereas Indians lived throughout the coastal plain.[52] The Colonial Office emerged from the constitutional conference with new respect for Jagan. It told the U.S. embassy in London that it found Jagan to be "genuine" and that it mistrusted Burnham and disliked his negotiating tactics.[53]

The Eisenhower administration theoretically should have been pleased with the outcome of the London conference. The devolution of colonial authority in British Guiana seemed to flow directly from Macmillan's memorable "Winds of Change" address in February 1960. Indeed, President Eisenhower had congratulated the prime minister, noting that he had been impressed by "your masterful address in Cape Town and your analysis of the forces of nationalism in Africa."[54] Throughout the latter part of the 1950s, the administration's leading figures again took up the anticolonial theme. In 1957, Secretary of State John Foster Dulles complained to the German ambassador that "the colonial powers tend to move slowly, in fact too slowly." At an NSC meeting in August 1959, President Eisenhower doubted that the United States could fully back France while it continued to wage war against Algerian nationalists. The president viewed U.S. history as "anti-colonial, and the French action in Algeria is interpreted by the rest of the world as militant colonialism." Eisenhower declared to his advisers that he United States had to pursue its own interests and not back Charles de Gaulle on Algeria, "because we are the most powerful country in the world, we are already considered a supporter of colonialism, and we had great difficulty disabusing countries like India of this impression." A year later, in a discussion with the U.S. ambassador to Portugal, Eisenhower recalled the advice he had given to Winston Churchill to set a firm date for colonial independence. The idea had "jolted" Churchill, but the United Kingdom would have made friends among colonized people if Churchill had accepted the president's advice. Portugal needed to learn from history, the president insisted, and set a date for the independence of its African colonies.[55]

However passionate President Eisenhower may have been on the issue of colonialism, neither he nor his chief advisers had resolved the dilemma of radical nationalism. Winston Churchill's wicked taunt still held: anticommunism trumped anticolonialism. And in the political discourse of the United States, the term "communism" was broadly and imprecisely defined. Against the advice of the African and Asian bureaus of the State Department, Eisenhower had, for example, acceded to Prime Minister Macmillan's request and ordered the United States to abstain on the December 1960 U.N. resolution calling for a speedy end to colonialism. The resolution passed by a vote of 89–0, with nine abstentions including those of the United States and the United Kingdom. Macmillan had assured Eisenhower that "we are making a tremendous effort by our colonial policy to get peaceful development in Africa and to keep communism out."[56] In its policy statements on colonial areas including the British West Indies, the Eisenhower administration called for "orderly progress toward independence."[57] In the context of the Cold War that meant that the United States demanded that anticommunist leaders guide nationalist movements.

CHEDDI JAGAN UNSETTLED U.S. policymakers not only because of his suspect political ideologies but also because he, his wife, and his political party became identified with the Cuban Revolution. For more than four decades, the United States has been obsessed with Fidel Castro's Cuba. Castro and his band of bearded guerrillas rode on tanks into Havana in the first days of 1959. Their triumphant entry into the capital city marked the culmination of Castro's six-year struggle against dictator Fulgencio Batista. The Cuban strongman had dominated national life since 1934 and had directly ruled since 1952. Castro and his youthful followers opposed Batista's tyrannical rule. They also envisioned a socially just, progressive Cuba that addressed the nation's problems of poverty and deep social and racial inequities. Like other educated Cubans, Castro held ambivalent views about the United States. He appreciated the wealth and technological prowess of the United States and admired its heroes, such as Abraham Lincoln. He also enjoyed U.S. popular culture, playing baseball and rooting for major league teams. But Cubans deeply resented the role that the United States had played in Cuba's history and political and economic life. After assisting Cuba's struggle for independence in the War of 1898, the United States attached the Platt Amendment (1903–34) to the Cuban constitution, giving the United States the right to oversee Cuba's internal affairs. U.S. military forces repeatedly invaded the island. With their money guaranteed by the bayonets of U.S. marines, U.S. investors came to dominate Cuba's economic life. With approximately $900 million invested in Cuba by 1959, U.S. investors accounted for 40 percent of the country's critical sugar production. U.S. companies also controlled public utilities, oil refineries, mines, railroads, and the tourist industry. Cubans took further offense that U.S. tourists considered Havana their playground for gambling, narcotics, and prostitution. Cubans also could not forget that the Eisenhower administration fawned over Batista and armed him with U.S. weapons, because the dictator protected foreign investments, voted with Washington at the United Nations, and professed to be anticommunist. In fact, the unscrupulous Batista quietly worked with the Cuban Communist Party.

Reforming Cuban society inevitably meant altering the U.S. presence in Cuba. Like many Cubans, Fidel Castro blamed the United States for Cuba's backwardness and international insignificance. His agrarian reform law, which was promulgated in April 1959, set the tone for U.S.-Cuban relations. The law expropriated farmlands of over 1,000 acres, with compensation to be paid in Cuban bonds and based on the land's declared value for taxes in 1958. Sugar barons, both foreign and domestic, had predictably undervalued their land in Batista's Cuba. The new law, which was to be administered by a Cuban Communist, Antonio Núñez Jiménez, also prohibited foreigners from owning agricultural land. Sympathetic observers judged agrarian reform as a legitimate effort to address the crushing poverty and injustice that characterized the Cuban countryside. But from Washington's perspective, the Agrarian Reform Law of 1959 smacked both of anti-Americanism and communism.

Fidel Castro only progressively moved toward communism. On 1 December 1961, he publicly declared, "I am a Marxist-Leninist, and I will continue to be a Marxist-Leninist until the last day of my life." Most historians do not believe that Castro was a Communist in the 1950s, although his compatriots included his brother Raúl Castro and the Argentine, Ernesto "Ché" Guevara, both committed radicals. The Cuban Communist Party did not initially embrace Castro's anti-Batista movement; the party only began to support Castro fervently after he took power. Castro gradually concluded that communism provided answers to Cuba's problems and that the Communist concept of the "dictatorship of the proletariat" would enhance his drive for personal domination of Cuba. As Castro reaped the animosity of the United States, he predictably turned to the Soviet Union. In February 1960, Castro hosted a Soviet trade fair in Cuba and signed a commercial agreement. The Soviets agreed to purchase one million tons of Cuban sugar over the next five years and to provide the Cubans with a $100 million credit to purchase Soviet equipment.

By the end of 1959, U.S. officials spoke of overthrowing Castro. The CIA official responsible for the Western Hemisphere, Colonel J. C. King, suggestively recommended that "thorough consideration be given to the elimination of Fidel Castro." On 17 March 1960, President Eisenhower gave formal approval to a "program of covert action against the Castro regime." The plan included launching a propaganda offensive, creating anti-Castro forces within Cuba, and training a paramilitary force outside of Cuba for future action. Through the rest of 1960, the administration attacked Cuba. The CIA broadcast anti-Castro diatribes from a radio station on Swan Island, a dot of land off the coast of Honduras. The administration tried to strangle the Cuban economy, cutting off sugar imports and banning U.S. exports to the island. The CIA began to train Cuba exiles in Guatemala with the mission of carrying out an amphibious invasion of Cuba. The CIA also contacted the criminal underworld of the United States, the "Mafia," urging organized criminals to carry out a "gangland-style killing" of Castro and his chief associates. The CIA reasoned that the Mafia resented Castro for having driven gambling interests out of Havana. On 3 January 1961, Eisenhower broke diplomatic relations with Cuba.[58]

Cheddi and Janet Jagan walked right into the middle of the U.S. war against Fidel Castro. They would become casualties of the conflict. In April 1960, shortly after the successful constitutional conference in London, the Jagans traveled to Havana to observe the Cuban Revolution, meet with Cuban leaders, and discuss economic ties. Cuban officials in London arranged the trip. Neither the Colonial Office nor the Foreign Office tried to stop the trip, although they judged it a "foolish" venture.[59] While in Havana, Jagan publicly praised the Cuban Revolution and recalled that the U.S. interventions in Iran and Guatemala "were preceded by an anti-Communist campaign seeking to represent the Governments of the countries as pro-Communist." Jagan predicted that the "imperialists" would try to do to Cuba what they had done to British Guiana in 1953. Apart from his public performance, Jagan met with Castro and with Ché Guevara at the Cuban National Bank. Jagan emerged from the talks with tangible results. Castro offered to lend British Guiana $5 million for hydroelectric projects. Jagan also laid the foundation for a Cuban agreement to purchase in cash substantial quantities of British Guiana's surplus rice production. The leaders further discussed cultural and student exchanges. Jagan left Cuba after a few days, although Janet Jagan stayed in Cuba for a longer period.[60]

Multiple interpretations can be offered about the journey to Havana by the Jagans. For U.S. officials, the trip confirmed their worst fears about the couple. They immediately concluded that any Cuban money that went to British Guiana originated in the Soviet Union. Using Cuba as its agent, the Soviet Union planned a new offensive in the Western Hemisphere. The State Department ordered its embassies in London, Moscow, Havana, and Georgetown to be on the alert. Janet Jagan stayed in Cuba because she was a "hard core" Communist and was probably "moving in Communist circles in Cuba for the purpose of obtaining support for Communist activity in British Guiana."[61] The United States accordingly asserted its hegemony. In September 1960, Secretary of State Christian Herter instructed the London embassy to inform the Colonial Office that "we presume the Cuban loan will delay British Guiana's independence." The United States felt certain that "Her Majesty's Government would be loath to leave the colony to the mercies of a Jagan-dominated policy and Communist-assisted economy." The United States and the United Kingdom should not give in to Jagan's "blackmail tactics" of playing the West off against the Communist bloc. Herter warned that "weakness at this stage" would only make the United Kingdom's tenure in British Guiana more difficult in the future.[62]

The Jagans undoubtedly admired the Cuban Revolution and saw themselves on the cutting edge in the global struggle against imperialism and international capitalism. But Western observers in London, Georgetown, and Havana offered more nuanced interpretations of British Guiana's relationship with Castro's Cuba than those born in Washington. Cheddi Jagan lived in the British Empire. In 1959–60, British diplomats in Havana did not depict Cuba as the command post for Communist subversion.[63] Despite vehement U.S. protests, the United Kingdom preserved its diplomatic and commercial ties with Cuba. Prime Minister Macmillan dismissed U.S. trade sanctions against Cuba as "ridiculous in itself," pointing out that Communist countries would learn to produce what the West denied them. With international trade accounting for 40 percent of its gross national product, the United Kingdom, wanted to expand its commercial ties with Communist countries.[64] Jagan's rice deal with the Cubans made economic sense for the colony and was politically advantageous to Jagan and the PPP. The rice producers were small landowners of Indian background who were thought to be "bourgeois" in their attitudes. Nonetheless, they would be naturally grateful to the PPP, if Jagan found new markets for their rice.[65] Jagan also extended his search for help beyond Cuba. In September 1960, he was in Caracas asking neighboring Venezuela, which was led by President Rómulo Betancourt, a stout anticommunist, to help develop British Guiana's timber industry and to contribute to the hydroelectric project to facilitate the colony's capacity to smelt its bauxite. Jagan further inquired about a deal for rice. He told the Venezuelans that he expected that the Colonial Office would not let him accept the Cuban loan, but he hoped that it would stimulate London to be more generous with its aid.[66] As to the issue of whether a Cuban loan would discourage U.S. support, the Colonial Office pointed out that Jagan would be unimpressed with the argument, because the United States had not aided British Guiana.[67] The new U.S. consul in Georgetown, Everett K. Melby, seconded the Colonial Office's reasoning and rejected the "blackmail" argument raised by Secretary Herter. British Guiana desperately needed capital and the United States would reap favorable publicity if it built roads and hospitals in the colony.[68] Although he hardly drew on a sophisticated line of reasoning, Governor Ralph Grey weighed in with his analysis of the Jagans and Cuba. He discounted speculation that Janet Jagan was plotting in Havana, suggesting instead that her "most vivid" impression of Cuba was "those splendid, virile young men with their flashing eyes and curling beards."[69]

Neither complex nor frivolous arguments about British Guiana swayed the Eisenhower administration during its last days in office. It initiated the campaign that accelerated during the Kennedy and Johnson presidencies to deny power to Cheddi Jagan and the PPP. The administration began to interfere directly in the colony's politics, covertly supporting anti-PPP groups. In August 1960, U.S. officials heard of a Catholic group, "Defenders of Freedom," linked to conservative businessmen led by Peter D'Aguiar. D'Aguiar, who was of Portuguese origin, sold soft drinks and brewed British Guiana's most popular beer, "Banks." The Defenders of Freedom was reportedly affiliated with an anticommunist group in Connecticut, "Americans Safeguarding Freedom." State Department officials immediately decided they would cultivate D'Aguiar and his supporters. They met in Washington with their representatives and promised to have the U.S. Information Agency, without attribution, provide them with anticommunist material.[70] D'Aguiar's friends asked for money. U.S officials did not respond directly to such requests but observed support could be obtained from Christian churches, especially the Roman Catholic Church, in the United States and from the Cuban exile community.[71] The CIA had previously worked with the Roman Catholic hierarchy in the United States and Guatemala in the 1954 destabilization campaign against the Arbenz government. The agency was also in the process of building a close relationship with anti-Castro Cubans.[72] In early January 1961, the State Department also hosted an associate of Forbes Burnham, who informed Washington that he would be seeking funds in the United States to help the PNC. U.S. officials did not ask Burnham's friend to comment on Consul Melby's earlier report that "Burnham is believed by some to be both anti-East Indian and antiwhite."[73] Cold War imperatives were about to overwhelm long-standing U.S. commitments to national self-determination, democracy, and racial justice.

AS PRESIDENT-ELECT John F. Kennedy prepared to take office on 20 January 1961, the United States and the United Kingdom were headed for a clash over the small, weak colony of British Guiana. The two Western powers had drawn different historical lessons from watershed events of the 1950s. To U.S. officials, the Cuban Revolution meant that communism was a clear and present danger in the Western Hemisphere. The region had become, in Kennedy's words, "the most dangerous area in the world."[74] British Guiana could not be permitted to endanger the United States. British officials believed, however, that the Suez Crisis had taught them to abandon atavistic imperial practices and that the United Kingdom's national security would be enhanced by quickly shedding its colonial possessions. From the British perspective, neither time nor money would be well spent holding on to a bothersome possession in South America that weighed little in the international balance of power.

CHAPTER THREE

COVERT INTERVENTION, 1961–1962

Iain N. MacLeod, who served as secretary of state for colonies in Prime Minister Harold Macmillan's cabinet, recounted an exchange that he had with President John F. Kennedy in the White House. "Mr. President," Macleod queried, "do I understand that you want us to go as quickly as possible toward independence everywhere else all over the world but not on your doorstep in British Guiana?" According to Macleod, Kennedy laughed and then responded, "Well, that's probably just about it."[1] The ironic banter between the two officials masked the grave consequences that portended for the small British colony in South America. In the name of anticommunism, the Kennedy administration took extraordinary measures to deny the people of British Guiana to right to national self-determination. U.S officials and private citizens incited murder, arson, bombings, and fear and loathing in British Guiana. Indeed, the covert U.S. intervention ignited racial warfare between blacks and Indians. By the end of 1962, the United States had forced the United Kingdom to accede to U.S. demands to find a way to deny power to Cheddi Jagan and the People's Progressive Party.

THE YEAR 1961 WOULD BE the last tranquil year that Guyanese would enjoy for more than three decades. The year would be characterized by peace, relative prosperity, free elections, and hope that British Guiana would soon win its independence. U.S. consular officials in Georgetown characterized 1961 as the "most prosperous year in British Guiana's history." Export sales of sugar and rice grew by 20 percent during the year. The colony opened its first manganese mine. Per capita income grew to $384. British Guiana remained poor, but its level of economic activity was substantially higher than many of its small Caribbean and Central American neighbors, whose per capita incomes were well below $200. Trade accounted for more than half of economic activity, with British Guiana remaining firmly tied to the West. The colony sold approximately 75 percent of its agricultural products and minerals to the United Kingdom, Canada, and the United States and purchased more than two-thirds of its imports from the same three countries. British Guiana also sold substantial quantities of its surplus rice to Cuba for cash, accounting for about 6 percent of its exports. Canadians in minerals and the British in sugar remained the key private investors in the colony. British Guiana's long-term prospects still depended on attracting outside capital, because the country had to spend extraordinary amounts of money on public works, keeping the coastal plain dry. The population, now about 600,000, continued to grow, especially in the countryside, as rural Indians reaped the benefits of successful campaigns to eradicate malaria. The antimalarial campaign involved the extensive spraying of the pesticide DDT.[2]

Cheddi Jagan interpreted the colony's economic growth as the "crowning achievement" of his rule since 1957. He was everywhere, seeking business and asking for help. At the end of 1960, Jagan was back in Washington looking for loans. The United States continued to review loan applications, maintaining only the small technical assistance program of $300,000 to $500,000 a year. The Colonial Office would not permit Jagan to accept the $5 million loan offer from Fidel Castro's Cuba, although it approved of the rice sales. In mid-1961, Jagan was back in Caracas trying to strike a rice deal. Jagan also contacted East Germany about rice milling equipment. East Germany had earlier offered scholarships for four students to study in Leipzig.

The Colonial Office thought that Guyanese students would find East Germany too different and perhaps too cold for their tastes. Jagan pointed out that he had operated elevators in the United States from midnight to 8:00 A.M. and added that "young men needed to learn to be intrepid."[3] British officials thought Jagan's efforts to obtain aid from the Soviet bloc would hurt British Guiana's image in the United States. On the other hand, as Patricia Hutchinson of the Foreign Office remarked, "there are a number of aid-recipient countries, India for instance, which still manage to obtain substantial American aid in spite of assistance from the Soviet Union."[4]

Jagan and the PPP's chief legislative goal for the first half of 1961 was the separation of church and state in education. As late as the mid-1950s, 269 of the 297 primary schools in the colony were church-affiliated schools. Hindu and Muslim children attended schools administered by Christian clergy. Indian teachers alleged that they were denied promotions. The Jagan government established state authority over fifty-one denominational schools. The measure sparked outbursts, protests, and charges of communism by Roman Catholic and Anglican bishops. Administrators and principals, who were primarily Afro-Guyanese Christians, feared the loss of their positions. Educational reform had the unfortunate effect of intensifying racial tensions in the colony. The Colonial Office did not express alarm, perhaps reasoning that the process of separating church and state began in eighteenth-century Europe.[5]

By 1961, the United Kingdom wanted to cut the imperial ties as quickly as possible. Governor Ralph Grey (1959–64) articulated British positions while richly fulfilling the role of the condescending colonialist. Sir Ralph told U.S. diplomats that his country "has fully accepted the fact that the days when it can run British Guiana are over and it would like to get out of the business of running the country as gracefully and honorably as possible." In Grey's opinion, British Guiana never amounted to much economically and lacked the natural potential to compete in international markets as an independent country. The colony "was hardly a good showpiece for what the 'old imperialism' either had accomplished or was capable of accomplishing." Grey also found the Guyanese wanting, labeling them "children" in dispatches to the Colonial Office. Governor Renison's expectation that the colonial subjects would mature with political responsibility had not come to pass. Grey judged "there has been time enough for the children to realize the increasing measure of responsibility they now have for their own destiny." Unless they came "to grips with their own destiny," the Guyanese would not be able to sustain their independence.[6] Some officials in London shared Grey's patronizing views. Commonwealth Secretary Duncan Sandys exclaimed to Prime Minister Macmillan that "the sooner we get these people out of our hair the better."[7]

Although Governor Grey constantly ridiculed the colonial subjects, he did not consider them an international menace. Grey never hesitated to tell London or Washington that Cheddi Jagan was not part of an international Communist conspiracy. He depicted Jagan as "a muddle-headed Marxist-Leninist socio-economist who dazes himself with hard work and too much turgid reading and many of his public utterances are arrant nonsense as well as being tediously dull." He conceded Jagan was dedicated to the people of British Guiana. But his favorite word for the PPP leader was "impractical." When he was not speculating on Janet Jagan's marital life and romantic affairs, Grey spoke favorably of her as being, unlike her husband, "intelligent and practical." Grey could not imagine that the Soviet Union would have any interest in the Jagans, the "muddlers" of the PPP, or insignificant British Guiana.[8] In part, Grey based his assessments of the Jagans and the PPP on the intelligence he received from the Special Branch. The Special Branch had thoroughly penetrated the PPP, receiving regular reports from agents. Governor Grey used colorful, often obnoxious language to describe British Guiana's political milieu.[9] But his assessment of the role of communism in colonial life mirrored the judgments of his predecessors, Governors Savage and Renison.

Governor Grey became especially exasperated when U.S. officials spoke of a link between the colony and Castro's Cuba. As he noted to the Colonial Office in early 1961, "I do not get very excited about all the Cuban business but it is perpetually in our local newspapers and the Americans are very hot about it."[10] He investigated alarms sounded by U.S. officials. In February 1962, for example, U.S. Consul Everett Melby relayed intelligence that a Cuban vessel, the *Bahía de Santiago de Cuba*, carrying fifty tons of arms, had docked in Georgetown's harbor. Grey ordered his security personnel to board the vessel. They found secondhand printing machinery on board. The ship left Georgetown after loading the rice that British Guiana's farmers had sold to Cuba. In another case, Cubans allegedly deposited an arms cache on the western coast of Venezuela, more than 1,000 miles from Georgetown.

U.S. officials suggested this Cuban aggression threatened British Guiana. Grey responded, "Do people who send out these reports look at maps?"[11]

However harshly Governor Grey spoke of the Jagans and the PPC, he and his colleagues in the Colonial Office saved their severest criticism for Forbes Burnham and the PNC. They believed they could work with Cheddi Jagan and actually hoped that he would triumph in the August 1961 elections. As Colonial Undersecretary Hugh Fraser observed, Jagan was not a "serpentine" character who hid his intentions "but rather one who is too open and talks too much."[12] By comparison, Burnham engendered a sense of foreboding among colonial officials. Grey dismissed Burnham as a "racist" who masked his radical political aims. The Colonial Office seconded Grey's assessment, labeling Burnham as "irresponsible" and one who acted "like a madman rather than a politician." It saw "Burnham's irresponsible racist agitation" as having the "greatest potential for triggering serious violence during and after the election."[13]

During the campaign that led to the 21 August 1961 elections, Forbes Burnham indeed called on his fellow Afro-Guyanese to vote their racial biases and fears. He warned that Jagan wanted to control the businesses, land, and shops of blacks. He referred to Janet Jagan as "that little lady from Chicago, an alien to our shores." Jagan rejected such base appeals, albeit PPP faithful chanted the Hindi slogan "Apan Jaaht!" or "Vote for your own." A relentless campaigner, the darkly handsome Jagan armed with his flashing smile and wavy hair made his campaign pitch in towns, like New Amsterdam, where blacks resided. He emphasized that progress, not domination by Indians, was the issue for Guyanese. He rejected religious intolerance, declining to associate with religious leaders who called on Hindus "to fight for their religion." The PPP ran a slate that included fourteen Indians and twelve blacks, with eight blacks given safe seats. The PPP's platform called for parliamentary democracy, freedom of religion, safeguards for private capital and investment, economic development, and a mixed economy based on the models of Ghana and India. Beyond his ideas, Jagan probably also impressed Guyanese, especially Indians, with the way he lived his life. As recounted by novelist V. S. Naipaul, who reported on the 1961 campaign, the Jagans lived in an "unpretentious one-floored wooden house standing, in the Guianese way, on tall stilts. Open and unprotected." What distinguished their house was the packed book shelves and magazine rack, which included the *New Yorker*.[14]

As it had in 1953 and 1957, the PPP had another big election win in 1961, capturing 20 of the 35 legislative seats. Burnham's PNC won 11 seats, and Peter D'Aguiar's United Front (UF) won the remaining 4 seats. The UF appealed to affluent Guyanese and Christians angry over school issues. Two of the UF seats were in the interior where Amerindians, who were closely associated with Christian missionaries, lived. The popular vote broke down along racial and ethnic lines and was close. The PPP won 42.6 percent, the PNC won 41 percent, and the UF won 16.3 percent. The PPP could have increased its raw vote total somewhat, if it had vigorously contested all 35 seats. The traditional "first across the post" system of vote counting gave the PPP a clear majority in the legislature. The Colonial Office was satisfied with the election, and Governor Grey asked Jagan to be prime minister and to form a cabinet. Jagan presented a multiracial cabinet that did not include Janet Jagan. The Colonial Office expected that the Jagan government would lead the colony to independence and scheduled an independence conference for May 1962.[15] Forbes Burnham, however, dismissed the electoral results, ominously remarking to U.S. Consul Melby that the "PNC controls Georgetown, civil service, police, trade unions and could shut down the country overnight." The bitter Burnham also warned the PNC faithful that, in the aftermath of the "Indian racial victory," bumptious PPP members were boasting that blacks would be dispatched to the sugar fields "to cut cane and pull punt."[16]

The John F. Kennedy administration tried to prevent Cheddi Jagan and the PPP's August 1961 electoral victory. With the Cold War coming to the Western Hemisphere in the form of the Cuban Revolution, the Kennedy administration would accept only those Western Hemisphere governments that unequivocally denounced communism and assented to U.S. foreign policy positions. As a senator, John Kennedy had garnered international praise for his 1957 speech in which he defended nationalism and denounced French colonialism in Algeria. He also had called for increased economic aid for nonaligned nations like India. As president, he often stated, including to Cheddi Jagan and President João Goulart of Brazil (1961–64), that the United States judged a nation on whether it was politically independent in the international arena, not on whether the United States agreed with its internal political and economic philosophies. He also claimed that he did not object if nations traded with the Soviet bloc, as long as they avoided economic dependence on Communist nations. The president proudly noted that the United States granted foreign aid to Yugoslavia, an independent Communist nation. In reality, however, the president excluded Western Hemisphere nations from this cosmopolitan approach. His administration launched, for example, a destabilization campaign against President Goulart of Brazil because the Brazilian pursued independent domestic and international policies that seemingly had the potential of giving aid and comfort to the Communists.[17]

In the case of British Guiana, the president's actions also belied his rhetoric about respecting nationalism. Kennedy saw Jagan and the PPP through the prism of revolutionary Cuba. The president had, in presidential aide Arthur M. Schlesinger Jr.'s words, an "absolute determination" to prevent another Communist bridgehead in the Western Hemisphere.[18] The president and his closest advisers persuaded themselves that the Jagans were wolves in sheep's clothing who engaged in democratic politics as means to an end. Once free of British colonial rule, they would openly embrace communism and ally with the Soviet Union. The United States would then be confronted with a "second Cuba" on the South American continent. As Attorney General Robert F. Kennedy saw it, what happened in British Guiana might determine the "future of South America." Kennedy conceded that it was a "small country," but Cuba was also small, and "it's caused us a lot of trouble."[19] Other administration officials saw historical parallels between Jagan and Castro. Deputy Under Secretary of State U. Alexis Johnson reminded British officials that "Castro had originally been presented as a reformer." He added, "We do not intend to be taken in twice." Secretary of State Dean Rusk agreed that, in view of "the prospect of Castroism in the Western Hemisphere," the United States was not inclined to give Jagan the same benefit of doubt which was given two or three years ago to Castro himself." President Kennedy also recalled the lessons of history. In a conversation with President Ramón Villeda Morales of Honduras, he observed that "experiences with Jagan, the Chinese, and Castro demonstrate that Communists frequently take over a Government in the guise of enlightened, democratic, revolutionary leaders, and not as Communists per se."[20]

The historical parallels and lessons that the president and his advisers drew on were often lost on intelligence analysts. In March 1961, the intelligence community, led by the CIA, produced its first "Special National Intelligence Estimate" on British Guiana. The analysts surveyed the colony's political scene and predicted that the PPP would likely gain a majority in the upcoming election. They could not predict what would follow. The analysts thought it unlikely that an independent state under Jagan "would proceed forthwith with an effort to establish an avowed Communist regime." They were even uncertain about Jagan's political leanings. Jagan never acknowledged being a Communist, "but his statements and actions over the years bear the marks of the indoctrination and advice the Communists have given him." They referred to the "ineffectual" Forbes Burnham as "a negro and doctrinaire socialist." The intelligence community's most informed guess was that an independent Guyana would align itself at the United Nations "with Afro-Asian neutralism and anti-colonialism." A Jagan government would be nationalistic, sympathetic to Cuba, and ready to establish political and economic ties with the Soviet bloc. Yet, Jagan wanted good relations with the West, because he needed economic aid from the United States and the United Kingdom.[21] However accurate and sophisticated these and subsequent national intelligence estimates were, they made little impression on the Kennedy administration and the successor Lyndon B. Johnson administration. Officials like Secretary Rusk actually took alarm from them, interpreting these cautious, restrained analyses as mandates for U.S. intervention in British Guiana. Cold warriors could not countenance a neutral nation in the traditional U.S. sphere of influence.

Within months of taking office, President Kennedy began plotting against Cheddi Jagan. On 5 April 1961, at a meeting in Washington, Kennedy briefly mentioned to Prime Minister Macmillan that the United States could not accept another Castro in the hemisphere and opposed Jagan leading an independent Guyana. The next day, Secretary Rusk reiterated U.S. concerns to Foreign Secretary Alexander Frederick Douglas (Lord) Home and other British officials. Rusk found the British baffled by the U.S. fear of Jagan. Ambassador Harold Caccia noted that "the Jagans provided the most responsible leadership in the country and they would be difficult to supplant." The British declined suggestions to undermine democratic procedures and refused to give the United States permission to launch a covert operation to prevent a Jagan victory. Instead, the British asked the United States to consider using economic aid as a way of fostering moderate policies in British Guiana.[22] The Kennedy administration essentially ignored the British arguments. On 5 May 1961, shortly after the Bay of Pigs debacle, the president ruled at an NSC meeting that the "Task Force on Cuba would consider what can be done in cooperation with the British to forestall a Communist takeover" in British Guiana. The administration had implicitly tied Cheddi Jagan and British Guiana to Fidel Castro and Cuba. The administration made it U.S. policy "to aim at the downfall of Castro" and would organize thereafter a massive sabotage and terrorism campaign against Cuba code-named "Operation Mongoose." The administration simultaneously ordered the veteran spy, Frank Wisner, who was stationed in London, to organize CIA activities in British Guiana.[23]

As had the Eisenhower administration, the Kennedy administration met with supporters of Burnham and Peter D'Aguiar. D'Aguiar himself met with Adolf A. Berle Jr., who was helping to plan the administration's bold, new economic aid program for Latin America, the Alliance for Progress. D'Aguiar warned that the Jagans would deliver British Guiana "lock, stock, and barrel to the Communist camp."[24] Jagan's opponents asked for U.S. help. State Department officials made no direct commitment but asked the consulate in Georgetown if Jagan's opponents needed financial assistance. The CIA likely passed money to conservative Christian groups, like the U.S.-based World Harvest Evangelism and the Christian Anti-Communist Crusade, who denounced the secularization of British Guiana's schools. Dr. Lloyd Sweet of Miami and the World Harvest Evangelism assured State Department officers that God guided him in his fight against Communists like Jagan. D'Aguiar's party also showed U.S. Information Service films with strong anticommunist and anti-Castro themes on Georgetown street corners.[25] This U.S. effort to shape the colony's public opinion was modest compared to what would follow in British Guiana and in other South American countries. Jagan alleged in his memoirs that the Christian Anti-Communist Crusade spent $45,000 in 1961. In 1962, the CIA spent $5 million supporting anti-Goulart candidates in Brazil, and President Kennedy authorized the CIA to spend over $200,000 to support the Chilean Christian Democrats, the rivals of the Chilean Marxist Salvador Allende.[26]

In early August 1961, the administration made a final effort to prevent Jagan's election. President Kennedy instructed his foreign policy team to concentrate on British Guiana. Secretary Rusk contacted Lord Home and reminded him that the United States judged that "Jagan and his American wife were very far to the left indeed and that his accession to power in British Guiana would be a most troublesome setback in this Hemisphere." Rusk wanted the British to arrange a confused electoral result to lay the basis for a future election by taking some unspecified action in four or five legislative districts. Rusk also consciously tried to instigate a showdown between the Colonial Office and the Foreign Office. The secretary of state understood that the Colonial Office oversaw British Guiana, but he wanted Foreign Secretary Home to consider the "foreign policy ramifications of a Jagan victory."[27] On 18 August 1961, in a "to Dean from Alex" reply, Home defended the principle of democratic electoral procedures and expressed guarded optimism about Cheddi Jagan. He predicted that, if the United States assisted the colony, "we think it by no means impossible that British Guiana may end up in a position not very different from that of India." The foreign secretary also diplomatically pointed to the hypocrisy inherent in the U.S. position on colonialism, noting that it was "true over the wide field of our Colonial responsibilities, we have had to move faster than we would have liked."[28] Rusk was unmoved by this British appeal to both his sense of justice and shame. On 26 August, he deplored the electoral results and called for a new round of Anglo-American discussions on the colony. Rusk reminded his friend Alex that he attached "importance to the covert side" in future courses of action.[29]

If there ever was a possibility of the United States working with Prime Minister Jagan, it occurred in September and October 1961. Colonial officials wished for "an ounce of sympathy" for Jagan, praying that the prime minister would make a good personal impression and win U.S. economic assistance, when he visited Washington and President Kennedy in late October. Governor Grey coached Jagan on how to sell himself to the U.S. public and the president. The governor fretted, however, that Jagan "may well get minced up at question time," when he appeared on the Sunday television news show, *Meet the Press*. Grey further worried that U.S. officials had lost perspective on the colony, equating British Guiana with the Soviet-American confrontation over Berlin.[30] U.S. Consul Everett Melby backed Grey's argument that Jagan desired good relations with the United States. Within the administration, Presidential aide Arthur Schlesinger responded positively to British pleas for understanding of Jagan and peppered the president with memorandums about British Guiana. Schlesinger was part of the liberal, internationalist wing of the Democratic Party led by luminaries like Eleanor Roosevelt and Adlai Stevenson, the U.S. ambassador to the United Nations. In the weeks before the Bay of Pigs fiasco, Schlesinger had bluntly warned Kennedy that a U.S.-backed invasion of Cuba would remind international observers of the brutal Soviet invasion of Hungary in 1956. Ambassador Stevenson worried that the United States would "undermine our carefully nurtured position of anti-colonialism among the new nations of Asian and Africa" if it opposed independence for British Guiana.[31] Canada, both a neighbor of the United States and a member of the British Commonwealth, also recommended that the administration work with Jagan. Secretary Rusk had forwarded the March 1961 intelligence estimate to Ottawa, reasoning that the Canadians would conclude that a PPP victory would jeopardize the substantial Canadian private investments in bauxite mining. Canadian mining companies assured their government, however, that they had substantial confidence in the Jagan government. Canadian officials gave Jagan a warm welcome in October 1961 when he visited Ottawa.[32]

Most of President Kennedy's advisers and supporters, however, unequivocally opposed a U.S. relationship with Jagan and the PPP. Secretary of State Rusk never wavered from his conviction that Jagan wanted to transform an independent Guyana into a Soviet satellite. Members of Congress agreed with Rusk. Senator Thomas Dodd of Connecticut led the assault against Jagan. Dodd, a leading member of the conservative, ferociously anticommunist wing of the Democratic Party, believed everything that Burnham and D'Aguiar told him about British Guiana. Dodd passed on to the administration documents, poorly forged by D'Aguiar's minions, purporting to prove that Jagan was on the payroll of the Soviet Union. The State Department eventually received 113 congressional letters critical of a policy of working with Jagan. Only Senator George Aiken spoke up for economic aid for British Guiana. Unlike his colleagues, the Vermont Republican had visited the colony.[33] Congressional sentiment reflected constituent pressure. African American members of the Democratic National Committee recommended that the administration support "the Negro leader," Forbes Burnham, who "is wholly committed to our cause." The small Afro-Guyanese community in New York City also lobbied on behalf of Burnham and the PNC.[34] Most important, labor union officials pressed their long-held views that the Jagans aimed to destroy the free trade union movement. Labor unions had campaigned hard for John Kennedy in 1960. Robert Alexander of Rutgers University, who had served Jay Lovestone of the AFL-CIO and repeatedly attached the Communist label to the PPP, helped design the Alliance for Progress. William Howard McCabe, who used the cover of the Public Service International, an international affiliate of the AFL-CIO, and was a CIA agent, conducted a fact-finding mission to British Guiana in October/November 1961. McCabe called on the AFL-CIO to fight to save freedom in British

Guiana. While in the colony, McCabe organized an antigovernment strike by the Commercial and Clerical Workers Union but kept his role hidden.[35]

In September 1961, President Kennedy approved a program that gave the appearance of a U.S. effort to accommodate the United Kingdom on British Guiana. When U.S. representatives went to London on 11 September to discuss British Guiana, they presented a dual-track policy. They promised British officials that Jagan would be given a friendly reception in the United States and offered economic assistance. An independent Guyana would be welcomed into the inter-American community. At the same time, the administration planned to develop a covert program to expose and destroy Communists in British Guiana, "including, if necessary, 'the possibility of finding a substitute for Jagan himself, who could command East Indian support'." As Schlesinger pointed out to Kennedy, the covert program had the obvious potential to conflict with the friendship policy.[36] The State Department highlighted that contradiction when it asked the Colonial Office to keep in mind the "possibility Jagan is Communist-controlled 'sleeper' who will move to establish a Castro or Communist regime upon independence."[37] The "sleeper" allegation suggested that State Department officers had perhaps persuaded themselves that Jagan embodied the central character in *The Manchurian Candidate* (1959), the Cold War political thriller by novelist Richard Condon. In any case, British officials emerged from the September 1961 Anglo-American meetings pleased that the United States had pledged to help British Guiana. They reluctantly agreed to joint intelligence gathering, but they refused to give the CIA permission to conduct covert operations in the colony. The British declined to accept the U.S. argument, as Ambassador to the United Kingdom David Bruce put it, that "various components of our program are parts of an inter-related package."[38] Events would prove that the Kennedy administration would not be bound by the ban on covert activity.

Prime Minister Jagan's talks in Washington in October 1961 with President Kennedy, Secretary Rusk, and other State Department officers seemingly went well. The State Department characterized Rusk's conversation with Jagan as being conducted in "an atmosphere of warmth and cordiality." Jagan thought Rusk "sympathetic and understanding" to his plans to help the rural poor and secularize education.[39] At the White House, Jagan emphasized to Kennedy that he believed in democracy, an independent judiciary, and independent civil service "in the British tradition." He called U.S. assistance "a political necessity for him." As Consul Melby had reported, Guyanese thought Jagan would come home with the "keys to Fort Knox." Jagan had grandiose ideas of spending up to $250 million on economic development. He envisioned receiving $40 million from the United States, which, on a per capita basis, would be far more than the United States offered any Latin American country under the Alliance for Progress. As a rule, Kennedy never discussed specific sums of money with foreign leaders. The president assured Jagan, however, that the United States could work with nations that pursued independent foreign policies.[40] Jagan left Washington disappointed he had received only a vague promise of a $5 million aid package. Nonetheless, Jagan reported to Governor Grey that he thought he had done well politically and that he communicated especially well with Kennedy and Under Secretary of State Chester Bowles. The prime minister wondered, however, whether the U.S. Congress would appropriate funds for countries "that do not fit into the American socioeconomic pattern."[41]

Cheddi Jagan misinterpreted his dignified audience with President Kennedy. As recounted by Schlesinger in his memoir of the Kennedy presidency, *A Thousand Days*, the president had already decided he could not abide Jagan governing an independent Guyana. He had watched Jagan's appearance on *Meet the Press*.[42] As Governor Grey feared, Jagan suffered a public relations disaster. Broadcaster Lawrence E. Spivak assumed the role of the redbaiting Senator Joseph McCarthy. Spivak's first question: "Are you or are you not pro-Communist." Spivak thereafter conducted an inquisition, grilling Jagan on differences between communism, Marxism, and socialism and demanding that Jagan denounce the Soviet Union. Jagan gave his customary imprecise, rambling answers to what the British embassy in Washington called Spivak's "character assassination." Spivak had made Jagan look "evasive and insincere," with television shots of Spivak "listening like a tightlipped and disbelieving schoolmaster to a shifty pupil." Other members of the panel, like veteran *New York Times* journalist Tad Szulc, treated Jagan with respect, asking questions about Jagan's plans for socioeconomic development. The Canadian press also gave Jagan sympathetic treatment, responding positively to Jagan's dream or fantasy of an independent Guyana joining both the Commonwealth and the Organization of American States and serving as a link between the Commonwealth, Latin America, and the United States.[43]

The *Meet the Press* interview gave President Kennedy an excuse for rejecting Jagan; U.S. taxpayers would dislike aiding a politically suspect leader.

Prime Minister Cheddi Jagan and President
John F. Kennedy at the White House, 25 October
1961. Photograph by Abbie Rowe, National Park
Service, JFK Library.

Kennedy would have to think hard about overruling his secretary of state and angering supporters like conservative Democrats, African Americans, and labor union officials. But even if Jagan had impressed the U.S. public, the president would have spurned him. With its $20 billion Alliance for Progress, the "Marshall Plan for Latin America," the United States proposed to build progressive, democratic, anticommunist societies throughout the region. In turn, the administration expected Latin American leaders to support U.S. foreign policies, and it insisted that they sever all ties with Communist Cuba. Presidential aide Richard Goodwin framed the issue squarely for Kennedy on 25 October 1961, the day Kennedy hosted Jagan. In August, Goodwin had attended the organizational conference, held in Punta del Este, Uruguay, for the Alliance for Progress. Goodwin had also had a lengthy exchange of views with Ché Guevara at Punta del Este. Goodwin warned the president that the United States could not permit neutralism in the Western Hemisphere. Jagan thought his country could "be an India, Ghana, or Yugoslavia." If Jagan received aid, it would be "an open invitation for other Latin American politicos to take the same line."[44] In the context of his relentless war against Fidel Castro, John Kennedy always took Goodwin's type of advice. The president's next task was to force Prime Minister Macmillan's government to accept the U.S. campaign against Cheddi Jagan.

GEORGETOWN, THE CAPITAL CITY of British Guiana, burned on 16 February 1962. Arsonists and bombers ignited "mammoth blazes" that consumed seven square blocks of the business section of Georgetown. Over fifty premises were destroyed by fire and another sixty were damaged and looted. Georgetown was especially susceptible to fire, because many of its important buildings were wood construction. Afro-Guyanese mobs attacked Indian merchants and looted their stores and stalls. With unemployment rates reaching 50 percent in Georgetown, crime was a major urban problem, with young blacks engaging in purse snatching and automobile theft. The young people proved ready to burn, loot, and murder when aroused by ruthless political leaders. Five people died and another forty were injured. Guyanese submitted claims to fire insurance companies of $6 million but damages amounted to more, because many merchants did not have riot insurance. Observers suggested damages totaled as much as one-sixth of British Guiana's gross national product. The colony's economy thereafter went into a steep decline. Surveying the damage, Governor Grey confessed to the Colonial Office that he was "sickened at its extent." U.S. Consul Melby shared Grey's dismay, lamenting that "whatever the immediate cause of the riots, they quickly took on an ugly racial tone in predominately African Georgetown."[45]

Prime Minister Jagan's opponents transformed a political debate into a political crisis in February 1962. Jagan proposed a budget based on the advice of Nicholas Kaldor, a Cambridge University economist who had been recommended to Jagan by the United Nations. Kaldor had previously advised governments in Ceylon, Ghana, and Mexico. In order to raise capital for roads and irrigation canals, the government would raise taxes on wealthy citizens and attach duties on nonessential imports. The government also devised a compulsory savings scheme, requiring wage earners earning as little as $60 a month to dedicate 10 percent of their wages to interest-bearing tax-free bonds redeemable in seven years. The Colonial Office accepted the rationale for Jagan's budget, pointing out that British Guiana needed money, the United Kingdom "was strapped for money," and the United States had refused to give a firm commitment of aid. London also knew that PPP leaders had tried and failed to obtain foreign aid from France, Italy, and West Germany. Both Iain Macleod and Reginald Maudling, the old and new colonial secretaries, dismissed allegations that the tax program was a Marxist program. The president of Booker Brothers defended the budget, calling it "a serious attempt by Government to get to grips with formidable economic problems." The Colonial Office judged that Jagan was acting thoroughly within democratic procedures, although it thought he could have done a better political job preparing Guyanese for sacrifices.[46]

Forbes Burnham and Peter D'Aguiar opposed the budget by resorting to violence. They played on the legitimate fears of Guyanese, such as civil servants, who could not see how they could afford new deductions from their already meager wages. Both Burnham and D'Aguiar recognized they could not defeat the PPP democratically and that Cheddi Jagan would lead the colony to independence. They, along with union leader Richard Ishmael, sought to bring the government down in the streets. Ishmael had informed the AFL-CIO that the movement toward independence could be delayed by strikes and asked U.S. union representatives in British Guiana for guns and dynamite.[47] Burnham repeatedly boasted that he controlled the levers of power in Georgetown. Both Burnham and D'Aguiar organized huge mobs, made incendiary statements to the mobs, and then declined to stop their

rampages. Both men were photographed brazenly shaking hands after leading an illegal march around government buildings. U.S. Consul Melby reported that Burnham "proved his skill at arousing Georgetown mobs."[48] A
subsequent Colonial Office judicial inquiry blamed the trio of Burnham,
D'Aguiar, and Ishmael for the violence.[49] The Jagan government could not
control the mobs, because the police force did not respond to his commands.
Virtually all police officers were Afro-Guyanese, because Indians had historically been denied the chance to join security forces. At Jagan's request,
Governor Grey restored calm by deploying British troops in the colony and
calling for reinforcements from Jamaica and the United Kingdom. Consul
Melby opined that British troops probably saved Jagan's life.[50] Jagan abandoned his budgetary proposals.

The CIA aided and abetted the rioters. The Kennedy administration had
decided to generate chaos in the colony to force the Macmillan government
to delay British Guiana's independence. At a meeting in Bermuda in late
December 1961, Lord Home stunned Rusk by informing him that an independence conference would take place in May 1962 and that British Guiana
would gain its independence within a year. State Department officers repeatedly implored the British to delay independence and schedule new elections. They "pointed out that Jagan won the previous election by a very
narrow popular majority and that precedents in other British colonies could
undoubtedly be found to support the concept of new elections." The British
refused and, in any case, Consul Melby predicted that the PPP would likely
strengthen its majority in a new election.[51] So frantic was the administration
to see Jagan out of power that it began to ask about the state of his marriage.
State Department officers in Washington instructed the consulate to check
press rumors that the Jagans were contemplating a divorce. In December
1961, the U.S. embassy in London reported that Janet Jagan had moved to
London with a Communist lover. Two months later, the embassy updated its
gossip, reporting that Janet Jagan's "amorous relationship" was over. Consul
Melby had already dashed the State Department's apparent hope that divorce
would leave Cheddi Jagan directionless, noting Cheddi Jagan's political support in British Guiana did not depend on his marriage to a white foreigner.[52]

With its diplomatic efforts rejected, the administration turned to violence. It infiltrated CIA operatives into British Guiana in imaginative ways.
On 12 January 1962 President Kennedy authorized the expansion of technical
assistance to British Guiana to a level of $1.5 million and agreed that U.S. aid

officials should go to the colony to study the feasibility of the $5 million aid package. Kennedy also informed Fowler Hamilton, the administrator for the Agency of International Development, that "I am also requesting immediate action to intensify our observations of political developments in British Guiana." As Hamilton subsequently explained, what Kennedy signaled in the words "observations of political developments" was that the technical assistance and study groups should include CIA people.[53] On 18 January, the administration raised the status of its representation in Georgetown from consulate to consulate general. The diplomatic staff would thereby be increased, providing increased opportunities for CIA agents to put on the cloak of diplomatic cover. The administration also intensified its contacts with Jagan's political opponents, trade union officials in British Guiana, and the AFL-CIO.

After the fires of 16 February, Jagan publicly raised the issue of CIA intervention and remarked to Consul Melby "that he realized the U.S. government worked in various ways." Administration officials categorically denied any role in the riots, with the State Department responding that it was "astonished" by Jagan's "accusations and remarks."[54] In response to a direct question from Colonial Secretary Maudling, Arthur Schlesinger replied that it was "inconceivable" that the CIA had stimulated the racial riots.[55] Union officials William Howard McCabe and Ernest Lee, the son-in-law of AFL-CIO President George Meany, assured Governor Grey that they had been in British Guiana for legitimate purposes. They added that they had rejected Richard Ishmael's request for guns and dynamite. Lee stated that he intended to raise money for the union workers of British Guiana who had lost their jobs in the aftermath of the riots.[56]

The CIA has claimed that it destroyed its records on British Guiana. U.S. government censors have withheld key documents. Tim Weiner, a correspondent for the *New York Times* who specializes in declassification issues, wrote in 1994 that government officials informed him that "still classified documents depict a direct order from the President to unseat Dr. Jagan." Weiner continued, "The Jagan papers are a rare smoking gun: a clear written record without veiled words or plausible denials, of a President's command to depose a Prime Minister."[57] Although the prosecuting historian cannot wave that proverbial smoking gun in front of a jury, the Kennedy administration would need the skills of a legendary lawyer like Clarence Darrow or

F. Lee Bailey to explain away in a court of law the evidence that the Kennedy administration encouraged and financed the attacks on the Jagan government. Two former CIA agents, Philip Agee and Joseph Burkholder Smith, have written of the CIA's involvement. Burkholder worked with associates of Forbes Burnham in February 1962.[58] Numerous sources have identified McCabe as a CIA agent, working under the cover of the American Federation of State, County, and Municipal Employees and its international affiliate, the Public Service International. McCabe arrived in British Guiana in the midst of the riots as a stowaway on an airplane carrying a blood bank from Surinam.[59] Since 1990, Arthur Schlesinger has repeatedly decried the CIA intervention in British Guiana.[60] Colonial officials, such as Undersecretary Hugh Fraser, similarly denounced the CIA intervention.[61] The administration's brazen words and actions immediately after the riots further incriminated them. On 20 February 1962, even as Georgetown smoldered, President Kennedy expressed to the United Kingdom's ambassador to the United States, David Ormsby-Gore, his "unhappiness" over British Guiana and his "regret" that Governor Grey and London "had moved so quickly in [a] manner which had [the] effect of shoring up [a] tottering Jagan regime."[62] Both the president and State Department officials also promptly called on the British to see the riots as a reason for delaying independence and scheduling new elections. One State Department officer went so far as to claim that the riots were "a spontaneous outburst of democratic opinion, a la Hungary, against Jagan."[63] No U.S. official, other than Consul Melby, expressed regret that racial warfare had broken out in British Guiana.

In case the United Kingdom officials could still not read U.S. intentions, Secretary of State Dean Rusk spelled it out for them in a message to Lord Home on 19 February 1962. Rusk informed the British foreign secretary that "it is not possible for us to put up with an independent British Guiana under Jagan." The secretary darkly noted that the February riots resembled "the events of 1953." The colony, Anglo-American harmony, and the inter-American system would all face "disaster" if Jagan continued in office. Rusk called for "remedial steps" leading to new elections. Rusk's virtual ultimatum to the United Kingdom flowed directly from the advice he had received the day before from his subordinate, William R. Tyler of the European Division. Tyler recommend a "go for broke" policy to unseat Jagan. He further suggested keeping the February demonstrations going by sending money through third countries and the labor movement. Tyler thought, however, that the United States should counsel Jagan's political opposition against violence.[64] On 8 March 1962 President Kennedy partially qualified Rusk and Tyler's demands when he issued National Security Action Memorandum (NSAM) No. 135. The memorandum noted that "no final decision" would be taken on British Guiana until Rusk met with Lord Home and British officials had the chance to conduct an "on-the-spot survey" of British Guiana. But the memorandum emphasized that the United States needed to explore ways to persuade the British to delay independence and schedule new elections.[65]

A range of emotions characterized the first reactions of British officials in London and Georgetown to Rusk's demand that Guyanese be denied their democratic rights. Prime Minister Macmillan told Home that he read Rusk's letter with "amazement" and found some of Rusk's phrases "incredible." The prime minister marveled, "How can the Americans continue to attack us in the United Nations on colonialism and then use expressions like these which are not colonialism but pure Machiavellianism."[66] In his sarcastic reply to Rusk of 26 February 1962, Lord Home reminded the secretary of state of the historic U.S. role as "the first crusader and prime mover in urging colonial emancipation." He also wondered how expressions such as "Jagan should not accede to power again" could be reconciled with democratic processes.[67] Colonial Office leaders, Iain Macleod and Reginald Maudling, tried reason on Arthur Schlesinger. Macleod, who did the talking for Maudling, rejected the charge of "Communist" that the United States leveled against Jagan. Instead, the former colonial secretary depicted Jagan as "a naïve, London School of Economics Marxist filled with charm, personal honesty, and juvenile nationalism." He further asserted that if he "had to make the choice between Jagan and Burnham as head of my country I would choose Jagan any day of the week."[68] Governor Grey, on the other hand, vented his frustration, bitterly complaining to a State Department officer visiting Georgetown that Washington had "offered no solutions other than to say no." John Hennings, who served as the Colonial Office's attaché in the embassy in Washington, contributed to the debate by initially labeling Rusk's message as a "somewhat saucy letter." He later decided that Rusk's letter merited the term "impertinent."[69]

Secretary of State Rusk was taken back by the United Kingdom's reaction and asked President Kennedy to write to Macmillan.[70] The president first asked Hugh Fraser to stop in Washington for a meeting. The Undersecretary of State for the Colonies went to Georgetown in early March to assess the colony's political milieu and survey the destruction. Fraser gave his all for queen and country during the more than three hours he spent with Kennedy. The president conducted ninety minutes of the meeting in a swimming pool heated to 92 degrees. Whereas the heat presumably soothed the president's troublesome back, it left Fraser with an "exhausting experience." Fraser emphasized that "racialism" between blacks and Indians was the central problem in British Guiana. He blamed Forbes Burnham and Peter D'Aguiar for exacerbating racial tensions. Fraser further suggested in his meetings with the president and other U.S. officials, including CIA Director John A. McCone, that the United States confused Jagan's nationalism with international Communism. He hoped that he "made it clear that a line can be drawn between these types of international communists and what I would call the anti-colonial type of communist which I pointed out to them Jefferson might well have been if the communist manifesto had been written in 1748 instead of 100 years later." In any case, Fraser ridiculed the idea that an independent Guyana would serve as a base for Communist expansion in the Western Hemisphere. The colony was a "mudbank," surrounded by forests and mountains and without natural communications with Latin America. Finally, Fraser reiterated the British position that the United States could orient Cheddi Jagan toward the West with economic development assistance.[71]

Fraser's mission to Washington failed, in the short term, to reduce the Anglo-American tension over British Guiana. Drawing an analogy between British Guiana and the American Revolution had not allayed U.S. concerns over Jagan. And British officials understandably resented the U.S. intervention in their colony. The Kennedy administration had violated the September 1961 agreement not to conduct covert operations in British Guiana. Prime Minister Macmillan or perhaps one of his aides placed two large exclamation points on the dispatch from Fraser, in which Fraser reported that CIA Director McCone told him that the CIA had taken no actions in British Guiana. Nonetheless, the Macmillan government realized it could not readily dismiss the U.S. position. Kennedy had given Fraser an extraordinary amount of presidential time. As Fraser concluded, that fact "makes it clear that the problem of B.G. in American eyes is regarded as one of critical importance."[72]

TWO MONTHS AFTER Hugh Fraser's trip to Washington, Prime Minister Macmillan made the conceptual decision to accommodate the United States by delaying independence and finding a scheme to deprive Cheddi Jagan and the PPP of power. The prime minister's decision came following Foreign Secretary Home's meeting with Rusk in Geneva in late March 1962 and his own conference with Kennedy in Washington in late April. As Macmillan noted to adviser Sir Norman Brook, discussions with the U.S. officials had persuaded him that the United States attached "great importance" to the colony. He interpreted the U.S. concern as being "moved by internal political considerations as much as by a genuine fear of communism." Nonetheless, the United Kingdom's interests were served by cooperation with the United States. Macmillan further reasoned that "in the future the Americans will have to carry the burden of British Guiana and so it is only fair that they should have a chance in shaping its future." On 30 May 1962, Macmillan wrote to President Kennedy, informing him he would postpone the independence conference and also try to persuade the political leaders of British Guiana to hold another election before independence.[73]

The prime minister's decision to permit the United States to have its way in a British colony flowed from multiple sources. Somewhat to Macmillan's surprise, he and Kennedy had become friends. Despite their obvious differences in age and experience, the two leaders found that they communicated well, that they shared similar insights on life and laughed at the same things. Kennedy once most famously shared with Macmillan his discovery that if he did not have sexual relations with a woman every three days that he would develop a terrible headache. The United Kingdom's representative in Washington, Ambassador David Ormsby-Gore, facilitated communication between the two men. The president asked the British to appoint Ormsby-Gore, a Kennedy family friend, to the position. Ambassador Ormsby-Gore and his family frequently socialized with the president and his wife on weekends, including at the family compound at Hyannis Port, Massachusetts. Ormsby-Gore also had the privilege of easy access to the Oval Office.[74]

Beyond personal ties, the prime minister made it a fundamental principle of his foreign policy to work closely with the United States. Macmillan had drawn many lessons from the Suez debacle. He believed that his country's wealth and power and its historical contributions to world civilization entitled it to a major say in international affairs. But Macmillan had learned from the Suez Crisis that the only way that the United Kingdom could pursue its foreign policy aims would be as the principal ally of the United States. Macmillan thought that he had created an "interdependent" relationship with the United States. President Kennedy also characterized the Anglo-American relationship as an interdependent one. The countries shared a common language and cultural tradition and had been wartime allies. But as historian Nigel J. Ashton has instructed, the two leaders differed on their interpretations of interdependence. Kennedy believed that he should consult with the British on major issues. For example, Ormsby-Gore became the first foreigner with whom Kennedy shared information about Soviet missiles in Cuba. The president also conferred with Macmillan throughout the Cuban Missile Crisis. But Kennedy never considered himself bound to take Macmillan's advice on the missile crisis or any other foreign policy issue, including the future of British Guiana. Macmillan desired, however, for the Anglo-American relationship to mean a partnership of equals. When conflicts arose with Washington, the prime minister always had to weigh the specific issue against his larger goal of a harmonious relationship with the United States. To be sure, the prime minister occasionally defied U.S. leaders. He refused to join the trade embargo against Cuba, for example, because he knew that his country's economic security depended on expanding trade.[75]

Bureaucratic and domestic politics also pushed Macmillan toward accepting the U.S. position on British Guiana. Consistent with its basic mission, the Foreign Office worked to promote good relations with the United States. British diplomats further believed that the Colonial Office failed to appreciate the nuances of international affairs. Foreign officers wrote of their "awkward" role mediating between the State Department and the Colonial Office and blamed the Colonial Office for not accepting that the United States had legitimate regional security concerns. Philip de Zulueta, a close adviser of Macmillan, agreed, telling the prime minister that "the Colonial Office still treats the place as if it were Africa or Asia whereas it is in the U.S. backyard and politically very important to the Administration with the midterm elections coming in the autumn."[76] The Macmillan government also did not want to spend scare public funds keeping troops in a colony the British considered difficult and worthless. British officials calculated that British Guiana cost $7 million annually and that the bill would rise to $20 million if London reimposed direct rule.[77]

Although Prime Minister Macmillan signaled to President Kennedy in May 1962 that he would follow the U.S. lead on British Guiana, it would take him more than a year to execute the anti-Jagan policy. British Guiana became a matter of serious debate within the United Kingdom. Government officials, especially in the Colonial Office, naturally resented the U.S. meddling. Moreover, many genuinely wanted democracy to take hold in British Guiana. Whereas they had mixed opinions about Cheddi Jagan, the British never wavered in their judgment that Peter D'Aguiar was irresponsible and that Forbes Burnham was a demagogue and a racist. Officials constantly dreaded that another racial conflagration would erupt in the colony. Domestic developments may have led the British to think hard about racial relations. During the 1950s, the population of West Indians and Africans in England had increased, mainly through immigration, by 450 percent. Racial tensions arose in major urban areas like London and Manchester.[78] The Macmillan government also had to consider the views of important former colonial possessions like India and Pakistan that would take note of the British sacrificing the Hindus and Muslims of British Guiana on the altar of Anglo-American amity. The prime minister could further count on its Labour opponents seizing on any appearance of kowtowing to the United States. Some element of calculation also went into Macmillan's delay. If he appeased the United States on British Guiana, he expected U.S. help on a knotty issue like the Congo or Southern Rhodesia.

While the British debated, the Kennedy administration readied itself for another election in British Guiana. In his 30 May letter to Kennedy, Macmillan had observed that the Western nations should generously support a new government, even if Dr. Jagan and the PPP once again won another election. The administration told itself, however, that the PPP could not be allowed to win a new election. As Dean Rusk reminded the president, the United States needed to base its policy "on the premise that, once independent, Cheddi Jagan will establish a 'Marxist' regime in British Guiana and associate his country with the Soviet Bloc to a degree unacceptable to us for a state in the Western Hemisphere." Rusk's 12 July 1962 memorandum to Kennedy included a plan for the CIA to manipulate the election. In the previous month, the Special Group, the administration's select committee that oversaw counterinsurgency activities, had received a six-page paper on

British Guiana. The president also authorized Richard Helms, the CIA's deputy director of planning, to confer with British counterparts. The planning for a covert operation made Arthur Schlesinger "nervous." The presidential aide had abandoned his personal campaign to persuade the administration to work with Jagan. He now agreed "there is no future in Jagan," although he also concluded, after a trip to British Guiana, that the colony "would be worse off with Burnham than with Jagan." Schlesinger also worried about the issue raised by National Security Adviser McGeorge Bundy. Bundy noted that "it is unproven that CIA knows how to manipulate an election in British Guiana without a backfire."[79]

DESPITE THE MISGIVINGS of aides, President Kennedy pushed the anti-Jagan policy forward. Ambassador Ormsby-Gore recalled that the president, from the summer of 1962 on, made it "very clear" to him that Jagan's rule in British Guiana "was unacceptable" to the United States.[80] On 18 August 1962, Kennedy met with CIA Director John A. McCone to review the covert campaign against Cheddi Jagan. The president secretly tape recorded the meeting. McCone noted that CIA agent Frank Wisner reported that the British had wanted to talk about alternatives to Jagan but not establish a policy. But McCone and Secretary of State Rusk had sent Assistant Secretary of State William C. Burdett to London to drive "the thing further along than I think the British expected." As a result, the British now agreed that "the Jagan government is undesirable and Communist oriented." Nearly four minutes of the tape recording remain classified. The meeting concluded with McCone leaving with Kennedy a "doctrine paper" on U.S. covert activities in eleven countries. McCone observed that the paper was highly classified, "because it tells all about the dirty tricks and we don't want to circulate it." National Security Adviser Bundy characterized the paper as "a marvelous collection or dictionary of your crimes." Laughter followed Bundy's quip.[81]

As it plotted against Cheddi Jagan, the Kennedy administration embraced Forbes Burnham. In March 1962, Burdett had conferred with Burnham in Georgetown. Burnham asked the United States to bypass the government and provide economic assistance directly to the people. Burnham further asked for U.S. financial support and for weapons. The United States should also persuade the United Kingdom to establish an electoral system based on proportional representation. He threatened a civil war, with the PNC having "to fight to defend itself," if the new electoral system was not established.[82]

Burnham would eventually receive all he asked. Upon Burdett's recommendation, the administration hosted Burnham in Washington in May 1962 and again in September. Burnham made a good impression on presidential aides and State Department officers. U.S. officials thought Burnham "presented PNC case in restrained manner typical of [a] British barrister." Indeed, the handsome Burnham never failed to impress with his dignified bearing and his impeccable British manners. Burnham's case included charging the Jagans as "thoroughgoing Communists," alleging that they received instructions from the British Communist Party in 1955, and warning that Cuba was sending arms to British Guiana. He emphasized that the PNC respected private enterprise. While in Washington, Burnham also met with Senator Thomas Dodd. Burnham returned with $100,000 in student scholarships, providing tangible evidence to Guyanese that Forbes Burnham, not Cheddi Jagan, could secure U.S. assistance.[83] Governor Grey noticed that Burnham had become cocky, boasting that he had the unlisted telephone numbers of presidential aides Schlesinger and Richard Goodwin and that he would now only speak to assistant secretaries or higher in the State Department.[84] In making Burnham the U.S. man in Georgetown, the Kennedy administration had to overlook the assessments of the intelligence community. In the 11 April 1962 National Intelligence Estimate of British Guiana, intelligence analysts wrote that "Burnham has a reputation for opportunism and venality." They added: "His racist point of view, so evident in the past, forebodes instability and conflict during any administration under his leadership."[85]

While in Washington, Burnham met with the leadership of the AFL-CIO. Indeed, among Burnham's boasts to Governor Grey, was the assertion that "a word to George Meany" would open important doors for him. Meany attended a luncheon for Burnham hosted by Serafino Romualdi. Labor officials also introduced Burnham around the United States, having him meet, for example, union representatives of the meat cutters in Chicago. The meat cutters promised to send men to train butchers in British Guiana. Andrew McLellan of the AFL-CIO's International Affairs Department began working with Richard Ishmael and CIA agent McCabe, promoting the issue of proportional representation to the Colonial Office. U.S. union officials also lobbied Kennedy administration officials, like Vice President Johnson, attesting that Burnham and the PNC "represent the democratic movement in British Guiana."[86]

The AFL-CIO also managed to increase U.S. influence in British Guiana while simultaneously enhancing Burnham's stature. In late 1961, the union established the American Institute of Free Labor Development (AIFLD). Romualdi served as president of the institute, and William Doherty Jr. became its chief operating officer. Doherty was the son of William Doherty, a union official who became the U.S. ambassador to Jamaica, which gained its independence in 1962. AIFLD's mission was to promote business unionism and combat any perceived "Castro-Communist" influence in the labor movement in Latin America. Between 1962 and 1967, the AIFLD received $15.4 million—89 percent of its budget—from Alliance for Progress funds. Contributions from U.S. corporations and labor unions made up the rest of the AIFLD's budget. In the period from 1961 to 1963, the AIFLD also reportedly received $1 million from the CIA through conduits like the Gotham, J. M. Kaplan, and Michigan Funds. Emissaries from the AIFLD were especially active in Brazil, training Brazilian unionists to organize strikes and demonstrations against the government of João Goulart.[87] In British Guiana, the AIFLD proposed building over 2,000 low-cost housing units for postal and government employees who belonged to a union led by Andrew Jackson. Jackson supported Burnham and the PNC. In 1962, the AIFLD also brought six Guyanese unionists to Washington for the AIFLD's first class on leadership training. The six returned to British Guiana and helped organize a massive, violent strike against the Jagan government in 1963. The six unionists remained on the AIFLD's payroll during the strike.[88]

If the Macmillan government had chosen to reject the U.S. demands and defend democracy in British Guiana, it could have cited international support for its position. Foreign corporations and governments argued that the United States had badly misjudged the political culture of the colony. The two major foreign investors in British Guiana, British sugar interests and Canadian mining operators, considered Jagan the best option for the country's future. Company representatives variously referred to Jagan as a "Christian Communist" and the "natural leader" of his nation. Both British and Canadian businessmen challenged the premise that political developments in British Guiana would have an impact in the Western Hemisphere.[89] Israel lobbied both the United Kingdom and the United States on behalf of Jagan, who had journeyed to Israel at the end of 1961. Israeli Foreign Minister Golda Meir told Foreign Secretary Home that "it was worth talking a risk and helping Jagan." Meir worried that, if the West spurned Jagan, extremists in the PPP would push Jagan toward the Communist bloc. Israeli diplomats in

Latin America delivered the same message to State Department officials. The Israeli ambassador to Venezuela thought Jagan a confused thinker but one who adhered to the rule of law and favored the West. Drawing on his own experiences in Israel's struggle for independence, Ambassador Arie Oron observed that "Dr. Jagan does not appear to think like a real revolutionary." Israel contemplated helping British Guiana train a local militia. The Kennedy administration politely but firmly rejected the Israeli advice, implying that Israel did not understand the politics of British Guiana. The State Department warned that if Israel aided Jagan it "would be regarded by [the] U.S. public as strengthening militarily a regime which has shown [a] consistent predilection for communism."[90] Succumbing to U.S. pressure, Israel dropped all thoughts of aiding Jagan and British Guiana.

The Macmillan government similarly acceded to U.S. wishes, delivering on its commitment to undermine Cheddi Jagan. In late October 1962, the Colonial Office hosted a conference in London on British Guiana's future. The conference had been scheduled for May and was originally designed to set a date for the colony's independence. In fact, the conference was part of the Anglo-American plot against Jagan. Duncan Sandys, who now held the joint position of secretary of state for Commonwealth and colonies, presided over the conference. Sandys had opposed the progressive colonial policies of MacLeod and Maulding. Within the Macmillan cabinet, Sandys had earned the reputation as a "hatchet-man," prepared to do Macmillan's unpleasant tasks.[91] Sandys later told a Macmillan biographer that the prime minister made it clear to him that the Anglo-American relationship mattered more than the future of British Guiana.[92] On 10 September 1962, Sandys informed the prime minister of his scheme. The conference would not focus on independence, as Jagan had hoped. Instead, Sandys would allow the conference to breakdown over the issue of proportional representation. The colony's political parties would continue squabbling at home, with no resolution. After a time, Sandys would call for a referendum on proportional representation, expecting that supporters of Forbes Burnham and Peter D'Aguiar would be able to muster 50 percent support for it. Sandys would then schedule new elections followed by an independence conference. Macmillan approved Sandys's intrigue and authorized Ambassador Ormsby-Gore to inform his friend President Kennedy. Ormsby-Gore's instructions included the caution to "please impress upon the President that no one at all knows of this plan and that it would be quite disastrous if it leaked out."[93]

The conference on British Guiana, which lasted from 23 October to 6 November 1962 and took place in the midst of the Cuban Missile Crisis, followed the course that Duncan Sandys had plotted. The parties deadlocked over the need for proportional representation. Jagan stressed the multiracial aims of his party and pointed to the PPP's multiracial support. He argued that British Guiana deserved the same electoral system that existed in the United Kingdom and throughout the Commonwealth. Burnham countered that politics in British Guiana was strictly on a racial basis, with the PNC being an African party and the PPP being a party of Indians. D'Aguiar also called for proportional representation, although he devoted his time to charging, without proof, that the Soviet Union financed the PPP. At the end of the conference, Sandys announced that the United Kingdom might have to consider imposing a solution if the parties could not reach an agreement in the future. Knowing he had the solid support of the Kennedy administration and the U.S. labor movement, Burnham predictably rebuffed Jagan's subsequent compromise proposals.[94] With its economy in ruins and its political system undermined, British Guiana was now, in the judgment of the Colonial Office, "in a parlous state."[95] New waves of racial violence would engulf the colony in 1963 and 1964.

BY THE END OF 1962, the Kennedy administration had gone a long away toward accomplishing the U.S. goal of destabilizing the Jagan government. It had damaged the colony's economy with the February 1962 strikes. It had also helped create a political climate of fear and tension between Indians and blacks. The administration had further found a Guyanese political leader who would seemingly do the U.S. bidding. What the administration needed was to ensure that the United Kingdom not waver from its pledge to remove the Jagan government from office. It would take two more years of covert intervention in British Guiana and constant U.S. pressure on the United Kingdom for the United States to achieve the dubious distinction of putting Forbes Burnham and the PNC into power.

proportional representation, 1963–1964

At the end of 1964, the United States achieved its objective of forcing Cheddi Jagan and the People's Progressive Party out of power. The United Kingdom delivered on the promises that Prime Minister Harold Macmillan had secretly made to President John F. Kennedy in 1962, mandating for British Guiana an electoral system of voting based on proportional representation. Forbes Burnham emerged from the new system as the leader of the colony. Although British officials kept Macmillan's word, the Kennedy and Johnson administrations resorted to extreme measures to maintain British resolve. British authorities found it difficult, even in the name of Anglo-American harmony, to deny their colonial subjects a democratic future. They further hesitated to exacerbate the racial and ethnic tensions that marred life in British Guiana. The United States needed once again to convince its ally that the imperatives of the Cold War had priority over democratic elections and racial peace.

AS DEVELOPED BY Colonial Secretary Duncan Sandys, the Macmillan government's scheme to undermine the Jagan government consisted of a two-step process. Sandys had taken the first step in October/November 1962, ruling that the colony could not attain independence until it held another election. Knowing that Jagan and the PPP would never agree to an election based on proportional representation, Sandys planned to impose a solution. But it would be another year before the colonial secretary carried out the second stage of his intrigue. Although Sandys was, in the words of a colleague, "a man of action" when it came to British Guiana, he faced formidable obstacles in implementing his plan "to tidy it up."[1] The United Kingdom's allies objected to delays in British Guiana's independence. British officials, both within and outside the government, further questioned the legality and morality of imposing a dubious electoral scheme upon colonial subjects.

In the aftermath of the failed independence conference of 1962, British Guiana became a subject of debate in international forums. Cheddi Jagan appealed to both the British Commonwealth and the United Nations for assistance. In early 1963, Commonwealth members of the United Nations proposed sending a commission to investigate British Guiana and to help resolve differences. The Macmillan government rejected the help, reasoning that the "Commission might quite likely come down on Jagan's side on the issue of the electoral system (since 'first past the post' is a more familiar and usual method of voting in Commonwealth countries than proportional representation) and this might prove embarrassing and even impede an ultimate settlement."[2] British authorities also worried that the Committee of Twenty-Four, the U.N.'s "Committee on Colonialism," would schedule public hearings on the status of British Guiana. At U.S. urging, Forbes Burnham made an appearance before the Committee of Twenty-Four in March 1963. Burnham's appearance was designed both to demonstrate that Jagan was not the only national leader and to win the support of black African nations. Despite Burnham's pleadings, the Committee of Twenty-Four voted to hold hearings on British Guiana at the 1963–64 U.N. session.[3]

Debate about British Guiana also intensified within the United Kingdom. In January 1963, Hugh Gaitskell, the leader of the opposition Labour Party, unexpectedly died. Gaitskell had generally supported Prime Minister Macmillan's foreign policies. The new Labour leader, Harold Wilson, launched sharp attacks upon the government, perhaps sensing that the public had grown weary of the Conservatives, who had governed since 1951. Wilson's criticisms quickly gained credence when, by March 1963, the John Profumo-Christine Keeler scandal began to envelop the Macmillan government. Profumo, the war minister, misled the House of Commons, asserting that he had not had a sexual relationship with Keeler, a prostitute. The affair evolved from a personal indiscretion into a matter of national security when the public learned that Keeler also had an intimate relationship with a Soviet military intelligence officer attached to the Soviet Union's embassy in London. In this new political atmosphere, Labour members of Parliament, like Anthony Greenwood, Arthur Bottomley, and Fenner Brockway, began to question the government's plans for British Guiana. Greenwood would become colonial secretary in the first Wilson government (1964–66). Parliamentary concerns about British Guiana were not limited to opposition politicians. Iain MacLeod, the former colonial secretary who retained his seat in the House of Commons, still held that the United States had succumbed to irrational fears about communism in British Guiana.[4]

Governor Ralph Grey doggedly opposed London's plan to undermine the Jagan government. As always, the view from Georgetown differed remarkably from those in Washington and London. In his years in the colony, Grey had not come to admire Jagan. He continued to report that Jagan was an inefficient manager who was leading the colony into administrative and economic chaos. Nonetheless, he judged Jagan to be a superior politician and a better human being than either Burnham or Peter D'Aguiar. He noted that Jagan remained popular in the countryside and that he was capable of defeating a referendum on proportional representation. Even if London dissolved the government, Jagan would remain on the political scene. Colonial authorities had the choice of either dealing with Jagan as "an ineffective leader or as an effective opposer." Grey asked, "Should we therefore avoid putting ourselves in any position from which it would be impossible, if all else failed, to 'make the best of Jagan,' as I was seemingly supposed to do when I was sent here?"[5] Career colonial officials in London quietly accepted Grey's arguments.[6]

The governor took special delight in ridiculing claims about international Communist activity in British Guiana. In the aftermath of the Cuban Missile Crisis, U.S. officials asked the British to check out every allegation of Cuban subversion raised by Cuban refugees in Miami. As Grey lamented, "I have always thought it unfortunate that the picture of this country that has the widest circulation overseas is of conditions very different from those that are apparent on the spot." Responding to U.S. intelligence, Grey's security agents boarded the Russian ship, *Mitshurinsk*, looking for arms. The ship allegedly had a cargo of "tomato paste," serving as cover for the arms. The governor's agents found neither arms nor tomato paste on the *Mitshurinsk*.[7] A Soviet trade mission to British Guiana in early 1963 proved similarly innocuous. D'Aguiar and his minions in the United Front thought the mission presaged a Soviet beachhead on the South American continent. The trade delegation found the visit disappointing, however, because the colony had little to offer that interested the Soviets. Jagan's government signed a few small contracts to sell rice and timber in exchange for Soviet tractors. Although the four Soviet trade emissaries left the colony without any major deals, they apparently provided Guyanese males with an evening to remember. The Soviets hosted a farewell party at their hotel, replete with vodka, crabmeat, caviar, and women. Governor Grey's office reported that "it was a very merry affair."[8]

Beyond sending his sardonic reports about life in British Guiana, Governor Grey made one last effort to break the political deadlock in the colony. He vouched for Jagan in his efforts to reach President Kennedy. On 16 April 1963, Prime Minister Jagan sent a lengthy, impassioned letter to the president. As the governor explained to the Colonial Office, "It is all too plain that the current American policy is getting us—and them—nowhere." In his cover letter to the State Department that accompanied Jagan's plea to the president, Grey emphasized that "this country seen at first-hand is very different from almost all things that it is reputed to be." Grey wanted U.S. officials to meet again with Jagan in the United States and to send an administration official, like Arthur Schlesinger Jr., to British Guiana. Grey even seconded Jagan's suggestion that President Kennedy should come to Georgetown.[9] Beyond extending invitations, Jagan in his letter to Kennedy pleaded for economic assistance, citing several cases in which the United States had made preliminary promises of help and then reneged on loans. The prime minister praised the Alliance for Progress and noted that he carried out the type of fiscal, tax, and agrarian reforms called for in the charter of the Alliance. He stated that he wanted a mixed economy for his country and that his party had no plans to nationalize the key bauxite and sugar industries. He denied that the economy of British Guiana had become closely tied to "any international conspiracy." In fact, the colony continued to sell most of its primary products to the industrial democracies. Jagan further reaffirmed his commitment to parliamentary democracy and his respect for the rights of citizens as guaranteed in the U.S. Constitution.[10] The Foreign Office deemed Jagan's letter "impressive" and predicted that President Kennedy would probably read it.[11]

Jagan's letter never made it to the Oval Office. Jagan merely received an acknowledgment from the president of his letter. The president's advisers and the State Department agreed that the United States would not respond in detail to the points Jagan raised in his twenty-five paragraphs. In their view, Jagan had made two erroneous assumptions in his letter. British Guiana was not eligible for Alliance for Progress funds, and it was not a democratic, progressive country. Jagan's Marxist beliefs belied his pledges of respect for parliamentary democracy. The State Department even suggested that Jagan had engaged in racial favoritism, claiming that his compulsory saving scheme would have fallen more heavily on black civil service workers as opposed to rice growers. The Kennedy administration's cold 3 June 1963 response advised Jagan to consult with Consul Everett Melby if he had issues to discuss with the United States.[12]

Prime Minister Jagan and Governor Grey's letters had arrived in Washington even as the administration plotted to intensify the pressure on Jagan and his colonial masters. Through National Security Adviser Bundy and then personally, President Kennedy asked Ambassador Ormsby-Gore in March and April 1963 about the United Kingdom's future plans for the colony. The British responded that the time was "still not ripe" for an intervention in British Guiana.[13] The Macmillan government, including Colonial Secretary Sandys, understood that it would have to overrule Governor Grey if it acceded to U.S. demands for action against Jagan. As Sir Hilton Poynton, the ranking career officer in the Colonial Office, lamented, formulating an overt policy was far more difficult than hatching a covert move against Jagan. Poynton also grumbled about pressure from the United States and the United Nations, "neither of whose business it really is."[14] The president's inquiries followed what the administration would have judged an alarming report from Consul Melby. On 14 March 1963, Melby warned his superiors that "time favors Jagan," because the PPP was strong and was working to solidify its political position. Melby correctly opined that the Macmillan government feared the international embarrassment that would accompany a move against Jagan. But the British were deluding themselves if they believed that the Jagan government would "disappear due to its own incompetence." Few governments fell "through stupidity," and in any case, Cheddi Jagan could count on "Janet Jagan and some of the men surrounding her" to provide the needed intelligence. Melby also warned that a new Labour government would likely not be interested in proportional representation and would accelerate the independence process.[15]

Consul Melby's dispatch helped spur the administration into action. It began immediate inquiries into Harold Wilson's views on British Guiana and vowed to inform him of the U.S. position on the colony when he called on Washington.[16] Administration officials also held, on 20 March 1963, a presumably critical meeting on British Guiana that remains classified.[17] CIA Director John McCone subsequently journeyed to London to discuss British Guiana with Prime Minister Macmillan. Whether Macmillan gave his approval for a new CIA campaign cannot be determined from available evidence. Poynton thought that his prime minister had satisfied McCone by explaining the United Kingdom's international and domestic difficulties.[18] The Colonial Office, however, may have been engaged in wishful thinking. In a 30 April 1963 message to Kennedy, Macmillan indirectly referred to clandestine activities, suggestively pointing to "our agreed plans." Investigative newspaper accounts later claimed that Macmillan and Sandys acquiesced in the CIA role in the British colony.[19] In any case, within a month after McCone's meeting with Prime Minister Macmillan, the Kennedy administration launched another full-scale covert assault on Cheddi Jagan and the PPP. Operating through the AFL-CIO, the administration organized and financed an eighty-day general strike in British Guiana.

The general strike, which was ostensibly led by Burnham, Richard Ishmael, and affiliates of British Guiana's Trade Union Council, began on 18 April 1963 and lasted until 8 July. The strikers claimed that the government's proposal to strengthen labor laws would undermine the free trade union movement. Jagan's party had reintroduced the labor bill it had first proposed in 1953, giving workers the right, upon a 65 percent approval, to decertify an existing union and join a new one. In introducing the bill, the PPP had an obvious political purpose, providing a vehicle for the mainly Indian sugar workers to leave the company union, the Manpower Citizen's Association headed by Ishmael, and join a new union associated with the PPP. Although the proposed legislation would benefit the PPP, it could be readily justified within the context of the international labor movement. In 1953, Burnham had supported the same legislation, which had been modeled on the Wagner Act (1935) of the United States. British trade union officials admitted to the Colonial Office that they did "not see any real dangers in the bill." They objected, however, to the growing influence of U.S. unions. British trade unionists further observed that the strike was "wholly political." One noted that "if Dr. Jagan had called me and told me that the unions could write their own demands and he would agree to them, the TUC [Trade Union Council] would still find reasons for not accepting." Governor Grey also did not find fault with the legislation.[20]

The strikers proved as lawless as the gangs and mobs that had destroyed Georgetown in the previous year. Widespread looting again broke out. Because the strike shut down fuel supplies, looters especially favored stealing bicycles, locally known as "tickers" for the sound made when a rider shifted gears. Bombs exploded at government buildings. Strikers hurled rocks and bottles at Prime Minister Jagan and other government officials. Jagan's bodyguard and a PPP legislator suffered serious injuries. Handbills were posted inciting strikers to violence. The handbills proclaimed: "Let us not be afraid to shoot!" As they had in 1962, Forbes Burnham and Peter D'Aguiar played to the mob. Burnham fired up crowds with denunciations of the government, and he led sit-ins at the entrances to government buildings. At one point in the strike, Burnham allegedly advised strikers to bring the agitation to "places where they grow rice." British Guiana's Indians grew rice. In response to unruly crowds, police apprehended strikers, loaded them into vans, and dropped them off outside of urban centers. D'Aguiar dispatched his brewery and soft-drink trucks to ferry the strikers back to the demonstrations.[21]

The strike added to the colony's economic woes and intensified racial hatred among its citizens. The strikers, which included civil servants, effectively shut the government down and immobilized transportation and communication facilities. Critical shortages of food and fuel developed. Potential foreign investors lost further faith in the colony. Per capita income declined by 20 percent from its 1961 high. Racial violence also became a daily feature of the general strike. Virtually all strikers were Afro-Guyanese who associated with Burnham's PNC. Mobs regularly attacked Indian merchants who stayed open for business and nonstriking Indian workers. Nine Guyanese died during the strike and scores were injured. In the midst of the strike in a speech in New Amsterdam, Burnham told PNC members that the racial violence was in the "nature of things," because the PPP practiced "political discrimination" against unemployed blacks in Georgetown. Burnham further alleged that the PPP aimed "to make Guiana a Soviet satellite." With the economy and society collapsing, the Jagan government withdrew the labor legislation and granted amnesty to the civil servants.[22] The colony's Indians unfortunately drew hard lessons from the fire bombings of 1962 and the strike of 1963, initiating attacks of their own. Wholesale racial warfare broke out after the strike, with hundreds of Guyanese casualties over the next eighteen months. As one scholar would note in the late 1980s, the agitation of 1962–64 "left a legacy of racial hatred that has permanently scarred the national psyche of the Guyanese population."[23]

The Afro-Guyanese strikers were sustained by a massive strike fund, estimated to be over $1 million, provided by the CIA through the AFL-CIO. Union President George Meany surreptitiously deposited funds in the Royal Bank of Canada.[24] The funds paid for the feeding of up to 50,000 people, providing them with a weekly ration that included salt fish, rice, sugar, flour, tin milk, cooking oil, split peas, potatoes, and bars of soap. The strike's organizers established food distribution centers in strategic locations throughout major areas such as Georgetown and New Amsterdam and in larger villages.[25] William Howard McCabe again organized the union's campaign in British Guiana and was aided by Guyanese graduates of the American Institute for Free Labor Development. McCabe kept Andrew McLellan of the union's International Division apprised of the course of the strike. Union officials, like Gerard P. O'Keefe and Tom Bornstein of the Retail Clerk's Union, assisted McCabe in British Guiana. Gene Meakins of the American Newspaper Guild later joined the effort, directing anti-Jagan propaganda campaigns over the radio. Guyanese would suddenly find new radio stations popping up on the colony's radio band. The American Newspaper Guild reportedly had access to substantial amounts of CIA money.[26] McCabe maintained a public profile during the strike. His purported international affiliate, the Public Service International, issued a special bulletin depicting McCabe heroically unloading food for striking workers.[27]

The AFL-CIO never publicly wavered from its stance that it joined the fight "to help save the trade union movement of British Guiana from being crushed by a totalitarian regime." It also claimed that both blacks and Indians supported the strike and that the union kept out of the colony's politics.[28] In fact, AFL-CIO representatives distributed, along with food, 25,000 pieces of PNC literature.[29] Although U.S. union leaders fervently believed that they were waging the good fight against communism, they expressed misgivings about the campaign in their internal documents. McCabe informed Ernest Lee, President Meany's son-in-law, that Indians were not safe in Georgetown and that a strike would inevitably lead to riots. McCabe also told the State Department that he found Burnham "unreliable."[30] Gene Meakins predicted to McLellan that, if the PNC gained power, it would try to gain control over Guyanese unions.[31] Nonetheless, the AFL-CIO forged ahead with its anti-Jagan campaign. After the successful strike, it convened a conference in late July 1963 in Barbados attended by Richard Ishmael and other union officials from British Guiana to conduct a postmortem on the strike and to plan agitation for the next year.[32]

Whereas U.S. union officials may have entertained doubts about British Guiana's future under Forbes Burnham, no such uncertainty characterized the Kennedy administration's war against Jagan and the PPP. During the strike, Kennedy became displeased with the British. On 4 June 1963, he wrote to Macmillan, recommending that his government take advantage of the turmoil in Georgetown, suspend the constitution, and restore direct British rule over the colony. He even advised Macmillan that, before intervening, "it might be desirable to let the local situation deteriorate still further." The president assured the prime minister that the U.S. public would support the action and that he was not worried about the reaction in the United Nations. He further reminded Macmillan that, "as you know, British Guiana continues to be a matter of greatest concern to me."[33] On 15 June Macmillan responded to Kennedy, pointing out that his government had no desire to bear the expense of direct rule and that it feared both the international and domestic uproar that would follow the removal of a democratically elected government in the British Empire. The British further antagonized Kennedy when they permitted Cuban ships to unload food and fuel in Georgetown during the strike. The petroleum products came to Cuba from the Soviet Union. The desperate Jagan had turned to the Cubans as a way of alleviating the effects of the general strike, after failing to obtain Venezuelan oil. The Macmillan government had no objection in principle to trade with Communist countries. Governor Grey reported that Jagan had bought oil from Cuba for practical rather than political reasons.[34]

A feverish anticommunism continued to inspire President Kennedy's war against British Guiana. In the aftermath of the Cuban Missile Crisis, Kennedy seemed ever more determined to destroy any sign of Castro's influence in the Western Hemisphere. In November 1962, the president had publicly pledged not to invade Cuba in return for Soviet Premier Nikita Khrushchev's agreement to remove ballistic missiles from Cuba. But the administration considered all measures, short of a military invasion of the island, to be available in its campaign against Fidel Castro. The administration developed an integrated program of propaganda, economic denial, and sabotage against Cuba. On 19 June 1963 at a meeting in the White House, for example, the president approved a sabotage program that included attacks on Cuban electric power plants, oil refineries, and sugar mills.[35] The administration commingled its suspicions about the Jagans and the PPP with its loathing of Castro. In July 1963, Secretary of State Rusk circulated to U.S. embassies around the world a list of charges against the pair and their supporters. Rusk found the Jagans guilty because they visited Cuba, spoke favorably of the Cuban Revolution, sold rice to Cuba, and permitted about sixty Guyanese students to study in Cuba. In the secretary of state's judgment, such beliefs and activities threatened U.S. national security.[36]

Secretary Rusk and President Kennedy dreaded a Soviet/Cuban outpost in South America and the spread of communism throughout the region. U.S. officials never explained, however, how an independent Guyana, led by English-speaking Indians of Hindu and Muslim faiths, would spread Marxist-Leninist doctrines in Spanish- and Portuguese-speaking lands populated by racially-mixed Roman Catholics whose ancestors were from the Americas, the Iberian Peninsula, and West Africa. Moreover, British Guiana's relations with its neighbors were strained or nonexistent. British Guiana and Venezuela had not overcome the boundary disputes of the nineteenth century. Indeed, so isolated was British Guiana from its continental neighbors that foreign and colonial officers actually tried to promote a Latin American presence in the colony. In 1963, the Foreign Office instructed its embassy in Rio de Janeiro to facilitate contacts between Brazilian and Guyanese academics and journalists. British diplomats in the Brazilian capital responded that Brazilians were self-absorbed, with little interest in their insignificant neighbor.[37] Impenetrable tropical rain forests helped, of course, to keep British Guiana and Brazil apart.

Hard thinking also did not characterize the Kennedy administration's analysis of racial relations within British Guiana. President Kennedy disdained racism and treated foreign leaders with dignity and respect. He especially enjoyed the company of Latin Americans and became a dear friend of President Rómulo Betancourt of Venezuela. Although not a fervent supporter of the U.S. civil rights movement, the president grew disgusted over the violence perpetrated by white southerners against African Americans seeking to exert their constitutional rights in states such as Alabama and Mississippi. In a moving, eloquent national address on 11 June 1963, Kennedy embraced the civil rights movement and pledged to introduce legislation that would strike down discrimination and segregation in U.S. life. Historians of U.S. foreign relations have aptly pointed out that the president also acted because he understood that discrimination against African Americans hurt the United States in the ideological struggle with the Soviet Union for the allegiance of the nonwhite people of Asia, Africa, Latin America, and the Middle East. Diplomats from these areas frequently encountered segregationist practices when they traveled through the U.S. South. Secretary of State Rusk made those points when he testified on 10 July 1963 in favor Kennedy's civil rights legislation. Rusk, a native of Georgia, repudiated the segregationist thinking of his fellow southerners.[38]

At the very moment that Kennedy and Rusk joined the struggle for simple justice in the United States, they were fostering policies that fueled racial hatred between blacks and Indians in British Guiana. Neither man, nor any other foreign policymaker in the administration, explored that contradiction, because they gave priority to the fight against communism. Forbes Burnham had persuaded U.S. officials that he was a reliable alternative to the suspect Cheddi Jagan. In other areas of the world, the administration also sided with racist non-Communists. For example, the administration opposed harsh sanctions against the apartheid regime in South Africa because it feared the association of Nelson Mandela and his African National Congress with the international Communist movement.[39] Although Burnham presented himself as a political moderate, it helped his case that he, unlike Jagan, had influential friends in the United States who also identified with the struggle for justice for black Americans. Both conservative northern Democrats and progressive African American Democrats spoke on his behalf. The AFL-CIO, which joined the U.S. civil rights movement, also embraced Burnham. Perhaps in the minds of some U.S. citizens, Burnham's drive for power coincided with the struggle for racial justice for African Americans. Such an association would become apparent in the mid-1960s during the presidency of Lyndon B. Johnson.

AS THE GENERAL STRIKE and racial violence raged in British Guiana, the Kennedy administration intensified its pressure on the Macmillan government. The administration worried that the British would renege on their mid-1962 promise to undermine the Jagan government. The British had not taken advantage of the strike by suspending the constitution and imposing direct rule. Moreover, U.S. officials charged that the British misrepresented the nature of the general strike. During question time in Parliament, Colonial Secretary Sandys conceded the obvious to his Labour Party inquisitors that the strike was not about the labor relations bill but was rather a political struggle between the two Guyanese political parties. Sandys suggested that the colonial subjects should peacefully settle the dispute. As Secretary Rusk saw it, Prime Minister Macmillan "has now reverted to the view UK should wash its hands of British Guiana by granting early independence, leaving the mess on our doorstep."[40] At a meeting on 21 June 1963 with his top advisors, President Kennedy made it clear that "British Guiana has become a major policy issue between the United States and Great Britain." Kennedy instructed Rusk to inform Macmillan that British Guiana "was the most important topic" on the Anglo-American agenda. Rusk, through U.S. Ambassador David Bruce, immediately sent a near ultimatum to Macmillan and Foreign Secretary Home. As scheduled, Rusk would come to England followed by the president at the end of June. Rusk insisted that British Guiana would be the principal subject of discussions. The British would not be permitted "to leave behind in the Western Hemisphere a country with a Communist government in control." The Foreign Office needed to exert its authority over the Colonial Office, because British Guiana was "not just a Colonial Problem but one with the highest foreign policy implications." The Macmillan government needed to appreciate "the deadly seriousness of our concern."[41]

The initial U.S. talks with the British, which lasted from 25 to 27 June 1963, proved inconclusive. British officials dismissed U.S. fears about communism, pointing to the strong internal opposition that confronted Jagan. Revoking the constitution and imposing direct rule would create too many problems. Members of the United Nations and the Commonwealth would be outraged. The action would make Jagan even more popular among Indians, who would soon be a numerical majority in the colony. In any case, direct rule would cost too much money. The British judged that they had no strategic interests in British Guiana and "the sooner we shed our obligations there the better." Because "we have other areas of greater importance to our interests in which to sink our money," the British sarcastically suggested that the United States should foot the bill if it wanted direct rule in British Guiana.[42]

President Kennedy brought the Anglo-American talks on the British colony to a conclusion. The president arrived at Birch Grove, Macmillan's country estate outside London, at the height of his international standing and power. Widely perceived as having forced the Soviet Union to back down during the Cuban Missile Crisis, the president had another Cold War victory in Berlin. On 26 June, he addressed a gigantic, delirious crowd of West Berliners from a platform mounted on the steps of the city hall. That morning Kennedy had seen the Berlin Wall for the first time. The president ensured that the wall, the hideous scar that divided Berlin, would forever symbolize the political and socioeconomic failures of communism. The president sent the crowd into a frenzy with his memorable proclamation that "today, in the world of freedom, the proudest boast is *Ich bin ein Berliner* [I am a Berliner]!" His answer to anyone who questioned the moral superiority of the West: "Let them come to Berlin!" The "Free World" had problems, "but we never had to put a wall up to keep our people in, to prevent them from leaving us!" Kennedy's triumphant performance in Berlin garnered the president adulation both at home and abroad.

President Kennedy's discussion with Prime Minister Macmillan and his advisers on 30 June 1963 must surely rank as one of the most extraordinary exchanges of views among allies during the history of the Cold War. The confident Kennedy politely listened as Colonial Secretary Sandys listed the colonial, racial, and parliamentary issues that bedeviled the government's relationship with British Guiana. Kennedy congratulated Sandys on his presentation and immediately shot back that "it was obvious that if the UK were to get out of British Guiana now it would become a Communist state." Kennedy then raised the stakes by adding that independence for the colony could precipitate a war in the Caribbean and perhaps a global conflict. A second Communist state in the region would "create irresistible pressures in the United States to strike militarily against Cuba." Embellishing the theme, Kennedy implied to the British that they had the power to prevent the election of a belligerent, rash person in the 1964 U.S. presidential race. Kennedy was presumably thinking of Republican Senator Barry Goldwater, the conservative anticommunist from Arizona. The president repeated "that the great danger in 1964 was that, since Cuba would be the major American public issue, adding British Guiana to Cuba could well tip the scales, and someone would be elected who would take military action against Cuba." Kennedy added that the "American public would not stand for a situation which looked as though the Soviet Union had leapfrogged over Cuba to land on the continent in the Western Hemisphere." The president promised that the United States would take a sympathetic approach to British problems with such colonies as Southern Rhodesia, but the British needed "to drag the thing out" when it came to independence for British Guiana. Kennedy recommended that the British cite "instability and the danger of racial strife" as rationales for delay.[43]

According to the memorandum of conversation, Prime Minister Macmillan did not respond directly to the president's strident lecture. Perhaps he had been stunned by his friend's aggressive approach. In his memoirs, Macmillan did not address the confrontation at Birch Grove other than to note that "on other difficult but really less important matters we were in agreement."[44] Macmillan concluded that his government could no longer delay in implementing the scheme to drive Cheddi Jagan from power. On 2 July, Duncan Sandys informed the Colonial Office that the United States would not accept an independent country under Jagan and ordered it to start working on a constitution that included proportional representation. On 18 July Macmillan wrote to Kennedy promising that his government would unseat Jagan.[45] Knowing that he would pay a domestic and international price for acceding to the U.S. demands, Macmillan took solace in reflecting on U.S. hypocrisy. As he told his diary on the day before he wrote Kennedy, "it is . . . rather fun making the Americans repeat over & over again their passionate plea to stick to 'colonialism' and 'imperialism' at all costs."[46]

Wanting to screw Macmillan's courage to the sticking point, Kennedy responded on 10 September 1963 to the prime minister's letter. He told Macmillan that the United States could fully assist his government if it informed the United States of the details of how it planned to suspend British Guiana's constitution and mandate a new election based on proportional representation. Kennedy pledged that the United States would steer Forbes Burnham and Peter D'Aguiar on the right path and would fund a "real economic development program" for the colony once Jagan was unseated. The president also promised that his administration would work on "creating and launching an alternative East Indian party" in British Guiana. The president concluded by acknowledging that "this problem is one in which you have shown a most helpful understanding of my special concern, and I am grateful to you and also to Duncan Sandys for your willingness to take hold of it when there is so little advantage in it for you."[47] On 28 September, Macmillan informed Kennedy that Sandys would call for a conference on October 1963 and then impose a solution. Macmillan warned, however, that the British scheme would collapse if Burnham and Jagan agreed to share power. The prime minister told Kennedy that he trusted "that your people will be doing what they can to discourage any joint moves, either for a coalition or an outside inquiry, either which might upset all our plans."[48]

Colonial Secretary Sandy's artful plan for British Guiana aimed at satisfying the United States and deflecting domestic and international criticism. Sandys presumed that the conference, which would be held in late October 1963, would deadlock on the first day, with Prime Minister Jagan insisting on setting a date for independence, with no new elections. Burnham and D'Aguiar would predictably demand a new electoral scheme. Sandys would then impose his solution of new elections based on proportional representation. The United States would support the United Kingdom's decision at international forums like the United Nations. But "in order to avoid disclosing the prior understanding between the two Governments, the U.S. Government will continue to refrain from comment on British Guiana until the British Government's decision has been announced." At the conference, Sandys would not raise the issue of communism but instead emphasize the racial tensions in the colony. Such an approach would provide cover from the allegation that the United Kingdom was merely responding to U.S. Cold War fears. After the conference, the United States would make an initial grant of $5 million to the colony with a "crash" program of economic aid to follow.[49]

The United States carried out its assigned role in the conspiracy. U.S. diplomats approached Chile, which served on the five-nation subcommittee on British Guiana of the U.N.'s Committee of Twenty-Four on colonialism, and advised Chilean officials that the United Kingdom should not be pressured, because British Guiana lacked the internal peace and order necessary for independence. Chileans were reminded that they represented the region's interests and could help prevent a "Congo-like situation developing" in the Western Hemisphere.[50] President Kennedy played his part by publicly downplaying the U.S. role in British Guiana. At a news conference in late August, Kennedy declined to answer a three-part question on Jagan and British Guiana, noting "I don't think it would be useful to respond." The president then added that is was "very important that we point out that this is primarily a British matter and we should leave the judgment to them."[51] While Kennedy was denying a U.S. interest, the U.S. Information Service prepared to launch a massive propaganda campaign in the colony. The agency assigned a second officer, described as "young, vigorous, and single with field experience in Brazil," to British Guiana. He and his colleague and the local staff of eight would flood the colony with anticommunist films, books, and pamphlets. They also planned to work with the U.S. information service in New Delhi and ship Hindi-language material to British Guiana.[52] Gene Meakins and the AFL-CIO also prepared to coordinate their anti-Jagan efforts in the labor field with the U.S. Information Service.[53]

Both British and U.S. officials rejected last efforts to save democracy in British Guiana. Jock Campbell, the head of Booker Brothers, told Sandys that British Guiana needed a "Trinidad-like constitution," which preserved the British "first past the post" voting system but also guaranteed a distribution of power based on race in key governmental posts. Campbell offered a solution meriting debate, because Trinidad and Tobago, which gained its independence in 1962 under the leadership of Dr. Eric Williams, had a multiracial society with blacks somewhat outnumbering Indians. The new constitution of Trinidad and Tobago protected racial minorities by requiring a three-quarter majority to amend critical clauses. The nation's constitution also provided for a nominated upper house, or Senate, to include "special interests" not elected to the lower house.[54] Governor Grey took the extraordinary step of going public with his opposition to the plot against Jagan. In September 1963, Grey gave an interview to a journalist based in Scotland, which subsequently appeared in newspapers throughout the United Kingdom. Grey especially criticized President Kennedy for refusing Jagan's repeated pleas for economic assistance. U.S. economic aid would have kept the colony firmly tied to West. As always, Grey ridiculed the idea that impoverished, resource poor British Guiana would be of any interest to the Communists or anyone else. The international press exaggerated Jagan's significance and once the colony gained independence "its importance in international affairs would be virtually non-existent." Speaking for the president, National Security Adviser Bundy complained to Ambassador Ormsby-Gore about Grey. The president assumed that the article accurately reflected the views of Grey and some in the Colonial Office. Although not upset by such views, the president believed that Grey's remarks added to "difficulties in handling the situation within the administration and within Congress." Ormsby-Gore relayed the president's complaint to Foreign Secretary Home and advised him to contact Duncan Sandys.[55] Shortly thereafter, Sandys transferred Governor Grey out of Georgetown.

Cheddi Jagan's final efforts to reach a compromise also proved futile. In September, Jagan asked Consul Melby what could be done to improve relations with the United States. He had concluded that the United States had adopted a policy of "Jagan must go." The prime minister asked for U.S. understanding and assistance in realizing his ideal of making his country the "first example of a socialist state created by non-violent means." Melby thought that Washington should at least talk to Jagan. Secretary Rusk instantly dismissed Jagan's overture and his consul's advice, instructing Melby that "we wish to avoid creating any impression, or enabling PPP to do so, that there exists real possibility of improving relations between PPP and USG."[56] The bitter Jagan thereafter protested to the Colonial Office that there was "some unholy agreement" between the United States and the United Kingdom to deny British Guiana its independence so long as he was in power. He lamented that "Americans saw things in black and white; anyone who was not wholeheartedly allied to the West was a Communist and had to be got rid of." Jagan knew that the United States was behind Burnham, and he feared that his life would be in danger with Burnham in power acting under U.S. direction. Despite his anger and fear, Jagan remained interested in a solution, like the Trinidad constitution, that would preserve majority rule and protect minority rights.[57]

The British Guiana Conference, which took place in London from 22 to 31 October 1963, exceeded Colonial Secretary Sandys's grandest expectations. The first days of the conference proceeded as scripted with Burnham, D'Aguiar, and Jagan debating whether the colony needed new elections and a new electoral scheme prior to independence. On 25 October, Sandys pronounced the conference deadlocked and offered to arbitrate the dispute. Burnham and D'Aguiar immediately accepted the offer, probably having already been quietly told by U.S. diplomats or by CIA agents to put their faith in Sandys. The colonial secretary's main concern had been "not to make a martyr or hero out of Dr. Jagan."[58] But Jagan surprised Sandys when he too agreed to sign a paper asking Sandys to arbitrate. Sandys carried out the pretense of thinking deeply about the issue for several days and then announced his decision on 31 October. Independence would not be considered, until British Guiana conducted new elections based on a system of proportional representation, with the entire nation a single constituency. Sandys also rejected Jagan's call for lowering the voting age from twenty-one to eighteen.[59] Burnham and D'Aguiar's supporters rejoiced at the decision. Richard Ishmael expressed to Consul Melby his "profound surprise that Sandys had not even thrown a crumb to Jagan."[60]

PPP members, including apparently Janet Jagan, criticized Jagan for trusting Sandys. Scholarly analysts of Guyanese politics have judged Jagan to have been politically naïve.[61] In his memoirs, Jagan wrote that he agreed to arbitration, thinking it was the only way to bring the British to fix a date for independence.[62] Jagan's mistake may have been more tactical than strategic. His domestic and international opponents would always make the propaganda point that Jagan had no right to complain about the results of subsequent elections based on Sandys's electoral scheme. But Sandys was going to impose the same solution no matter what Jagan agreed to at the conference. Prime Minister Jagan could have hardly known that President John F. Kennedy and Prime Minister Harold Macmillan had personally conspired against him, his wife, his political party, and his little nation.

In November and December 1963, Secretary of State Rusk, "filled with admiration for the way Mr. Sandys had handled the British Guiana problem," reviewed Jagan's defeat with British leaders. The British cynically noted that they found it "slightly awkward that Dr. Jagan had given so little trouble" at the conference. Rusk observed that it had been "very difficult for the Americans to keep their mouths shut about British Guiana." He added that "it was vital" that British Guiana not "become an internal issue in the United States." Colonial Secretary Sandys assured Rusk that the colony's election would take place after the November 1964 U.S. election. He happily predicted that the new electoral system would encourage splinter parties, because a party would need to win less than 1/35 of the total vote to win a seat in Parliament. Nonetheless, the British could not guarantee that the PPP would fail to win 50 percent of the vote. British Guiana needed those splinter parties to draw Indian votes away from Jagan. Sandys advised that "it would be a good thing if the American and British agencies concerned were to get together on this point."[63] Indeed, Rusk had already ordered the consulate in Georgetown to conduct a demographic analysis of British Guiana and to predict "the eligible voters based on race."[64] The United States would also begin to search for an Indian political figure who could serve as an alternative to Jagan.

In parliamentary debates, Labour members Arthur Bottomley and Fenner Brockway attacked Sandys for doing U.S. bidding, heightening racial tensions, and undermining electoral fair play in British Guiana. Sandys rejected the charges and answered that "my sole aim" was "to put an end to racial politics which is the curse of British Guiana." The colonial secretary ventured that, under a system of proportional representation, political parties would become multiracial, as they competed for voters across ethnic and racial lines, trying to win 50 percent of the vote.[65] Nonpartisan students of British Guiana's political milieu rejected Sandys's sophistry. Governor Ralph Grey, Consul Everett Melby, and Jock Campbell of Booker Brothers agreed in their separate analyses of the London conference that proportional representation ensured the continuation of racial politics and that parties would organize on strictly racial lines. So worried was Melby about British Guiana's future that he suggested in his last dispatch from Georgetown that the colony needed to be placed under the supervision of an international body like the Organization of American States. In one of his last dispatches, Governor Grey also noted that Indians would never waver in their support for Cheddi Jagan.[66]

By 1 November 1963, three weeks before his death, President Kennedy had essentially achieved his goal of preventing Cheddi Jagan and the PPP from governing an independent Guyana. In the president's analysis, he had exercised "international responsibility," in preventing a second Cuba in the Western Hemisphere.[67] Kennedy had, however, paved the way to power for Forbes Burnham, a political leader who had exacerbated racial tensions in British Guiana. What the president would have thought of Burnham's two decades of misrule cannot be determined. But the president's fervent admirers, like Arthur Schlesinger, subsequently regretted the administration's opposition to democracy in British Guiana.

THE YEAR 1964 PROVED critical for the people of British Guiana. Vicious racial warfare ravaged the colony. Amidst the violence, citizens voted in a national election at the end of the year under the system of proportional representation. The U.S. presidential administration of Lyndon Johnson worked feverishly to ensure that Guyanese did not again choose Cheddi Jagan as their leader. The administration also demanded that the Labour Party of Harold Wilson support British Guiana's electoral system.

New men in Washington, London, and Georgetown directed policy for British Guiana. Although not as personally involved in the British Guiana issue as Kennedy, President Johnson maintained U.S. policy and relied on Kennedy men, like Secretary of State Rusk and National Security Adviser Bundy, to carry it out. Within a month after Johnson became president, the State Department informed the British that it worked from the assumption that the understandings between Kennedy and Macmillan held and added that "President Johnson is just as concerned with this problem as his predecessor because he feels as strongly that we cannot have another Communist state in the Western Hemisphere."[68] The message went to a new prime minister. Weakened both by his own poor health and by the Profumo sex and espionage scandal, Macmillan resigned in mid-October 1963, just before the opening of the London conference on British Guiana. Foreign Secretary Home resigned his peerage and took over the leadership of the Conservative Party in the House of Commons. He left Duncan Sandys in charge of colonial affairs. The new prime minister visited Johnson in February 1964 and briefly discussed British Guiana with the president. Johnson reminded Prime Minister Sir Alec Douglas-Home of the Kennedy-Macmillan agreements and, according to Bundy, "the Prime Minister at once replied that he understood this agreement and supported it."[69]

Colonial Secretary Sandys replaced Governor Grey with Richard Luyt, a native of South Africa and a career colonial officer. Luyt had primarily served in the African posts of Kenya and Northern Rhodesia (Zambia) and had developed a good relationship with Kenneth Kaunda, the nationalist leader of Zambia. Unlike Grey, Luyt accepted proportional representation and principally defined his role as supervising a new election. Luyt, who had a reputation as a tough anticommunist, quickly took, however, the position of his gubernatorial predecessors—Savage, Renison, Grey—that international Communism did not threaten British Guiana. In his first comprehensive report to London, Luyt noted that Indians feared "hooliganism" by blacks more than they feared communism. Luyt also dutifully checked out reports of automatic weapons on Cuban ships that docked in Georgetown. His agents found sugar and rum but no weapons. Grey assured the Colonial Office that he saw no evidence to sustain U.S. allegations of Cuban influence in the colony. Luyt soon became exasperated, informing the Colonial Office that he understood that his mission was "to bring British Guiana peacefully and constitutionally to independence." If his primary mission was to frustrate communism, "he should be told."[70]

Beginning in March 1964, Consul General Delmar R. Carlson reported to Washington from Georgetown. The State Department had extended Everett Melby's tour of duty so that he could report on the London conference and its aftermath. Carlson's arrival in British Guiana was a routine transfer of personnel. Carlson, a career foreign service officer from Colorado, served in Germany and Canada and the State Department's Office of British Commonwealth and Northern European Affairs. Carlson fully adopted the contempt of his boss, Secretary Rusk, for Cheddi Jagan. Upon arriving in Georgetown, he conspicuously called on Forbes Burnham and Peter D'Aguiar before meeting with Jagan, the popularly elected prime minister of British Guiana. Although he accepted that "the defeat of Jagan is consonant with U.S. interests," Carlson initially displayed no fondness for Jagan's opponents. He opined that British Guiana was "a country outstanding for the perversity of its politics and the paucity of its leadership." He thought Burnham "a racist and probably anti-white," who "remembers slights and repays them; at the same time he takes advantage of people who treat him softly." Carlson judged D'Aguiar, the millionaire brewer and soft-drink maker, as being meticulous, pedantic, colorless, and a poor speaker, with a family life that was "not exemplary." D'Aguiar allegedly kept mistresses in British Guiana and abroad. Carlson excused D'Aguiar, however, noting "that for a respectable member of the community to have mistresses is a common situation in British Guiana."[71] Such charity had not previously characterized U.S. and British comments on Janet Jagan's alleged extramarital relationships.

Governor Luyt and Consul Carlson witnessed horrific violence in British Guiana in 1964. After the London conference, tension mounted in the country, with Jagan and PPP members denouncing Sandys's decision. Jagan implied that the decision was void, because Sandys had not set a date for independence. The British responded that the colonial secretary had made no promises when Jagan agreed to arbitration. Guyana's seawalls were transformed into billboards with slogans such as "Kill to Prevent PR [Proportional Representation]" or "PR or Death." Strikes in the sugar fields and demonstrations in cities and villages descended into violent riots. Unlike the horrors of 1962 and 1963, when principally Indians suffered attacks from blacks, both groups perpetrated violence against the other. Friends and neighbors battled one another in villages named "Bachelor's Adversity," "Vigilance," "Friendship," and "Valley of Tears." PPP members conducted "Freedom Marches" from the country districts to Georgetown. Residences and businesses were burned near where the marchers encamped. Freedom House, the headquarters of the PPP, was bombed, killing or injuring several party members, including Janet Jagan, who was cut by flying glass. The Jagans' young daughter, Nadira, was twice beaten up at school by Afro-Guyanese students. The parents sent Nadira to live with relatives in Chicago and dispatched her brother, Cheddi Jr., to Barbados. Two appalling incidents especially burned into the country's historical memory. In late May 1964, Guyanese blacks responded to the mutilation and murder of a black couple by attacking the Indian village of Wismar, beating residents, raping women, and torching their homes. The retaliation ruined 200 homes and left 1,800 people homeless. In June, two bombs exploded at the home of a senior Afro-Guyanese civil servant. The civil servant and seven of his nine children were consumed in the inferno.[72]

The end-of-the-year accounting of the political violence made for grim reading in a country of only 600,000 people. Two hundred Guyanese had died and 800 suffered injuries in the colony's 368 political/racial clashes. The violence had left 13,000 Guyanese as refugees. Security officials calculated 1,600 cases of arson, 226 explosions, and 675 illegal discharges of firearms. Between 1957 and 1961, British Guiana had an average of 2,000 indictable offenses per year. The figure rose to 4,000 indictable offenses in 1964. Little wonder that 5,000 blacks and Indians, aghast at the interracial turmoil, submitted a petition to Governor Luyt calling for a partition of the colony. In fact, in the aftermath of the violence, formerly multiracial villages became effectively partitioned.[73]

Although nominally in authority, Prime Minister Jagan had no power to control the violence. Forbes Burnham had underscored Jagan's helplessness when, in April 1964, he threatened that "if it comes to a showdown, the East Indians must remember that we could do more killing than they could."[74] The police force, which consisted of 1,320 blacks and only 164 Indians, ignored government orders. Police Commissioner Peter Owen, a colonial officer, defended the racial imbalance by observing that "the African group in the population tends to be more aggressive, are tougher physically, and have more stamina as police material than do the Indians." Consul Carlson joined in the racism, telling Washington that "environmental reasons favor blacks in attaining physical and educational requirements."[75] Owen and Carlson were perhaps unaware that independent India had built an impressive army that caught the attention of neighboring China and Pakistan. In any case, the Indians of British Guiana could not pass police examinations, because they had historically been denied educational opportunities in the colony's Christian schools. With the colony in chaos, Governor Luyt assumed emergency powers in late May and began ordering the arrest of PPP and PNC loyalists. He conceded to the Colonial Office that Indians had no confidence in the racially biased police force. Luyt rejected, however, a Colonial Office idea that he throw Burnham, D'Aguiar, and Jagan in jail and form a "National Government."[76] The governor's assumption of emergency powers had the effect of further limiting Jagan's authority.

Students of Guyanese politics have long known that outside actors like the CIA stimulated the riots and strikes of 1962 and 1963. They have assumed, however, that non-Guyanese played no leading roles in the violence of 1964.[77] Whereas the lack of access to CIA records makes a definitive judgment difficult, Department of State, White House, and AFL-CIO records point to substantial U.S. responsibility for the ugly events of 1964. Although overjoyed by the results of the London conference, President Johnson's national security team was disappointed by what immediately followed. In his correspondence with President Kennedy, Prime Minister Macmillan had suggested that, after Sandys had imposed his proportional representation scheme, a distraught Jagan would resign as prime minister. The United Kingdom would "renew direct rule for a period of six months to a year while a new constitution is introduced and new elections held under it."[78] But Jagan failed to fulfill expectations. He immediately began to plead his country's case to Caribbean neighbors like Barbados and Jamaica, Commonwealth members like Canada, Ghana, and India, and to the United Nations. Jagan elicited international sympathy, albeit little practical help, for his wronged nation and party. Wanting to "minimize international and domestic criticism of the UK," State Department officials proposed to McGeorge Bundy that the United States force a confrontation between Jagan and the British.

In a series of mid-December 1963 papers, William Burdett of the European Division wrote that "harassment of Jagan should be started immediately with a view to driving him to the conclusion that he has no alternative but to resign." Burdett suggested a covert psychological campaign, spreading rumors and having the U.S. Information Service personnel in British Guiana antagonize Jagan.[79]

Other U.S. officials also wanted to attack Jagan. In February 1964, in a background memorandum on British Guiana for President Johnson, Bundy reported that "our professionals are somewhat more hardnosed than the British and would like to see the British resume direct government and throw Jagan out." Bundy noted that neither he nor Rusk "feels as strongly on this" as did the "professionals" in the CIA. Nonetheless, Bundy worried that Colonial Secretary Sandys's busy schedule kept him from focusing on British Guiana. He warned Johnson "that an independent Jagan government would be literally unacceptable to us and we would have to make sure that it was overthrown, by hook or by crook."[80] In February, the Joint Chiefs of Staff, responding to a White House order, actually developed contingency plans to parachute 1,400 troops and land eight tactical fighter aircraft and six tactical reconnaissance planes in British Guiana within a day's notice. The U.S. military's mission would be to support the British "in preventing Communist or anti-West uprisings or movements." Maxwell Taylor, the chairman of the Joint Chiefs, reported to Secretary of Defense McNamara that the United States now had invasion plans for three countries in Latin America: Cuba, Panama, and British Guiana.[81]

The CIA closely monitored the political/racial confrontations of 1964. Richard Helms sent detailed reports to Bundy about the strikes in the sugar fields. The agency blamed the PPP for the country's violence, terrorism, and racial antagonism. But the CIA probably went beyond just monitoring the violence. It sent intelligence about the PPP to U.S. union activists in British Guiana.[82] The CIA's man in the labor movement, William Howard McCabe, encouraged the Manpower Citizen's Association, the company union of sugar workers, to engage in "counter violence with self protection." McCabe organized twenty-man security teams or "Vigilance Committees" to resist the PPP's alleged use of violence and terror. The AFL-CIO also paid the wages of twenty-seven organizers who worked for the Manpower Citizen's Association.[83] Gene Meakins, who earned $200 a week from the AFL-CIO, trained members of British Guiana's Trade Union Council to work in radio and in the news. Meakins's operation defended Burnham and the PNC and attacked Jagan and the PPP. In 1963–64, Meakins produced 624 ten-minute radio broadcasts, the "Voice of Labor," and fifty-two issues of the *Labor Advocate* newspaper. Between April and July 1964, Meakins reported that he had spent $25,000 on program expenses. Andrew McLellan of the AFL-CIO's International Division pointed to the union's massive role in British Guiana when he noted that "I know that more assistance has gone into British Guiana in the last two or three years from the International Trade Unions which includes the AFL-CIO than any other country in Latin America, including Brazil which is almost as large as the United States and has a population of well over 70 million people."[84]

Although U.S. officials and labor leaders perceived British Guiana as a critical Cold War battleground, they continued in 1964 to lack hard evidence about Soviet and Cuban influence in the colony to confirm their prejudices. U.S. intelligence reports unwittingly sustained Governor Luyt's judgment that international Communists could not be found in British Guiana. The State Department listed as a nefarious activity the charge that a music band from British Guiana had toured Cuba.[85] U.S. officials constantly sounded the alarm about Jagan selling rice to Cuba. But the United Kingdom and the rest of the British Empire angered President Johnson by continuing to trade with Castro's Cuba. Such dubious evidence perhaps prompted National Security Adviser Bundy to admit in March 1964, in a telephone conversation with Under Secretary of State George Ball, that "we don't rate him [Jagan] a Communist; we just think he's hopelessly imprisoned. If we knew how to spring him we would." Bundy added that "we know our man [Burnham] is no good."[86] Doubts never, however, pierced Secretary of State Dean Rusk's mind. Rusk responded to the argument that Canadian investors in British Guiana spoke highly of Jagan with the historical analogy that "there had been German businessmen who had thought they could control Hitler."[87]

Sustained by unpleasant perceptions of the past, the Johnson administration worked tirelessly to ensure that Guyanese rejected Cheddi Jagan in the national election, scheduled for December 1964. The administration aimed to prevent the PPP from garnering 50 percent of the national vote and thereby winning 27 of the 53 parliamentary seats. In a parliamentary system, the party that wins the most seats is customarily given the first opportunity to form a government. But presuming the PPP could be kept short of 27 seats, the Anglo-American plan was to have Governor Luyt tap Burnham, whose party was expected to finish second, to form a government with Peter D'Aguiar and his United Front Party. Although an archconservative who adamantly opposed the socialist policies of the PNC, D'Aguiar shared Burnham's hatred of Jagan and the PPP. The Johnson administration focused on enhancing the organizational abilities of the PNC and UF and creating splinter parties to draw Indians away from Jagan and the PPP.

Richard Helms, the CIA's deputy director of plans, directed the administration's anti-Jagan campaign in British Guiana. He reported to Bundy that his agents believed that an alternative Indian party could be formed by appealing to the professional classes and civil servants. By March 1964, the agency had produced a fifty-six page political survey of the colony based on interviews with over 1,400 Indian voters. The survey suggested that nonleftist Indians should be told that they could win political power in a system of proportional representation. The survey further called for informing moderates that another Jagan victory would discourage foreign investment and job creation and bring "political oppression, and the economic chaos and misery characteristic of Communist countries."[88] The CIA settled on Jai Narine Singh and Balram Singh Rai to lead the new Justice Party. Jai Narine Singh asked the United States for $75,000 a month in campaign expenses to be deposited in the Royal Bank of Canada. In conjunction with the British, the CIA also helped create a political party for Muslims, the Guiana United Muslim Party, or GUMP, led by Hoosein Ganie.[89] Throughout 1964, the CIA analyzed voter registration lists and polled the Guyanese electorate, sending the results to Bundy and the NSC. Most reports found the CIA "cautiously optimistic" that the PPP could be kept at under 50 percent of the vote and fewer than 27 seats. In its last report on 7 December 1964, the CIA estimated that the PPP would be held to 22 seats and that the Justice Party and GUMP would win a total of 3 seats. As Gordon Chase of the NSC noted to Bundy, "this, of course, would be a delightful outcome."[90]

The CIA also assisted the two main opposition parties—the PNC and UF—with money, advice, and campaign propaganda. Recognizing the superior capabilities of the PPP, the CIA focused on improving the organizational capabilities of the two parties. After perusing a U.S. study on "methods of influencing the election result," a Foreign Office official noted to colleagues, perhaps wryly, that the PNC and UF "are receiving good advice on organization." As did the Justice Party, the PNC asked for U.S. financial assistance.[91] The AFL-CIO also campaigned for the PNC. Gene Meakins's operation distributed campaign literature that promoted the PNC. At the suggestion of President George Meany, Andrew McLellan stopped in British Guiana in October 1964 to assess the election prospects of the PNC.[92] The Johnson administration also pledged to Burnham that his nation would receive in 1965 over $10 million in U.S. economic aid dedicated "to repairing some of the damage caused by Jagan's neglect and poor administration." Burnham confidently made predictions to the electorate about what magic the United States would perform in British Guiana, after he took power. In turn, Burnham assured U.S. officials he would never recognize the Soviet Union and would sever all ties with Cuba.[93] As the election neared, the CIA worked on ensuring a big turnout of opposition parties, making certain that anti-Jagan voters had access to absentee and proxy ballots and that the PPP did not intimidate voters.[94] The CIA followed National Security Adviser Bundy's vow that, whether "by hook or by crook," Cheddi Jagan would never again exercise power.

In a December 1964 intelligence memorandum, the CIA noted that the PPP "reportedly" received $500,000 from Cuba and Algeria. The agency did not identify the source of the report and provided no evidence to confirm the report.[95] How much the CIA spent in British Guiana supporting the opposition parties falls into the realm of educated guess. CIA documents on British Guiana can be found in the National Security Files of the Johnson Presidential Library, but the agency has refused to declassify all documents. In the 1970s, however, a congressional investigative committee declassified documents on the CIA's 1964 presidential campaign in Chile. President Johnson authorized the agency to spend $3 million dollars to ensure the election of Eduardo Frei Montalva of the Christian Democratic Party and the defeat of Salvador Allende Gossens, leader of the Marxist left. CIA money accounted for about half of Frei's campaign chest. As it did in British Guiana, CIA agents in Chile spent money on polling, posters, advertisements and anticommunist projects designed to appeal to targeted constituencies.[96] The CIA probably spent less than $3 million in British Guiana, because Chile's population of approximately 6 million people was considerably larger than British Guiana's population.

The Johnson administration left unexamined the ironies inherent in the massive U.S. intervention in the 1964 campaign in British Guiana. President Johnson would become identified at home by his promotion of civil rights and his Great Society social welfare programs. But in British Guiana, the administration backed a racially divisive figure in Burnham and a relic of nineteenth-century laissez-faire capitalism in D'Aguiar. The administration also promoted religious intolerance. Some of the indentured servants who arrived in British Guiana from colonial India had been Muslims. Hindus and Muslims did not divide on nationalistic or religious grounds, because sectarian conflict would hurt their common aspirations for a better life in British Guiana. Both communities voted for Jagan and the PPP in 1953, 1957, and 1961. In the 1960s, Hindus and Muslims did not take sides in the bitter India-Pakistan confrontation.[97] But the U.S.-backed Muslim party, GUMP, made explicit religious appeals to Muslims to reject Jagan and the PPP. In creating the Justice Party, the CIA resorted to a crude Marxist analysis, reasoning that propertied and educated Indians would vote their economic interests and reject the left-wing PPP. Veteran observers of the colony's political culture, like Governor Grey and Consul General Melby, had ridiculed such notions. Cheddi Jagan inspired devotion among Indians, because he had risen from poverty on a sugar plantation, flourished in the colony's Christian schools, and triumphed in prestigious universities in the United States. He had transformed his educational achievements into political power and had become an actor on the international stage. Blinded by their anticommunist zealotry, U.S. officials failed to see that voters in many countries would respond positively to such an inspiring story. Grey and Melby proved prescient about the Indian electorate. Despite the CIA's best efforts, the Justice Party and GUMP garnered less than 1 percent of the total vote and no parliamentary seats in the 1964 election.

As the Johnson administration managed the political campaigns of the four parties opposed to Jagan, it rebuffed entreaties for peace and compromise. First through the High Commissioner of India and then twice directly with Consul General Carlson, Jagan again pleaded for U.S. understanding. He rehashed the arguments of the past. He had "laid my cards on the table" when he met President Kennedy in 1961; he thought he had "passed the test." He reiterated his beliefs in socialism and parliamentary democracy, pledged again not to nationalize the bauxite and sugar industries, and vowed never to ally with the Soviet bloc. He envisioned his country pursuing a neutral course based on the Austrian model. Jagan also engaged in self-pity. He decried that "no matter what I try to do; I can get nowhere." He further lamented that "I am opposed by everyone, including the CIA, which I suppose is the American Government."[98] Jagan's pleas left officials in Washington unmoved. At a meeting attended by Bundy, Helms, and State Department officers, the group conceded that talking to an emissary from Jagan "might conceivably cool down the British Guiana security problem." But the officials rejected the idea, concluding that meaningful dialogue was impossible, "since we would have very little to say to Jagan."[99]

The Johnson administration also rebuffed international mediators. In early 1964, Jagan had aired his case at a meeting of Caribbean heads of state. The leaders of Barbados, Jamaica, and Trinidad and Tobago criticized Jagan for his relationship with Cuba and for not respecting the Cold War concerns of the United States. Reflecting his habitual refusal to accept the reality of his country being within the U.S. sphere of influence, Jagan responded that India accepted economic aid from both East and West and maintained its neutrality. Despite their exasperation with Jagan, the Caribbean leaders, led by Eric Williams of Trinidad, unanimously opposed proportional representation. Caribbean diplomats also judged Burnham "superficial, opportunistic, and wanting in statesman-like qualities" and thought that D'Aguiar secretly yearned for perpetual colonialism.[100] The State Department rejected the help of Caribbean nations, warning Trinidad and Tobago to take care to "ensure its mediation efforts give no aid and comfort to Jagan's maneuvers to perpetuate his hold on British Guiana government with attendant danger of spreading Castro infection in Eastern Caribbean."[101] The administration similarly scoffed at a Colonial Office peace proposal. Frantic with fear that the colony was descending into civil war, Colonial Secretary Sandys actually proposed in July 1964 creating a Burnham-Jagan coalition to rule until the December elections. U.S. officials instantly denied the British request, pointing out that a coalition now would establish an unacceptable precedent for the postelection future.[102]

Winning the acquiescence of the Labour Party to proportional representation proved the most critical test for the Johnson administration in its drive for victory in British Guiana in 1964. British Guiana had long been an issue of contention within the Labour Party. Between 1953 and 1960, for example, Labour's National Executive Committee had received more resolutions on British Guiana than any other colonial subject. Left-wing members of the party resented Labour leaders' decision in 1953 not to denounce Prime Minister Winston Churchill's overthrow of Jagan and his PPP government. With national elections certain in 1964, Labour parliamentarians made British Guiana a political attack point against the Conservatives. They called proportional representation the worst thing possible—"un-British." They decried CIA influence in the colony and charged that the CIA controlled Forbes Burnham. In a speech in the House of Commons, Robert Edwards of the Labour Party implied that the CIA fomented violence in the colony. In June 1964, Labour leader Harold Wilson criticized Prime Minister Douglas-Home, noting he had no "confidence or trust for a simple British Guiana solution, least of all on the basis of what we regard as a fiddled Constitution; fiddled by the right honorable Gentleman."[103] Wilson had previously sent a personal emissary, John Hatch, to Georgetown to investigate. Hatch had served as Labour's Commonwealth Officer from 1954 to 1961. In thoughtful, analytic pieces published in the *New Statesman*, Hatch saw tragedy in British Guiana's racial dilemmas. Blacks had long assumed they would have status and power once independence came. Racial tensions had arisen when Indians moved into middle-class occupations and showed success in commerce. The author thought that the process of social mobility would produce an integrated Guyanese society but in the short term it provoked racial antagonism. Hatch blamed U.S. officials, "goaded by their hysterical feelings toward Cuba," for intensifying racial tensions. He judged Jagan a poor administrator but infinitely superior to Burnham, who would "collapse without CIA propping." Hatch also feared that British Guiana faced "an ever more violent future" under the system of proportional representation.[104]

Labour leaders lacked the courage of their convictions. In February 1964, Patrick Gordon Walker, Labour's "shadow" foreign secretary, assured the State Department that Labour recognized the primacy of U.S. interest in British Guiana and did not want to confront the United States over the issue. Gordon Walker added, however, that the United States "exaggerated" the menace of Jagan, pointing out that Jagan did not control Georgetown. In April, Christopher Mayhew, a Labour spokesman on foreign affairs, informed Washington that two schools of thought existed within the party. Led by Arthur Bottomley, the shadow colonial secretary, members upheld the traditional Labour policy of bringing colonies to independence under chosen national leaders. These members denied that Jagan was a Communist and depicted him as the natural leader of the future racial majority. On the other hand, Mayhew reported that Gordon Walker stressed Anglo-American relations and would be prepared to accept proportional representation. Mayhew reasoned that Harold Wilson would have to decide the issue. In fact, although Wilson sharply criticized Sandys's electoral scheme, he took care in parliamentary debate never to say he would delay or cancel the December 1964 election. Assuming a Labour victory soon that would make him prime minister, Wilson neither wanted to commit himself to a policy for British Guiana nor alienate the United States. One Labour leader privately confessed to a U.S. diplomat in London that Labour had no idea how to bridge the colony's racial divide.[105]

The Johnson administration prepared for a Labour victory. In its discussions with Labour representatives, it emphasized that the United States would not accept another Castro in the hemisphere. It also asked the AFL-CIO to speak with friends in the Labour Party and Trade Union Council about British Guiana. As the October 1964 election approached, administration officials discussed ways "to advise Harold Wilson of the importance that President Johnson attaches to events in British Guiana." One official suggested that President Johnson should raise the subject of British Guiana in his congratulatory telephone call to Wilson. The CIA took a less alarmist tone, predicting that Labour would win the general election but that it would not fundamentally change the Conservatives' plans for the colony.[106] The CIA proved prescient on both points. Labour squeaked out a narrow victory with a parliamentary majority of five seats, ending twelve years of Conservative rule. Harold Wilson became prime minister on 16 October 1964.

The Labour Party's victory electrified Cheddi Jagan and the PPP. Having attentively followed political debate in the United Kingdom, Jagan surmised that Labour would either delay or perhaps cancel the December election. He headed for London at the end of October. Jagan could have saved his airfare. Within days after the Labour victory, the United States began to lobby the new government. Taking note of Jagan's expected mission to London, Ambassador Bruce spoke to Foreign Secretary Gordon Walker, who promised to relay U.S. concerns to Prime Minister Wilson. The foreign secretary assured Bruce that Labour recognized the U.S. government's "particular interest in safeguarding British Guiana against Communist subversion." The Johnson administration also inquired about Wilson's appointment of Anthony Greenwood to lead the Colonial Office. Wilson had put Arthur Bottomley in charge of Commonwealth affairs. Greenwood had been less outspoken than Bottomley on the issue of British Guiana, although he had expressed sympathy for Jagan's plight. U.S. officials concluded that Wilson and his foreign secretary would control Greenwood.[107]

The Johnson administration moved its lobbying campaign from London to Washington, hosting Foreign Secretary Gordon Walker in late October 1964. In a 23 October letter, Colonial Secretary Greenwood asked the foreign secretary to be firm with the United States, for the "Americans must not be allowed to think that we shall be willing for their sake to delay the grant of independence to British Guiana, or to ensure that it becomes independent only under a government which they regard as acceptable." Gordon Walker avoided responding directly to Greenwood, but he did note that the December elections would not be postponed.[108] In Washington, Gordon Walker proved amenable to U.S. policy concerns. Secretary Rusk reiterated the points that it would be an "intolerable situation" for Jagan to win the election and transform the colony into a "base for Communist subversion." If Burnham took power, however, Rusk promised a massive U.S. aid package. So pleased was Rusk with the new government's cooperative attitude that he informed President Johnson that he would not have to raise the British Guiana issue with Gordon Walker when he met him in the Oval Office on 27 October.[109] The Wilson government had no desire to confront the United States over the future of a troublesome but insignificant colony. With its minuscule majority in Commons, the new prime minister wanted to strengthen Labour's position for new elections by focusing on economic issues. He needed international help in addressing the United Kingdom's staggering balance of payments deficits. During his eight years as prime minister, Wilson avoided opposing U.S. Cold War policies. Although he resisted U.S. entreaties for troops, he disappointed Labour faithful by publicly supporting the U.S. war in Vietnam.

Among the numerous political batterings that Cheddi Jagan took in the years after his audience with President Kennedy, his meeting with Prime Minister Wilson on 29 October 1964 probably proved the most painful. The December elections would go forward as scheduled. The prime minister conceded that he had criticized the new electoral system in Commons but added that he never promised to change it once in power. His government "had to deal with the facts as they found them." Wilson suggested that Jagan and Burnham could cooperate in a new government. Jagan dismissed Wilson's naïve idea, noting that a coalition was "not acceptable to Burnham doubtless because it was not acceptable to the US Government." Jagan predicted "that independence under Burnham could very easily lead to the sort of right-wing dictatorship which was familiar in Latin America." Wilson thrice pledged that he would not approve of independence for British Guiana until blacks and Indians showed that they could work together. He further promised to end the racial imbalances in the police force and to send a Commonwealth team to ensure fair elections. From Jagan's perspective, Wilson did not understand the underlying realities of what was about to unfold. The United States "would do anything" to keep him and his party from power. Jagan concluded his difficult time with Wilson by observing that "elections are the end of the road; while you think they are the beginning."[110]

Prime Minister Wilson apparently believed that he could bring peace and justice to British Guiana. In subsequent meetings in November with Gordon Walker and Greenwood, the three leaders agreed that they disliked both Jagan and Burnham. But they continued to speculate that they could persuade the Johnson administration to support a Burnham-Jagan coalition. Wilson asserted that the timing of the colony's independence "is entirely a matter for us" and that his government would ensure "that there is no interference with the election" and would see to the "ending of external pressures as soon as possible." He also intended to make good on his promise to end racial imbalances in the police, security services, and civil services.[111] At the end of November, Wilson informed Washington that British Guiana would not "receive independence for a good many years to come." Wilson wrongly calculated that he would have a free hand in British Guiana after the December elections. Perhaps Foreign Secretary Gordon Walker better understood Jagan's "end of the road" metaphor than his prime minister. Speaking with Rusk on 7 December 1964, election day in British Guiana, the foreign secretary remarked that if Jagan won, "we might be driven to try to promote some kind of coalition government; so it might be better for Burnham to win."[112]

The 7 December electoral results generally met CIA expectations. Jagan and the PPP made an impressive showing, winning 45.8 percent of the vote, up from the 42.6 they won in 1961. But under proportional representation in the single national constituency, the PPP merited only twenty-four of the fifty-three parliamentary seats. About the same percent of the electorate as in 1961, 40.5 percent, voted for the PNC, whereas D'Aguiar's UF fell from 16 percent to 12.4 percent. Governor Luyt asked Burnham, who controlled twenty-two parliamentary seats, to form a government in conjunction with D'Aguiar, whose party earned seven seats. The Burnham-D'Aguiar coalition took power in British Guiana on 15 December 1964. In his postelection analysis, Luyt conceded that the PPP, under the traditional "first across the post" electoral system and the old electoral map, would have won a solid victory, garnering twenty of the thirty-five seats. The governor also admitted that proportional representation had made racial voting more evident and that multiracial parties had not materialized, as Duncan Sandys had predicted.[113] The CIA wasted its money on the Justice party and GUMP. At most, the splinter parties cost the PPP one parliamentary seat. Nonetheless, Philip Agee, the former CIA agent, recalled that Jagan's defeat represented "a new victory for the station at Georgetown" and the culmination of a five-year effort.[114]

Scholars have depicted the December 1964 elections as the last election that Guyana would have for the next three decades in which there were no widespread voting irregularities.[115] The Commonwealth team of electoral observers did ensure that votes were counted accurately. But elections are not normally judged fair and free when external actors, like the CIA and the AFL-CIO, interfere. Violence also marred the electoral process. Consul General Carlson reported on an incident in late November when the correspondent of *Time* risked his life to save a female PPP supporter who was attacked by a mob. The journalist, Mo Garcia, a U.S. citizen, acted because the police stood by and did nothing. The conduct of proxy voting also raised questions. Over 6,000 Guyanese cast their votes by proxy, with the PPP winning less than 9 percent of those votes.[116] Burnham and the PNC would steal future elections by manipulating the proxy voting system. What perhaps can be accurately said about the 1964 election is that it served as the vehicle by which the United States accomplished its goal of driving Cheddi Jagan and the PPP from power.

WHEREAS THE UNITED STATES had achieved its foreign policy objective in British Guiana by the end of 1964, it could not assume its victory was complete. Demographic developments favored Indians and the PPP. Cheddi Jagan and his party could possibly win 50 percent of the vote in the next election in an independent Guyana. Over the next four years, the Johnson administration would focus on bolstering Forbes Burnham and the PNC and sustaining the U.S. war against Jagan and the PPP. U.S. officials would conclude that the imperatives of the Cold War required that the United States overlook Prime Minister Burnham's destruction of democracy in Guyana.

CHAPTER FIVE

Guyana,
1965–1969

During the period from 1965 to 1969, the
United States achieved its enduring and immediate foreign policy goals for British
Guiana. The United States traditionally favored national self-determination and opposed European colonialism in the Western
Hemisphere. On 26 May 1966, the British
colony in South America became the independent nation of Guyana. The U.S. man in
Georgetown, Forbes Burnham, presided over
the independence ceremonies. The United
States had effectively deprived Cheddi Jagan
and his party of any meaningful political role
in Guyana. But the United States customarily
promoted democratic procedures and liberal
economic policies. It now preached the virtues
of racial equality both at home and abroad. In
showering Burnham with praise and economic
assistance, the Lyndon Johnson administration aided a political figure who trampled on
democratic procedures, plundered the nation,
and denied Indians their basic political and

human rights. After 1969, Burnham also transformed his nation into a bizarre state aligned with violent, radical movements. The people of Guyana paid a terrible price for the Cold War victory of the United States.

THE LYNDON JOHNSON ADMINISTRATION moved rapidly to bolster the new government of Forbes Burnham and Peter D'Aguiar, which took power in mid-December 1964. On 18 December, the administration proposed that an Anglo-American study team immediately go to British Guiana. Prime Minister Harold Wilson, wishing to maintain his options, opposed the idea, but the British soon thereafter permitted an officer from the U.S. Agency for International Development into the colony.[1] The United States made good on the promise frequently given by Secretary of State Dean Rusk that the United States would generously aid the colony, once Jagan exited the political scene. In 1965, the United States provided $12.3 million, of which the first $5 million was in the form of a direct grant. The grant was unusual, for under the Alliance for Progress, the United States gave low-interest loans to Latin American nations. Only the poorest countries, Haiti and Paraguay, received grants in 1965. The United States dedicated the initial grant to road building, airport improvement, and sea defenses. Construction began on projects that the Eisenhower administration had initially promised to help build. Over the next three years, the United States provided an additional $25 million to the coalition government. By comparison, the United States had provided a total of less than $5 million in economic assistance from 1957 to 1964, the Jagan years. The United Kingdom supplemented the U.S. efforts, offering about $5 million in development assistance in 1965.[2]

U.S. officials bluntly informed officers in both the Colonial Office and Foreign Office that the U.S. aid was conditioned on keeping Jagan out of power. As William Tyler of the State Department put it, the United States "would not be able to swallow such a coalition or help a government in which Jagan was a member." In the immediate aftermath of the election, the Colonial Office continued to believe that a rapprochement between Jagan and Burnham could foster racial harmony in British Guiana. U.S. officials rejected the argument, holding that Jagan's past record did not justify the assumption that racial harmony could be achieved through a rapprochement. Instead, they urged that Burnham be encouraged to appoint Indians to government and that U.S. aid be directed at helping rural Indians. Contrary to the results of the 1964 election, they further argued that an alternative

Indian political party could succeed in the future.[3] The British did not accept U.S. reasoning, but officials, especially in the Foreign Office, wanted U.S. money. As one British diplomat noted, U.S. aid "will support Dr. Jagan's contention that he has been deprived of office as a result of American pressures and that Mr. Burnham is a stooge of imperialists. On the other hand, there is a great deal that needs to be done in British Guiana, and we cannot afford to look a gift horse in the mouth." The Foreign Office became so convinced of the need to conciliate the United States that it actually passed to the State Department memorandums by career officers in the Colonial Office who opposed U.S. policies in British Guiana.[4]

Dissenters in the Colonial Office undoubtedly would have liked access to U.S. documents. In January 1965, the CIA Office of National Estimates issued a special study, "Prospects for British Guiana." It found that "the outlook for British Guiana remains bleak." The polarization of Guyanese politics along racial lines had not diminished. Further racial clashes were "probable." The intelligence analysts further took note that Burnham had appointed two ministers to his cabinet who had a history of racial militancy. Indians also resented that blacks continued to control the police force and the civil service.[5] The Johnson administration did not share such deep forebodings with the British. Anticommunist fears triumphed over racial concerns. The administration reminded British diplomats stationed in Washington that Burnham "may not be the ideal Premier but he is the only present alternative to Jagan and the PPP." William Tyler addressed the concerns of Cecil King, publisher of the *Mirror*, a London daily, about Burnham. The United States "was under no illusions" about Guyanese politicians. King might be right that Jagan was "simply a bewildered dentist." Nonetheless, the U.S. legislators and citizens regarded Jagan as being vulnerable to Communist subversion and would deny economic assistance to any government that included him.[6]

As promised, the U.S. urged moderation upon Burnham. In 1965, with its money flowing into British Guiana, the United States essentially pushed the United Kingdom out of its colony. Consul General Delmar Carlson, described as a "ball of fire" by his superiors, dropped his initial distaste for Guyanese politicians and became a personal advisor to Burnham and D'Aguiar. Carlson essentially replaced Governor Luyt as the source of colonial authority, although he consulted with Luyt twice a week. Carlson defined his mission as "making Burnham a success and Jagan a failure," which required "continued U.S. influence and manipulation." Carlson urged Burnham to work with

D'Aguiar and to issue conciliatory statements on race relations. When, in April 1965, D'Aguiar threatened to quit the coalition in a dispute over budgetary matters, Carlson interceded, warning that a collapse of the government would hand British Guiana to Jagan on a "silver platter." He flattered the conservative D'Aguiar, congratulating him on saving the colony from communism.[7] Carlson also planned to have Burnham travel to Washington in May 1965 and meet President Johnson. Secretary Rusk and National Security Adviser Bundy planned an impressive ceremony for Burnham "as a factor in a process which we hope will protect us from the tragedy of another serious Communist threat in the Hemisphere."[8] Domestic political uncertainties kept Burnham from making the visit in 1965. In turn, Burnham tried to please, acceding to U.S. demands on the international front. He severed ties with Cuba, including the rice trade, and agreed not to have contact with the Soviet Union. In a midyear review, Consul Carlson happily reported that Burnham was "doing better than expected" and was "amenable to U.S. influence." Carlson wondered, however, how Burnham would govern an independent Guyana. Carlson worried that the "ambitious" Burnham "has an inferiority complex with racial overtones" and that he could be "unscrupulous."[9]

U.S. money, more than U.S. advice, accounted for Prime Minister Burnham's success. The colony's economy nearly collapsed during the period of political and racial violence from 1962 to 1964. With U.S. development assistance, British Guiana's economy grew by 8 percent in 1965. Burnham increased the colony's budget for capital spending by 266 percent, increasing employment in the public works sector. The new contracts to build roads and seawalls provided lucrative opportunities for Burnham and his henchmen to profit personally. Their coalition partner, Peter D'Aguiar, would grow increasingly concerned about the growth in government spending and the widespread financial corruption. Nonetheless, the new economic growth gave the appearance of peace and prosperity to outside observers. The Canadian aluminum companies increased their investments in the bauxite mining industry.[10]

Cheddi Jagan and his party took no part in the colony's new political culture. The PPP adopted the motto that it had been "Cheated Not Defeated." Until mid-1965, PPP legislators boycotted the new assembly. Jagan and the party also refused to cooperate with colonial authorities. Militant PPP members argued that the war against their party justified resorting to violence. At stormy party meetings, Jagan persuaded members to reject that option.

But over the next four years, Jagan exerted little leadership. He and the party seemed content to wait for the next election, when Indians would comprise about 50 percent of the electorate.[11] In late March 1965, Jagan arrived in Cuba, staying for several weeks. The Cubans did not, however, give him a grand reception, and Cuban officials assured British diplomats stationed in Havana that Cuba had no intention of interfering in British Guiana.[12] Jagan busied himself, composing his diatribe, *The West on Trial: The Fight for Guyana's Freedom* (1966), the verbose, self-pitying, but largely accurate account of what had happened to British Guiana, the PPP, and Janet and Cheddi Jagan during the past twenty years. Accounts of Jagan's apparent resignation reached Washington. Cheddi Jagan and his wife now appeared beaten and demoralized to Western diplomats. U.N. Ambassador Adlai Stevenson reported that at a chance meeting with Governor Luyt at the airport in San Juan, Puerto Rico, the governor observed that he was now shocked at Jagan's appearance. Jagan "appeared just like another scrawny little Indian." General Consul Carlson joined in the appraisal of the Jagans, relaying a remark that Janet Jagan "looked quite old, graying, and even somewhat dumpy." The State Department further insulted Cheddi Jagan in late 1965 when it denied him a visa to the United States to attend a "teach-in" on the war in Vietnam on the campus of the University of California at Berkeley. U.S. officials decided that Jagan, being "hopeless and beyond salvage," could offer no "constructive criticism" to the debate on Vietnam.[13]

For the colonial masters, Burnham's triumph and Jagan's defeat posed new questions. Prime Minister Wilson's Labour government entered 1965 assuming that the 1964 elections marked a way station and not the final destination for British Guiana. The government had pledged that independence awaited the two communities in British Guiana demonstrating that they could coexist peacefully. As indicated in conversations with U.S. officials, including President Johnson, in December 1964, Wilson thought it might take years to achieve racial harmony. The United States did not object to the United Kingdom staying, as long as it kept Jagan out of power. But the Labour government received strong criticism from its former colonies about the 1964 election and proportional representation. Canada, India, and Trinidad and Tobago all pointed out that the elections had increased racial tensions in the colony. Kwame Nkrumah, the leader of Ghana, summarized the collective dismay when he observed that proportional representation had substituted one racial party for another, and "he did not see how this could be regarded as an adequate and appropriate basis for independence." Commonwealth countries further lamented that the United Kingdom had succumbed to U.S. pressure.[14]

The Wilson government attempted to address the concerns of Commonwealth members as well as those of Labour parliamentarians who continued to object to the 1964 elections in pointed questions now directed at Wilson's own ministers. In January 1965, the Colonial Office submitted a series of papers on British Guiana that included the recommendation that a Burnham-Jagan coalition would promote racial harmony and might be the only way to prevent further bloodshed in the colony. Foreign Secretary Patrick Gordon Walker reacted angrily, telling Colonial Secretary Anthony Greenwood that "I feel strongly that we cannot consider such a coalition and must exclude it from our minds." He reiterated the Foreign Office's position that "cooperation with the United States on British Guiana is absolutely essential to good relations." Prime Minister Wilson informed Greenwood that he was unhappy with both the Colonial Office and Gordon Walker and dispatched the colonial secretary to Georgetown to investigate.[15] Colonial Secretary Greenwood's February 1965 mission to British Guiana proved a miserable failure. He informed Burnham that independence was conditioned on peace and racial justice. Burnham took the position that the glaring inequities in the civil service and security forces "was not the result of injustice but solely that of incapacity or preference" and that he would "oppose preferential treatment for members of any particular race in order to make artificial adjustments in the racial balance which emerged from sound reasons of the past." Cheddi Jagan matched Burnham's intransigence, refusing to consider attending a conference on British Guiana's racial issues that included Burnham. When he returned to London, Greenwood reported on his mission to correspondents who covered Commonwealth issues and declared, "I hope never to see another small country so torn by fear and mistrust between different races."[16]

Since the Waddington Commission report in 1951, the United Kingdom's position on the future of British Guiana had oscillated wildly, as it reacted to international events and diplomatic pressures from the United States. The recommendation that Colonial Secretary Greenwood delivered to Prime Minister Wilson marked another radical shift in policy. He tacitly admitted that he had no solution for British Guiana's problems. On 22 March 1965, the colonial secretary summarized his thinking for Wilson. The colony was doing well economically under the Burnham-D'Aguiar coalition, although Indians remained wary. Jagan remained uncooperative. The threat of violence persisted. These developments led Greenwood to reason that "on the assumption that the races will never cooperate effectively so long as we are there to hold the ring, there is much to be said for a constitutional conference later thus year leading, if all goes well, to independence in 1966." Greenwood further proposed that the International Commission of Jurists, an international body recognized by the United Nations, should study the colony's racial imbalances and offer solutions. Once the Burnham government accepted the report, the United Kingdom would offer independence to British Guiana.[17] In effect, Greenwood asked his prime minister to reverse the policy on British Guiana that he had enunciated a few months ago.

After some deliberation, Prime Minister Wilson accepted Greenwood's plan. He conceded to his cabinet at a 29 March meeting that "he had personally assured President Johnson that we did not intend to grant independence until the communities in British Guiana could live together." But the warring bureaucracies, the Colonial Office and Foreign Office, finally agreed on policy. The Foreign Office seconded Greenwood's argument that "the demand for racial harmony gives Jagan an opportunity to stir up racial discord." Wilson reasoned that the Johnson administration would probably not object to "an early grant of independence if this was likely to strengthen Mr. Burnham's position, since their main concern was to keep Dr. Jagan out of power."[18] On 1 June 1965, Wilson announced in the House of Commons that the United Kingdom would hold an independence conference in the fall. Nevertheless, Wilson apparently thought himself trapped by the course of events. In a telephone conversation with Greenwood, Wilson conveyed his "anxiety" about Burnham and raised "Dr. Jagan's repeatedly expressed fears about a police state." When informed that Forbes Burnham resisted receiving the International Commission of Jurists, Wilson noted on the dispatch that "we've been on the run ever since the constitution was fiddled. If Burnham's the angel he is made out to be he would have agreed."[19] Prime Minister Wilson now perhaps implicitly understood that Jagan had been prophetic in warning that the December 1964 elections would be "the end of the road."

Beyond believing that independence under Burnham would please the United States, Prime Minister Wilson and his ministers had other reasons for abandoning a racially divided colony to its fate. Labour traditionally supported the rapid end of colonialism. When he appointed Greenwood to the cabinet, Wilson instructed the colonial secretary to work himself out of a job.[20] The Wilson government, facing severe domestic economic difficulties, also had no enthusiasm for spending money on a poor, troublesome colony. The government wanted to cut the cost of maintaining the two battalions of troops stationed there to maintain the peace. The government further persuaded itself that Burnham, in conjunction with U.S. development assistance, might bring a semblance of peace and prosperity to an independent nation. Greenwood predicted to Wilson that "East Indians would find themselves fairing a good deal better than they did under the inefficient Jagan government." The Conservatives, led by Duncan Sandys and Nigel Fisher, seconded that view in speeches in the House of Commons.[21] Labour leaders understood that they would have Conservative support for early independence, albeit they would disappoint some of their party faithful. Finally, both Wilson and Greenwood probably took insult that Jagan no longer trusted British authorities and that he boycotted all mediation efforts. Greenwood opined that Jagan, unlike Burnham, did "not grasp how British Guiana fits into the wider scheme of things."[22]

The International Commission of Jurists, under the direction of Secretary-General Sean McBride of the Republic of Ireland, visited British Guiana for two weeks in August, took testimony, and issued its report in October 1965. Consul General Carlson, at Governor Luyt's request and with Washington's approval, pressured Burnham to accept the commission.[23] Jagan refused to cooperate with the jurists. In its report, the commission readily documented the wide racial and ethnic disparities in the colony's security forces and civil service. For example, Indians comprised only 300 of British Guiana's 1,600 police officers. The jurists took a largely uncritical tone, noting that the Indian population had grown rapidly and therefore felt disproportionately underrepresented. Although they rejected quotas, the jurists recommended affirmative efforts to recruit Indians into the public services, suggesting that 75 percent of recruits into the police force over the next five years should be Indians. They further called for the appointment of an ombudsman to address allegations of racial discrimination. The jurists believed, however, that economic development and growth would resolve problems by creating more employment for all. On 20 October 1965, in a national address, Burnham accepted the report and promised that he would work for a racially integrated society in an independent Guyana.[24]

Shortly after pledging to work for racial equality, Burnham headed for

London and the independence conference, which convened on 2 November 1965. Burnham's acceptance of the report of the International Commission of Jurists provided the cover for the Labour government to assert that it was not abandoning the colony to racial warfare. Despite a personal plea from Colonial Secretary Greenwood, Cheddi Jagan and the PPP refused to attend the conference, calling British Guiana "virtually a police state" and comparing it to Rhodesia under the white minority rule of Ian Smith. In a letter drawn up by Greenwood and signed by Prime Minister Wilson, the British rejected the Rhodesian analogy and tartly observed to Jagan that "if your party or their supporters were concerned about the actions of the present British Guiana Government, and had genuine fears for the future, the place to express that concern and those fears was at the constitutional conference."[25] At the conference, Burnham and D'Aguiar agreed that an independent Guyana would become a member of the Commonwealth, with the monarch as the nominal head of state. The next elections would take place in December 1968. Thereafter, Guyanese could decide whether they wanted to form a republic and leave the Commonwealth. The new constitution retained the single legislative body and the nationwide system of proportional representation. The constitution also incorporated the recommendation for an ombudsman to investigate racial discrimination. The conference fixed the date of independence for 26 May 1966. PPP members subsequently cried insult, pointing out that 26 May 1966 would be the second anniversary of the horrific attack on the Indian village of Wismar.[26] In any case, Forbes Burnham would lead the nation to independence.

As Prime Minister Wilson had predicted to his cabinet, the Johnson administration welcomed independence for British Guiana, because the process left its man in power in Georgetown. Administration officials wondered, however, whether Burnham could maintain order and hold onto power, once the British withdrew from Guyana. In August 1965, Richard Helms of the CIA warned National Security Adviser Bundy that Jagan retained the loyalty of Indians and that strikes and violence might ensue. Gordon Chase of the NSC staff offered a contrasting judgment to Bundy, noting that compared to Africans, Indians were "timid." Without the protection of British troops, "they might be even more timid," and "Jagan himself may decide to bug out." Prime Minister Burnham affirmed Chase's stereotypical, racist thinking, confidentially telling CIA agents that Indians' loyalty to Jagan did not extend to violence. Burnham spoke with the confidence of a leader who

knew that the security forces were composed of PNC stalwarts.[27] For insurance, the Johnson administration asked the Wilson government to retain
British troops in Guyana after independence. The British reluctantly agreed
to keep one battalion of troops there until October 1966, although they
dismissed the fear that Jagan and the PPP would mount an insurrection.[28]

The United States concluded its years of confrontation with British au-
thorities over British Guiana in Washington in meetings with Colonial
Secretary Anthony Greenwood in mid-October 1965. Greenwood pleased
Secretary Rusk, opining that Burnham had gone out of his way to be econom-
ically fair to Indians. He further predicted that the two communities would
learn to live together once independence came.[29] Greenwood's meeting with
Bundy turned out more curious than his time with Rusk. An aide advised
Bundy that doubts existed about Greenwood because he "is an avid reader of
The Invisible Government" (1964). In that book, David Wise and Thomas B.
Ross became the first authors to provide credible evidence of CIA covert
activities around the world. Bundy decided not to question the colonial
secretary's reading habits. Instead, he complimented Greenwood "on his
excellent handling of a difficult problem" and twice reminded him of "the
continuing Presidential interest in British Guiana—President Kennedy's as
well as President Johnson's."[30] Bundy need not have worried about the colonial secretary's commitment to the Cold War. Greenwood had proved as
willing, as Duncan Sandys had been, to do U.S. bidding.

In its confidential analyses, the Johnson administration took a less san-
guine view of Guyana's future than did Greenwood. Back in Washington in
October 1965 for consultations, Consul Carlson told the NSC that the United
States had not succeeded in establishing an alternative Indian party or finding a leader to supplant Jagan. Carlson further doubted that Burnham could
woo British Guiana's largest community to his side. He predicted that "Burnham will probably do whatever is necessary to win the election in 1968,"
including establishing literacy tests to disqualify Indians. CIA analysts also
took a pessimistic view of Guyana's racial future. In late October 1965, the
CIA's Office of National Estimates reported that Jagan remained popular
among Indians, although his appeal was racial and not ideological. It further
noted that Indians had shown little inclination for organized violence and
that "Jagan has always been more of an ideologist than insurrectionist." Still,
the CIA predicted renewed communal violence. In December 1965, the CIA's
Richard Helms informed Bundy "that the basic division of the country along

racial lines would continue." Burnham hoped that a growing economy would induce blacks from the Caribbean islands to immigrate to Guyana. He wanted U.S. help for his plan. Burnham told Helms that immigration was the "only possible course of action which would prevent Jagan returning to power with the support of the Indian community."[31]

Despite concluding that Burnham and his supporters would perpetrate political crimes against the majority Indian community, the Johnson administration went forward with its policy of embracing the prime minister. The administration nominated Consul Delmar Carlson to be the first U.S. ambassador to an independent Guyana. Burnham had asked Secretary of State Rusk to make the appointment.[32] Cynical observers from the PPP might have jeered that Carlson had become a virtual member of Burnham's cabinet. The administration also named Burnham's friends in the U.S. labor movement to the U.S. delegation to the independence ceremonies. It asked AFL-CIO President George Meany to attend. Meany declined, asking Joseph Bierne, leader of the Communication Workers of America, to take his place. The administration also sent William Doherty Sr., the former president of the National Association of Letter Carriers. Doherty was the father of William Doherty Jr., who directed the activities of the American Institute of Free Labor Development in British Guiana.

Although union leaders represented the United States at Guyana's independence ceremonies, they no longer shaped U.S. policy toward the South American nation. In 1964, the Jagan government had managed, after years of legal maneuvers, to force William Howard McCabe to leave British Guiana. Thereafter, the CIA man lost his cover from the American Federation of the State, County, and Municipal Employees. In 1964, Jerry Wurf replaced Arnold Zander, who had cooperated with the CIA, as president of the union. Wurf found the union bankrupt and deeply in debt. He also found "cloak and dagger types" working out of the fourth floor at union headquarters in the "International Relations Department." Wurf fired the lot when he concluded that they had nothing to do with union business. The department head, presumably McCabe, used the pseudonym of "Harold Gray." Wurf's subsequent investigations revealed that his union had served as a conduit for the transfer of $878,000 in CIA funds to Latin America from 1957 to 1964. Wurf did not publicly disclose his findings. A White House acquaintance asked Wurf to meet with a CIA man at a "safe house" in Maryland. Wurf agreed to keep quiet but told the CIA that his union would no longer handle covert funds. Three years later, investigative journalists and major newspapers like the *New York Times* would expose the CIA-labor connection.[33] In the aftermath of President Wurf's inquiries, McCabe announced, on 18 September 1964, to his "brothers" in the union movement the closing of his department for "financial and structural reasons."[34]

Gene Meakins, ostensibly of the American Newspaper Guild, directed the CIA-union effort in British Guiana through 1964. Since 1963, the Jagan government had tried to deport Meakins, but with the assistance of the U.S. consulate, Meakins had fought the deportation order in the colony's courts. Meakins left British Guiana on 9 December 1964, two days after the 1964 elections. Meakins had worried through 1964 that he would be killed by a bomb, writing to Andrew McLellan of the AFL-CIO that "people have told me I am high on the PPP's list."[35] After Meakins's departure, the only visible union activity in Guyana was the American Institute of Free Labor Development's project, first announced in 1962, to build low-cost housing for Guyanese unionists. Director William Doherty Jr. thought that with Jagan out of the way, the American Institute could proceed with its plans. By 1969, Doherty had to report to the American Institute's directors that the $2 million loan had been lost and that the 568 housing units had not been built. Guyanese union officials, who were associated with Burnham and the PNC, had stolen the money through exorbitant salaries and personal loans.[36]

On 26 May 1966, in an impressive ritual, the United Kingdom transferred power to Forbes Burnham and the new nation of Guyana. The independence ceremony had been preceded by a visit to the colony by Queen Elizabeth II. Colonial Secretary Greenwood led the United Kingdom's delegation. Duncan Sandys, the official who had mandated the proportional representation scheme, was Burnham's guest of honor at the ceremonies. The PPP boycotted both the queen's visit and the independence celebrations, although Jagan attended the flag-raising ceremony. Continuing his policy of trying to project an inclusive attitude, Burnham embraced Jagan at the flag-raising ceremony.[37]

In his last dispatch from Georgetown, Governor Richard Luyt pronounced the United Kingdom's 153 years of colonial rule a success. Guyana, he concluded, "goes forward with a fair chance of a peaceful and prosperous future." He called Burnham "statesmanlike" for accepting the report by the International Commission of Jurists and suggested that Burnham would rectify the racial imbalances in the security forces. He further thought that racial tensions would diminish in an independent state. His reading of Guyana's evolving demography led him to estimate that the PPP would win 49.4 percent of the vote in the next election, if racial bloc voting persisted. Indians might, however, choose other parties if Burnham could deliver peace and some prosperity. Luyt placed his bet on Burnham holding his coalition together and winning the next election. The governor attributed this rosy scenario to the decision to conduct the 1964 election under the system of proportional representation.[38] Luyt left Georgetown with an obvious sense of satisfaction that he had been the official who had overseen the implementation of proportional representation. Subsequent developments in Guyana's political culture would demonstrate that Governor Luyt had deluded himself about his contribution to the colony's future.

PRIME MINISTER BURNHAM did not seize the opportunity to foster a healthy and harmonious political culture in the new Guyana. Burnham was not merely in office, as Cheddi Jagan had been under British colonial rule. Burnham exercised real power. He took control of a richly diverse society. According to tabulations done in December 1964, 641,500 people, a 12 percent increase in population in the 1960s, resided in Guyana. The survey showed that Indians with 320,000 and blacks with 200,000 made up the two largest communities in the nation. People classified as mixed race constituted 79,000 of the population followed by Amerindians with 29,500. Portuguese, Chinese, and other Europeans accounted for another 13,000 people.[39] For the first time in the country's history, Indians constituted an absolute majority of the population, but they were excluded from exercising power in the parliamentary system dominated by Burnham and the People's National Congress and Peter D'Aguiar and the United Front. Burnham had pledged to treat all communities fairly and to implement the recommendations on racial justice of the International Commission of Jurists. But as Jagan had appropriately asked Colonial Secretary Greenwood in 1965, "Who will compel the coalition government to carry out its promises if it fails to do so?"[40] In fact, Burnham ignored the report on racial justice. The police and security forces did not reflect a broad cross section of Guyanese society. At the end of the 1960s, blacks still made up 75 percent of the personnel in police and military. Officers in these security forces were closely tied to Burnham and the PNC. Shortly after independence, Burnham's government passed a National Security Act, which empowered the government to suspend the writ of habeas corpus and detain Guyanese on national security grounds. Burnham constantly looked for an excuse to arrest Cheddi Jagan and his key followers and to proscribe the People's Progressive Party. U.S. intelligence analysts confirmed this when they reported in late 1967 that Jagan "knows that Burnham needs scant excuse to jail him, or to outlaw his party, and that the Negroes are generally more adept than his own East Indian followers in the tactics of violence."[41]

Beyond intensifying racial discrimination in Guyana, Burnham began to bankrupt the nation through mismanagement and financial corruption. As during the colonial period, the nation's economy depended on the sale of sugar, bauxite, and rice. Booker Brothers produced the sugar on fifteen large plantations, and the Canadian aluminum companies mined the bauxite. On small plots of land, Indian farmers produced the country's surplus rice. The United Kingdom remained Guyana's major trading partner. Prices for these primary products fluctuated wildly. The prices also declined relative to the cost of imported manufactured goods. Nonetheless, Guyana managed to achieve a small surplus of trade in the 1960s. The nation supplemented that income with significant amounts of foreign aid from 1965 through 1969. Burnham's budget for 1969, for example, counted on $46 million in grants and loans from the United States, the United Kingdom, Canada, and the United Nations, with the United States providing about 60 percent of the aid. Despite the aid and small trade surplus, Guyana enjoyed only a minuscule rate of economic growth in the second half of the 1960s. At the end of the decade, per capita income was still below that of 1961, the last peaceful year in the colony's history. Unemployment remained stubbornly high at 20 percent. Poor prices for exports combined with rapid population growth burdened Guyana's economy.[42] But Burnham and his henchman also stole from the nation. In 1967, Peter D'Aguiar discovered that approximately $580,000 had been illegally spent on a highway and that the director of audits could not account for another $11.7 million in government spending. D'Aguiar became further incensed as Burnham padded the job rolls in the civil service, judiciary, and police with PNC faithful. In September 1967, D'Aguiar quit Burnham's cabinet in disgust.[43]

Jagan and the PPP observed but did not participate meaningfully in Guyana's political life from 1966 through 1968. After independence, Jagan took his seat in the legislature. In his inaugural speech, Jagan charged that the method of independence had been unfair and would perpetuate divisions in

Guyanese society. Jagan predicted that the PPP would win a free and fair election. Jagan understood, of course, that Guyana's demographic evolution favored the PPP. Jagan also repeatedly protested that he did not expect a fair election in 1968. Outside observers agreed that Indians remained devoted to Jagan. The CIA noted that Indians "idolized" Jagan. Ambassador Carlson apparently thought that the CIA exaggerated, for he characterized Jagan "as only a demigod to Indians." Carlson further observed that Jagan had become increasingly bitter about Guyana's political life and more of a doctrinaire leftist. In November 1967, Jagan attended in Moscow the fiftieth anniversary celebrations of the Bolshevik Revolution. Despite Jagan's purported leftward drift, no one anticipated revolutionary upheaval in Guyana. The CIA thought violence unlikely, "given the docile nature of the East Indians, plus their fear of the Negroes."[44] The new British representative in Guyana, High Commissioner T. L. Crosthwait concurred, noting Indians held "a common fear of Negro domination."[45] Such comments underscored the limited freedom Jagan and the PPP had in independent Guyana. With his control of security forces, Burnham had created a repressive dictatorship, with the trappings of a parliamentary democracy.

The United Kingdom watched Guyana's descent into tyranny. British diplomats focused on bilateral trade and investment issues, recognizing from June 1966 on that effective influence on Guyana and Burnham would have to come from the United States. High Commissioner Crosthwait and career officials in the Commonwealth and Colonial Office took a pessimistic view of Guyana's future. They rejected the rosy scenario that Governor Luyt had created in his last dispatch. They believed that Guyana's vicious racial divisions would persist. They also discounted Luyt's prediction that some Indians would forsake Jagan and the PPP. Furthermore, Burnham could be counted on to withdraw from his alliance with D'Aguiar. British officials assumed that Burnham would either rig the next election or find a pretext for crushing his political rivals. If Jagan was permitted to win an election and gain power, they expected that the United States would intervene in Guyana. In fact, in July 1966, Walt Rostow, President Johnson's new national security adviser, brusquely informed an aide to Prime Minister Wilson that the United States "would be very concerned" if Jagan returned to power and that the British should disabuse themselves of any other conclusion. As Sir John B. Johnston in the Commonwealth Office summarized the British dilemma, "It is not a pleasant prospect to contemplate our continuing to support an authoritarian regime which has departed from a democratic constitution because the alternatives would be worse." Johnston conceded, however, that his government had already adopted such a policy in regard to Pakistan, Uganda, and Nigeria.[46] In Guyana, also, the Wilson government backed an authoritarian. With U.S. encouragement, British military officers provided training and assistance to the Guyana Defense Force, reasoning that a trained and equipped army would prevent disorders in Guyana.[47] An effective Guyana Defense Force would also presumably bolster the Burnham regime.

Unlike the Wilson government, the Johnson administration spent little time questioning Burnham's rule in Guyana. Only intelligence analysts based in Washington told the truth about Burnham, repeatedly warning that Burnham was determined to hold on to power and would find the best "legal" way to perpetuate his rule. The CIA and State Department's Office of Intelligence and Research based their judgments on solid evidence. The CIA had sources in the upper echelons of the PNC who reported on the machinations of Burnham and his henchmen.[48] Ambassador Carlson dominated the debate, however, about Burnham. He dispatched positive reports about Guyana and explained away Burnham's crimes. At Burnham's request, the ambassador also ordered his embassy staff to have no contact with Cheddi Jagan. According to Carlson, Guyana had followed a "remarkable" pro-West line, and its economy thrived under Burnham's direction. In 1967, Burnham toyed with the idea of establishing diplomatic relations with the Soviet Union. Carlson reminded Burnham that "he had given me his word that when he came to power he would not recognize the Soviet Union." Carlson happily reported that Burnham dropped the idea. Carlson also kept Washington apprised of Guyana's voter rolls. In mid-1967, he estimated that the Burnham-D'Aguiar coalition would win 5,436 votes more than the PPP. By the end of 1967, he feared that the PPP could win 50.1 percent of the vote.[49]

The Johnson administration found no fault with Ambassador Carlson's positive assessments of Burnham. In July 1966, President Johnson met Prime Minister Burnham in Washington, greeting him on the south lawn of the White House and hosting a luncheon for him. Thereafter, the White House arranged for Burnham to take a trip across the United States on Air Force Two. National Security Adviser Rostow briefed his president, telling Johnson that Burnham had done a "highly commendable" job in alleviating racial tension and promoting economic growth. Rostow added: "What most concerns him—and us—is to increase his political base sufficiently to win a clear majority over Jagan in the 1968 election." Burnham emerged from the White House in a jubilant mood. Burnham told Carlson that he supported Johnson's policies on civil rights and the war in Vietnam, and Johnson, in turn, approved of his plan to attract black emigrants to Guyana. According to Burnham, Johnson declared, "Remember you have one friend in this corner going for you and his name is Lyndon Johnson."[50] The bountiful economic aid package for Guyana that Johnson approved, dubbed a "golden handshake" by State Department officers, gave substance to those words. The administration also dispatched agents from the Public Safety Program of the Agency for International Development to train Guyanese police. No U.S. official questioned Burnham as to why he had reneged on his pledge to fulfill the report of the International Commission of Jurists and desegregate the police force, although CIA analysts documented the continued discrimination. Burnham undoubtedly impressed U.S. officials with his commitment to racial justice when he gave in April 1968 a fine speech, "To a Martyr," in tribute to Dr. Martin Luther King Jr. Burnham also led a candlelight procession through Georgetown in memory of the slain civil rights leader.[51]

Although the United States supplanted the United Kingdom as the dominant power in Guyana, U.S. citizens did not become leading players on the Guyanese stage. U.S. investors and traders continued to have negligible interest in the independent nation. Ambassador Carlson reported that only 600 U.S. citizens lived in Guyana in mid-1967. Shrimp fishing constituted their most important commercial enterprise. U.S. missionaries, about 150 Christians, constituted the largest group of U.S. citizens in Guyana.[52] Many propagated their faith in interior villages populated by Amerindians. Carlson also noted that representatives of the Christian Anti-Communist Crusade had returned to Guyana. Jagan had expelled the organization in the early 1960s for interfering in the colony's domestic political affairs. As it had since 1953, the U.S. officials thought of Guyana almost solely within the context of the Cold War. The Johnson administration accepted the finding of the Eisenhower and Kennedy administrations that an independent Guyana led by Cheddi Jagan would enhance the power of the Soviet Union and diminish the security of the United States.

The absolute determination of the United States to keep Jagan from returning to power can be assessed in a conspiracy discussed at the end of 1966 in the State Department's Division of American Republic Affairs. After

Prime Minister Forbes Burnham and
President Lyndon Johnson outside the
White House, 21 July 1966. Photograph
by Yoichi Okamoto, LBJ Library.

Guyana gained independence, the State Department moved responsibility for Guyana from the Division of European Affairs and the Bureau of North American Affairs over to its Latin American section. In a memorandum to his boss, Robert Sayre, the director of American Republic Affairs, Harry Fitzgibbons noted that the United States wanted Jagan to be exiled from Guyana and that it might be able to achieve that objective by encouraging Jagan "in the kind of activities which would support (politically if not legally) a move to exile him." Fitzgibbons assumed that Jagan would "involve himself in subversive activities including terrorism," if he learned that Burnham, with U.S. and United Kingdom support, planned to rig the next election. Fitzgibbons proposed various ways to "leak" disinformation to Jagan. He suspected "that Cheddi will decide that he can't afford the luxury of insulating himself from the planning and preparation, if not the execution, of the PPP's counterattack."[53] Whether the Johnson administration played the part of an *agent provocateur* cannot be established by available evidence. When Jagan actually learned that Burnham would violate basic democratic procedures, he walked out of the Guyanese legislature, but he did not encourage or engage in violence. The United States did, however, aid and abet Burnham in his plot to conduct a fraudulent election.

By mid-1968, Burnham had a comprehensive plan to steal the election. His scheme to encourage blacks from the Caribbean islands to immigrate to Guyana had not worked out. Guyana's high unemployment rate discouraged everyone. Instead, Burnham told party leaders that he planned to limit the registration of Indians and register underage supporters of the PNC. In addition, he would increase the use of proxy voting, arrange for Guyanese overseas to vote, and provide false voter registration cards for Guyanese living in the United Kingdom, Canada, and Caribbean islands. Burnham no longer wanted to deal with his coalition partners, Peter D'Aguiar and members of the UF. The CIA reported that, at the closed party meeting in early June, "Burnham said that he will rig the election in such a way that the PNC will win a clear majority."[54] Burnham had already publicly signaled his intentions, surprising party members in April 1968 at the annual PNC congress with the promise that he would seek an absolute majority in the next election. Burnham's manipulation of voter registration rolls became apparent as the December 1968 election approached. The domestic register of voters showed nearly a 24 percent increase from the 1964 register. In one PNC stronghold, the number of registered voters increased by over 100 percent.

The manipulation of the domestic voter rolls paled compared to the scams Burnham and his acolytes carried out abroad. The overseas register listed 70,541 eligible voters, with 45,000 of them living in Great Britain. British census figures demonstrated that approximately 20,000 Guyanese lived in Britain in 1968. Such fraud prompted D'Aguiar to join Jagan in late October 1968 in walking out of Guyana's legislature. D'Aguiar subsequently went to Great Britain to investigate the overseas voting rolls.[55]

British journalists, both in the print and electronic media, exposed Burnham's deceptions and confirmed D'Aguiar's suspicions. Guyana had become a subject of public debate, for in 1967 in two comprehensive articles, the *Sunday Times* of London had revealed how the Kennedy administration and the CIA had, with the acquiescence of Prime Minister Macmillan and Colonial Secretary Sandys, destabilized the Jagan government.[56] On 9 December 1968, the Granada Television Company produced a thirty-minute documentary, *The Trail of the Vanishing Voters*. The documentary opened showing two horses grazing at 163 Radnor Street in Manchester, where "Lilly and Olga Barton" were registered to vote in Guyana. Using the resources of the Opinion Research Centre, a respected polling organization, the television producers demonstrated that only 150 voters had valid registrations out of a sample of 1,000 voters. Many of the addresses listed on the rolls did not exist. Granada's journalists checked 550 names in London and found only 100 valid voters. After Guyana's election, Granada's journalists tried to analyze the domestic voter rolls, but Burnham barred their entry into the country. The journalists decided instead to examine the voter lists in New York City and again found that most of the people and addresses did not exist. A second documentary, *The Making of a Prime Minister*, appeared in early January 1969, just as Burnham arrived in London for a Commonwealth meeting. The documentary presented authorities testifying that Burnham's fraud was unprecedented in the history of Commonwealth nations.[57]

The Johnson administration did more than explain away Burnham's destruction of Guyanese democracy; it knowingly helped the prime minister commit his political crimes. On 21 November 1967, Thomas Hughes, the director of the State Department's Division of Intelligence and Research, presented the "dilemma" for the United States to Secretary of State Rusk. Analyzing the voter roles, Hughes could not guarantee that Jagan and the PPP would not win the 1968 election. He further observed that "the Negroes presently have no intention of surrendering power, and they might not surrender it even if Jagan wins the election." But if Burnham did lose, Hughes wondered whether the United States "could support Burnham's illegal self-perpetuation in power with consequent damage to the growth of democratic processes in Guyana."[58] Rusk indirectly addressed Hughes's observation by aiding Burnham. The State Department asked its embassies around the world about absentee voting laws. Burnham employed a U.S. firm, Shoup Registration Systems, Inc., to enroll voters. Scholars have asserted that the company had ties to the CIA. Paul Kattenberg, who served as the deputy chief of mission in the U.S. embassy in Georgetown, confirmed those assertions in an oral history interview in 1990, when he related that the Johnson administration authorized a "very costly and considerable" clandestine operation to assist the PNC in the 1968 elections. Kattenberg characterized the operation as "absolute baloney" and informed Ambassador Carlson that he would not take part in it. Unlike Carlson, Kattenberg judged Cheddi Jagan to be "a fairly reasonable politician."[59] In January 1968, Rusk arranged for Burnham to visit again with President Johnson. Burnham was in Washington to have his throat examined at the Bethesda Naval Hospital. Rusk reminded the president that Burnham "was well aware that we support him because he is virtually the only Guyanese who has the popularity and political acumen to lead a democratic government in Guyana and keep Communist-oriented Cheddi Jagan from power." Johnson again had a pleasant discussion with Burnham, although at Walt Rostow's urging, Johnson advised Burnham to keep his coalition with D'Aguiar together.[60]

As the extent of Burnham's manipulation of the voter registration lists became known, the State Department suggested moderation to Burnham. John Calvert Hill, who had served as the department's liaison with the CIA, asked Ambassador Carlson to speak with Burnham. On 29 June 1968, Carlson told Burnham that friends of Guyana in Washington feared that he would use "Tammany Hall tactics" and "embarrass" the United States. Burnham wanted to know what was "reasonable." Carlson artfully replied that "the matter was not one of any precise equation but simply one of dimension." The ambassador added, "We wanted him to win, we had backed him to the hilt; neither of us wanted a scandal." The amenable Burnham accepted Carlson's point and noted that he would register 50,000 new voters overseas, with 30,000 of them voting. Burnham expected to win 75–90 percent of the overseas voters. His new law allowed the descendants of Guyanese mothers and the wives of Guyanese to vote. Carlson concluded from this colloquy that

Burnham's "intentions were much more reasonable than had been feared" and that Burnham "is not planning or expecting a massive rig." Writing for Rusk, Assistant Secretary of State for Latin American Affairs Covey Oliver congratulated Carlson on his performance and seconded his decision not to press Burnham further on electoral issues.[61]

As the 16 December 1968 election approached, the CIA and the State Department's Division of Intelligence and Research kept administration officials fully informed of Burnham's electoral machinations. Embassy officials in London also provided details on the Granada Television documentary. Thomas Hughes calculated that, in a fair election, the PNC would win only 39 percent of the vote. Burnham had taken personal control of the ballot machinery, while simultaneously maintaining a "dignified, statesman-like posture." Hughes also reported that neither Cuba nor the Soviet Union aided the PPP.[62] Reports of electoral fraud did not disturb President Johnson and his aides. In July, President Johnson approved a $1 million PL 480, "Food for Peace," loan and an additional $2.5 million of supporting assistance. As National Security Adviser Rostow explained to the president, "the overriding consideration is to give Mr. Burnham additional resources with which to carry on development projects with high political impact." On 23 November 1968, three weeks before Guyana's election, Johnson approved a $12.9 million loan to modernize the rice industry. William Gaud of the Agency for International Development recommended the loan to Johnson, noting that the loan made economic sense and would ameliorate racial tensions by persuading Indian rice farmers to vote for the PNC. He opined that Burnham directed a "moderate, efficient government" and that the PPP had run a "radical, inefficient, racial" government. Gaud wanted the loan approved immediately so as to influence the election but not to appear to be doing so. Rostow agreed with Gaud, telling Johnson that "the rice loan project plays a key part in Burnham's electoral strategy" and would help to guarantee his election. Rostow arranged for Ambassador Carlson to announce the loan in Georgetown during the last week of November 1968.[63]

Prime Minister Burnham and the PNC claimed a massive victory in mid-December 1968. Electoral officers announced that the PNC had won 55.8 percent of the vote and deserved thirty of the fifty-three seats in the legislature. The PPP garnered only nineteen seats and the UF won four seats. The PNC built its victory by allegedly winning most of the 19,297 proxy votes and 94.3 percent of the 36,745 overseas votes. Electoral officials did not explain whether Lilly and Olga Barton, the grazing horses of Manchester, also favored the PNC. Beyond creating votes, Burnham's henchman, led by Minister of Home Affairs Llewellyn John, took other measures to rig the election. Guyanese had traditionally counted ballots in electoral districts. Minister John ordered ballot tabulations to be conducted on three locations, providing opportunities for PNC operatives to tamper with ballot boxes while in transit. PNC thugs also intimidated Indian voters.[64]

Despite overwhelming evidence of electoral fraud, Ambassador Carlson did not judge the election "a massive rig." After analyzing the vote, he told Washington that allegations of fraud were an "exaggeration." Carlson's superiors agreed with his judgment. The State Department recommended that President Johnson congratulate Burnham, noting the election "went off remarkably smoothly." It further claimed that "Burnham's largely Negro party for the first time made substantial inroads into the East Indian community which Jagan leads." The United States had finally achieved its long sought objective in Guyana. Summarizing U.S. policy for Johnson, the department cheered that "Burnham's election victory caps four years of intensive effort to concentrate his government democratically against the Jagan threat." U.S. support "has been extremely important to Burnham throughout this period." President Johnson, who was soon to step down from office, accepted the recommendation, sending a personal note of congratulations to his friend, Forbes Burnham.[65]

Peter D'Aguiar, the erstwhile anticommunist ally of the United States, did not delude himself that democracy and racial justice had triumphed in his homeland. Both in an interview with John Calvert Hill of the State Department and on the Granada Television documentary, *The Making of a Prime Minister*, D'Aguiar confessed his sins and bewailed the fate of Guyana. In January 1969, he told Hill that the recent elections were "fraudulent without finesse." Hill agreed but responded that it would be "inappropriate" for the United States to take a stand on the issue. D'Aguiar further observed that Jock Campbell, the chairman of Booker Brothers, accepted his assessment that Burnham would now establish a dictatorship. D'Aguiar cried that "U.S. support had enabled Burnham to establish a firm position from which he could probably not be dissuaded from following extreme policies against other races." D'Aguiar blamed himself for cooperating with Burnham, although he did not apologize for his complicity in the violence of 1962. On television, D'Aguiar reiterated his opposition to communism but lamented that Burnham's crimes would create a pretext for violent revolution. Disgusted and humiliated, the wealthy D'Aguiar retired from Guyanese politics.[66] His prophesy about dictatorship and racial tyranny in Forbes Burnham's Guyana came to pass.

FORBES BURNHAM AND HIS People's National Congress practiced the politics of squalor in Guyana. Burnham, who created a personality cult, dominated the nation until he died from a heart attack in August 1985. The PNC, under Burnham's henchman, Desmond Hoyte, carried on until 1992. Burnham and his followers perpetrated despicable crimes against the Guyanese. They rigged elections, murdered political opponents, persecuted Indians, stole money, ruined the economy, and impoverished the nation. They created a society of crime, misery, fear, and hunger. International observers began to compare the squalid nature of life in Guyana to that in Haiti under the crazed dictator François "Papa Doc" Duvalier (1957–71) and his venal son Jean-Claude Duvalier (1971–86).

The PNC motto was that "it is either we or the coolies who will run Guyana." The party transformed the denial of political power to the majority Indian population into an art form dubbed "fairytale elections."[67] The government conducted national elections and referendums in 1973, 1978, 1980, and 1985. Each announced electoral result seemed more ludicrous than the previous one. In 1973, electoral officials claimed that the PNC share of the vote had risen from 55.8 percent in 1968 to 70.1 percent. By 1985, the PNC claimed over 80 percent of the vote and forty-two of the fifty-three seats in the legislature. The party used the electoral tricks of 1968—overseas voting, proxy voting, centralized counting—to compile its majorities. Instead of relying on government officials to carry out the fraud, Burnham and the party assigned the army to oversee elections. Military men provided the additional luxury of being able to intimidate Indian voters. In 1980, opposition parties invited an international team of human rights advocates to observe the elections. In their report, the observer team noted that a local calypso artist sang the lyric that "the elections in Guyana will be something to remember." The team concluded that the singer had made an ironic point, for Guyana's elections served "as an example of the way an individual's determination to cling to power at all costs can poison the springs of democracy."[68] That report confirmed what Burnham had once said to the United Kingdom's representative in Georgetown. Guyana's prime minister responded to allegations of electoral fraud by noting that "I read the Holy Bible regularly and I can assure you that there is nothing in it about one man, one vote."[69]

Beyond scriptural teachings, Burnham relied on security forces and the civil service to preserve his dictatorship. After 1964, Burnham rapidly expanded the size of security forces in Guyana. In 1964, British Guiana had approximately 2,000 police and soldiers. By 1980, the number of armed personnel exceeded 20,000, with 4,500 in the police force and 7,500 in the Guyana Defense Force. Another 8,000 belonged to paramilitary groups like the Guyana National Service and the People's Militia, which were closely tied to the PNC. The security forces were essentially segregated units, with Afro-Guyanese comprising over 90 percent of the personnel. Burnham continued to violate the pledges he had made to the International Commission of Jurists to seek a racial balance in the civil service and security forces. The paramilitary units proved especially vicious, inflicting a reign of terror on Indians. Known in Guyana as "kick-down-the-door gangs," these armed units employed commando tactics in invading Indian homes. The gangs robbed family members, assaulted the males, and raped women and young girls. Indian housewives in rural areas took to congregating by the public roads during the day, because they feared being attacked in their isolated homes. The robberies served as a form of PNC patronage. Young thugs were permitted to rob and terrorize Indian families in return for their loyalty to the regime. Such lawlessness characterized life in Burnham's Guyana. By the 1980s, Guyana had the second highest crime rate in the world, exceeded only by the crime rate in war-torn Lebanon. Common criminals favored the technique known locally as "choke and rob."[70]

Cheddi Jagan and the PPP characterized the racial tyranny of Guyana as a "Rhodesia in Reverse," referring to that state's white minority government. A more apt African comparison was Uganda, where the grotesque dictator Idi Amin drove 80,000 Asians, mostly Indians and Pakistanis, out of the country in 1972. Burnham never ordered Indians to leave Guyana but he made their life intolerable. After the electoral fraud of 1973, 5,000 to 7,000 people a year left Guyana. In 1978, 13,000 people fled the country, which was an extraordinary number of emigrants for a country of 700,000 people. Emigrants included educated Indians and blacks, and they headed for Canada, Great Britain, and the United States. In 1990–91, the census takers in Canada and the United States counted 181,000 Guyanese living in North America. Others estimated that 400,000 Guyanese lived abroad by 1991.[71] Burnham did not, however, direct his political repression solely at Indians. In the mid-1970s, a new political organization, the Working People's Alliance (WPA), began to challenge the PNC, calling for a boycott of the 1978 referendum. The WPA, initially founded by blacks, began to appeal to Indians and declared itself a political party in 1979. On 13 June 1980, an individual associated with the Guyana Defense Force gave Walter Rodney, the leader of the WPA and a prominent historian, a bomb disguised as a walkie-talkie. After Rodney's assassination, the Burnham regime continued to repress WPA activists, arresting Dr. Rupert Roopnarine, for example, nineteen times between 1979 and 1986.[72] The American Historical Association posthumously awarded Walter Rodney the prestigious Beveridge Prize for his study, *A History of the Guyanese Working People, 1881–1905* (1981).

Burnham had other inducements for PNC faithful not inclined toward violence. He padded the civil service rolls with his supporters. At times, the payroll for the civil service consumed 50 percent of the government's budget. Burnham created enormous new opportunities for lucrative employment, graft, and corruption in the 1970s. After eliminating the capitalist-oriented United Front party from the government in 1968, Burnham began to pursue what he labeled "cooperative socialism." Neither international nor domestic analysts could define Burnham's new theory of political economy. In practice, it meant nationalizing the economy. Burnham expropriated the foreign enterprises, the Canadian and U.S. bauxite mining companies and the sugar estates of Booker Brothers of the United Kingdom. He also nationalized foreign and domestic banks, the pharmaceutical distribution system, and private schools. By the end of the 1970s, the government controlled 80 percent of the economy. A prerequisite for employment in the new government enterprises was a PNC membership card.[73] As U.S. Ambassador John R. Burke, who served in Georgetown from 1977 to 1979, recalled, Burnham mandated that the government control the economy, because he feared that the Indian majority of Guyana would flourish in a free, open, competitive economy.[74]

Burnham and his criminal gang repeatedly demonstrated that they knew how to manage an election. Their skill at electoral fraud did not, however, translate into business acumen. In the 1970s and 1980s, Burnham and the PNC turned Guyana into an economic facsimile of Haiti, the region's poorest nation. After the nationalization of foreign enterprises, the country became starved for outside capital, technology, and managerial talent. In fact, Guyana transferred significant financial resources abroad as it compensated the British, Canadian, and U.S. companies. Burnham also spurned foreign aid for a time, arguing that international lending agencies acted selfishly and that foreign aid was incompatible with his vision of cooperative socialism. The major export industries—sugar, bauxite, rice—predictably collapsed, with significant declines in output and exports. In the 1960s, Guyana had managed small balance of trade surpluses. In the 1970s and 1980s, Guyana almost always bought significantly more than it sold. As the economy disintegrated, Guyana began to borrow heavily from private banks and international agencies. By the 1980s, the servicing of the debt consumed over 30 percent of the government's budget, leaving little money for investment in human and physical infrastructure. To be sure, poor global prices for bauxite, sugar, and rice and the rapid rise in oil prices after the Arab oil embargo (1973) and the Iranian Revolution (1979) compounded Guyana's problems. But gross economic mismanagement combined with the wholesale corruption of Burnham and his cronies caused the country's financial debacle.[75]

The collapse of Guyana's economy reduced the population to absolute misery. Georgetown experienced periodic breakdowns of electricity and water supply. Sewage systems deteriorated, leading to a rapid increase in gastrointestinal diseases. The government failed to maintain seawalls, canals, and dikes. When floods inevitably followed, Hamilton Green, the minister of public works, blamed PPP saboteurs for the disasters. Inflation raged out of control; prices rose over 450 percent between 1970 and 1983. The unemployment rate shot up to 30 percent. The minimum daily wage amounted to less than $1.00. Doctors and other medical personnel fled the country; government-owned hospitals became breeding grounds for disease. Short on foreign currency, the Burnham government banned the import of essential foodstuffs like wheat even as the domestic output of rice declined. It actually became a crime in Guyana to be in possession of a loaf of bread. PNC minions distributed scarce food at party-controlled outlets. Malnutrition increased, with one mid-1980s study showing that 71 percent of children under five years old had confirmed symptoms of malnutrition.[76]

As Guyanese starved, Prime Minister Forbes Burnham celebrated his personality. He preferred being addressed as "Comrade Leader." Although he had no military training, Burnham appeared in public in military uniform, bearing the insignia of a general. According to British diplomats, one story that circulated at Georgetown Christmas parties related that "our Great Leader has decided that he no longer wishes to be known as the P.M. As everything begins with him, he wants in the future to be known as the A.M."[77] Burnham had indeed assumed the role of King Louis XIV of France. He had become the state of Guyana. As the economy and social services crumpled around him, Burnham commanded a costly national celebration of his sixtieth birthday in 1983. Burnham's delusions of grandeur persisted even after his death. His sycophants, apparently carrying out Burnham's last command, displayed his embalmed body in a glass casket. But in the Guyanese heat, the body deteriorated and had to be buried.

Burnham's Guyana became a haven for bizarre, weird movements. One religious cult, the House of Israel, served as a private army for the PNC. The House of Israel, which claimed a membership of 8,000, had no relationship to the state of Israel or to Judaism. It was a black-supremacist group that held that blacks were the original Hebrews and that Jews living in Israel were imposters. David Hill, an African American who had fled criminal charges of blackmail, larceny, and tax invasion in the United States, headed the cult. Other fugitives from U.S. justice joined the group. House of Israel brutes broke up anti-PNC strikes and demonstrations and, in one case, murdered a Roman Catholic priest. U.S. citizens also formed Guyana's most notorious cult, the People's Temple of Christ led by the Reverend Jim Jones. Jones and over 900 disciples committed mass suicide on 18 November 1978 at the "Jonestown" compound. Before the mass suicide, the People's Temple had been intimately involved with the PNC. It lobbied on behalf of the PNC, and Jones's disciples probably voted in the 1978 referendum. Temple leaders also arranged sexual affairs for PNC officials with female members of the cult. In truth, the People's Temple also developed ties with respectable sectors of the Guyanese community, such as the Guyanese Council of Churches.[78]

Burnham's international policies proved as disastrous for his country as his domestic initiatives. International observers remarked that the ambitious Burnham yearned for a leading role on the international stage and that he craved international recognition. He also apparently felt embarrassed that he was widely perceived as the product of CIA machinations.[79] Burnham's debut occurred in September 1970, when he attended the Lusaka Conference of Non-Aligned Nations. Guyana was the only Western Hemisphere nation to participate fully in the conference. At the conference, Burnham pledged that

Guyana would make a $50,000 annual contribution to back those working to overthrow white minority rule in southern Africa. While in Africa, Burnham and his entourage happily observed the development of one-party rule in African states like Ethiopia and Uganda. In 1972, Burnham hosted a lavish meeting of foreign ministers of the nonaligned movement in Georgetown. Delegations from seventy-nine nations attended. Also in 1972, Georgetown was the scene of a Caribbean cultural festival. Diplomats in Georgetown noted that "Burnham's government lost no opportunity to cash in on Guyana's brief moment of glory."[80] Guyana could scarcely afford such expenditures on international affairs.

Burnham's conception of cooperative socialism and nonalignment ultimately and ironically led him into the Communist camp. Burnham committed every sin that U.S. officials had warned that Jagan was capable of carrying out. He denounced U.S. economic aid and evicted Peace Corps volunteers from the country. By the mid-1970s, he had opened diplomatic and economic relations with the Soviet Union, Eastern European nations, the People's Republic of China, and Fidel Castro's Cuba. U.S. diplomats reported that Guyana became "inundated" with foreign Communists, including operatives from the militant Communist nations of Bulgaria, East Germany, and North Korea.[81] Burnham also accepted economic aid from the Communist nations. He traveled to Beijing and Havana and hosted Fidel Castro in Georgetown. He even flew to a conference in Algeria with Castro on Castro's airplane. In 1976, he began to permit Cuban airplanes to refuel in Guyana on their way to transporting Cuban troops to Angola. He also denounced the 1983 U.S. invasion of the Caribbean island of Grenada. He spoke of the virtues of Marxism-Leninism.[82] The U.S. man in Georgetown had seemingly created the only Marxist state in South America, although a cynic might have assigned the label "kleptocracy" rather than "Communist" to characterize Burnham's misrule. When asked about his apparent change in political philosophy, Burnham protested that "I did not try to fool the United States government or anybody," adding that he had always been a socialist.[83]

Analyzing how the United States reacted to Burnham's antics is beyond the scope of this study. In any case, documentary evidence concerning U.S. foreign policy for the 1970s and 1980s remains unavailable for research, although U.S. diplomats who served in Guyana have recalled their experiences in oral histories. The United States did not make a sustained effort to destabilize the Burnham regime. As evidenced by U.S. efforts against the Chilean Salvador Allende (1970–73), the overthrow of the New Jewel Movement in Grenada, and the relentless 1980s campaign against the Sandinistas of Nicaragua, U.S. officials had not renounced the policy of confronting leftist movements in the Western Hemisphere that they perceived as endangering U.S. national security in the Cold War. But U.S. officials forecast that an unseating of Burnham would lead to Cheddi Jagan and the PPP taking power. Ambassador Clint A. Lauderdale, who served in Georgetown from 1984 to 1987, deplored Burnham and concluded that U.S. national security interests would not be threatened by the democratic election of Jagan. Nonetheless, Ambassador Lauderdale noted that Jagan, with his long-standing Communist affiliations, presented a "public relations" problem for U.S. policymakers. They worried that the U.S. public would react strongly to another political leader in the Western Hemisphere who accepted the label "Communist." Burnham continued to play on these fears. During the last fifteen years of his rule, Burnham rarely spoke to U.S. officials. When he did, he told them not to "forget when you evaluate my regime that my opposition is the Communists."[84]

Jagan confirmed long-standing U.S. suspicions when, in June 1969, he attended the World Conference of Communist and Workers Parties held in Moscow. Jagan enrolled the PPP as a pro-Soviet Communist party. At the conference, Jagan admitted, however, that he came to his open embrace of the international Communist movement only after both the Conservative and Labour governments of the United Kingdom had betrayed the PPP.[85] Thereafter, Jagan did not wield significant influence at home or abroad. He counseled his party against violence, recognizing that resistance would give Burnham the excuse to massacre Indians. He continued to trumpet his belief in parliamentary democracy, having his party compete in Burnham's sham elections. At times, Jagan and PPP legislators boycotted the Guyanese legislature, protesting Burnham's latest outrage. On the other hand, Jagan supported Burnham's nationalization of the economy, suggesting that it was putting Guyana on the path to true socialism.[86]

Although U.S. policymakers during the Cold War declined to call for the free elections in Guyana that Cheddi Jagan would inevitably win, U.S. presidential administrations, especially the Republican governments of Richard M. Nixon, Gerald R. Ford, and Ronald Reagan, expressed disdain for Forbes Burnham in a variety of ways. In 1971, the Nixon administration cut off economic aid to Guyana. The administration's ambassador in George-town, Spencer King, referred to Burnham as a "racist demagogue" in con-versations with diplomatic colleagues.[87] Henry A. Kissinger, Nixon and Ford's secretary of state, pithily dismissed Guyana as being "invariably on the side of radicals in Third World forums." Kissinger sent tough messages to Cuba about its adventures in Africa through Guyana, knowing the two na-tions shared a close relationship. Kissinger also apparently asked Venezuela and Brazil to threaten Guyana in 1976 when Burnham began to assist Castro with his African adventures.[88] The Jimmy Carter administration tried to improve relations, offering economic aid on humanitarian grounds to the beleaguered nation.[89] After the Jonestown tragedy of 1978, the Carter ad-ministration withdrew its interest in Guyana. The Reagan administration closed down the U.S. economic aid program, with the Burnham regime again ridiculing U.S. assistance.[90] Beginning with the Carter administration, the United States began to issue annual human rights surveys. These reports documented the political oppression and human misery of Guyana.[91]

U.S. policy toward Guyana underwent a remarkable change during the period from 1990 to 1992. With the breaching of the Berlin Wall in November 1989 and the collapse of the Soviet Union in the summer of 1991, any linger-ing fear that Guyana could become a Cold War battleground had obviously dissipated. U.S. policymakers could now focus on the appalling misery of a little country with a minuscule population in an isolated, largely uninhabi-table region of the Western Hemisphere. By 1990, the country's economy was prostrate. The production of sugar and bauxite had fallen by more than 50 percent since 1970. Electrical output had similarly declined by 50 percent. Guyana had a staggering external debt of $1.5 billion. Its currency was vir-tually worthless. With a per capita income in 1991 of only $290, Guyana had the lowest per capita income in the Western Hemisphere. International agencies, like the International Monetary Fund and World Bank, informed PNC leader Desmond Hoyte that Guyana could expect no financial help unless it pursued a course of political and economic liberalization. Nongovernmen-tal organizations, like the Caribbean Conference of Churches, similarly pres-sured Hoyte to hold free elections. The George H. W. Bush administration also promoted free elections. With the Cold War over, democratic values had supplanted anticommunism as the driving force in the U.S. approach to its southern neighbors. The United States no longer embraced anticommunist military dictators like General Augusto Pinochet of Chile (1973–90). The

Bush administration further hoped that a policy of democracy would isolate the region's last Communist, Fidel Castro of Cuba.[92]

Former President Carter and his Carter Center oversaw Guyana's transition to democracy. The desperate Hoyte implied that he would permit a free election and invited Carter to Georgetown in September 1990. Carter laid down strict guidelines for the election, including, for example, ending the PNC scheme of counting votes at a central location. The Hoyte regime delayed elections for two years, realizing that Jagan and the PPP would easily win and end nearly three decades of PNC tyranny. In October 1992, Guyana's first free election since 1961 finally took place. The Carter Center sent sixty-six observers to Guyana. The British Commonwealth also sent observers. Deputy Assistant Secretary of State Donna Hrinak represented the Department of State. On the evening of the election, Carter had to intervene personally with Hoyte when a mob of Afro-Guyanese threatened to storm the headquarters of the electoral commission. Mobs were also attacking Indian merchants and looting their stores. Carter, who subsequently earned the Nobel Prize for Peace for promoting democratic practices and respect for human rights throughout the world, displayed courage and conviction in Guyana. According to U.S. Ambassador George F. Jones, Carter told Hoyte that he did not fear for his own safety, because he had Secret Service protection. Carter warned, however, that Guyana would suffer international opprobrium if the election commission was attacked. Hoyte relented, sending police and armored personnel carriers into the streets to preserve order. Jagan and the PPP routed the PNC, winning 53.5 percent of the vote, an 11 percent margin of victory.[93] In one of the great ironies in the history of U.S. foreign relations, U.S. citizens helped put Cheddi Jagan and his party in power thirty years after Secretary of State Dean Rusk had declared that "it is not possible for us to put up with an independent British Guiana under Jagan." Indeed, President Jagan attended a luncheon for Caribbean leaders hosted at the White House by President Bill Clinton in August 1993, thirty-two years after his fateful White House session with President Kennedy.

Jagan had not renounced the political faith that Kennedy and Rusk found so objectionable. Even after the shattering of the Communist world, Jagan still believed that "the old Thomas More and Marxist Utopias are still alive." As a Communist, he envisioned building "a society free from exploitation and governed by those who produced the wealth." Jagan told Ambassador Jones that communism had never really been tried. "The Soviet Union had

Cheddi Jagan and Janet Jagan in Guyana a
few days after the 1992 presidential election
victory. Courtesy of Nadira Jagan-Brancier.

messed it up."[94] Such views did not discourage Jones, who was stationed in Guyana from 1992 to 1995, because he found Jagan to be a pragmatic politician. Jagan appreciated President Carter's assistance, and he expressed no public bitterness about his past treatment by the United States. Jagan remained a keen student of U.S. affairs, regularly listening to the official radio broadcast, the Voice of America. In essence, Jones discovered the same person that United Kingdom officials, like Colonial Secretary Iain MacLeod, had previously described. Ambassador Jones judged Jagan to be a democrat with a genuine concern for the poor. Jones applauded Jagan for ending the PNC's censorship of the media. And as he had demonstrated during the period from 1957 to 1964, Jagan again showed that he understood that his country's economic fate depended upon cooperation with the United States. Jagan welcomed the return of U.S. economic assistance and the Peace Corps to his country. Ambassador Jones also found nothing to fear from Janet Rosenberg Jagan, although he thought her more ideological than her husband. He described the Jagans as "charming" grandparents. The Clinton administration actually offered to restore Janet Jagan's U.S. citizenship, which had been revoked twice during the anticommunist hysteria of the 1950s and 1960s.[95]

In March 1997, after suffering a heart attack, Cheddi Jagan died in Walter Reed Army Hospital in Washington, D.C. Although he had established democratic procedures, Jagan had not solved the country's pressing socioeconomic problems. In part, Jagan fulfilled the assessment of him offered by the Colonial Office in 1950s and 1960s that he was impractical when it came to economic development. Jagan talked about selling off government enterprises to foreign investors, but he could not bring himself to do it. In any case, economic progress would have been difficult in a country that had been racially polarized since the violence of the early 1960s. And Forbes Burnham and his clique had left a ravaged country.

THOSE WITH A HISTORICAL consciousness could perhaps best appreciate what happened to Guyana during the Burnham years. In his memoir of the Kennedy administration, *A Thousand Days* (1965), Arthur Schlesinger concluded his discussion of his president's policy toward British Guiana with the ambiguous observation that "with much unhappiness and turbulence, British Guiana seemed to have passed safely out of the Communist orbit." Twenty-five years later, Schlesinger decried the course of events and publicly apologized to Cheddi Jagan.[96] That "unhappiness and turbulence" marred life in Guyana under Forbes Burnham should have perhaps been anticipated by those who were not professional historians. From 1953 to 1969, U.S. and United Kingdom officials had repeatedly used words like "unscrupulous," "opportunist," "demagogue," "madman," and "racist" when they spoke of Forbes Burnham.

conclusion

The U.S. intervention in British Guiana/
Guyana from 1953 to 1969 confirms the well-
known reflection of Thucydides on international relations—large nations do what they
wish, while small nations accept what they
must. Through overt political and economic
pressures and covert conspiracies, the United
States achieved its goal of depriving Cheddi
Jagan and the People's Progressive Party of
power and insuring that Forbes Burnham and
his People's National Congress dominated the
newly independent nation. U.S. policymakers
generated political instability and economic
chaos and incited racial warfare in the British
colony. They also succeeded in overawing
British officials, demonstrating to the British
that they could not control British Guiana
without U.S. cooperation. Like the Indians of
Guyana, the British had to accept the extension
of U.S. power and accede to U.S. demands.

U.S policy in British Guiana violated the
sacred principles of U.S. foreign relations.

Thomas Jefferson, the first secretary of state (1789–94), established U.S. support for the right of national self-determination, insisting that the United States should keep its diplomatic ties with revolutionary France. The Monroe Doctrine (1823) anticipated the end of European colonialism in the Western Hemisphere. So powerful, however, was the U.S. opposition to Jagan and the PPP that the Eisenhower, Kennedy, and Johnson administrations actually favored the United Kingdom retaining its colony in South America for the foreseeable future. The United States consistently recommended to other nations the concepts of majority rule, democratic procedures, and civil liberties inherent in the U.S. Constitution and Bill of Rights. But the proportional representation scheme served as a vehicle for depriving Indians of political power. In 1968, the Johnson administration assisted Burnham and the PNC in manipulating or "rigging" the electoral results. The United States customarily stood for religious freedom and tolerance, and in the second half of the twentieth century, it preached the virtues of racial peace, harmony, and justice. In spite of these traditions, U.S. officials encouraged religiously-based parties in British Guiana, setting Muslims against Hindus. They further embraced Forbes Burnham, who persecuted the Indians of Guyana. After 1968, Indians fled the country, because Burnham and his criminal friends stole their basic human rights.

The Eisenhower, Kennedy, and Johnson administrations foresaw communism taking hold in British Guiana. They imagined the Soviet Union establishing a beachhead in South America and transforming British Guiana into a Communist center for subversion in the Caribbean and South America. Cheddi Jagan might permit the Soviets to build a military base in independent Guyana. The United States perceived the British colony as a potential Cold War battleground; U.S. leaders acted to save the United States. U.S. intervention in British Guiana can be located within the foreign policy structure—the containment thesis of George Kennan, the Truman Doctrine (1947), and NSC 68 (1950)—built by the Harry S. Truman administration during the early years of the Cold War. To be sure, the Truman administration focused on the Soviet threat to Europe and Asia, but the Eisenhower, Kennedy, and Johnson administrations extended Truman's anticommunist foreign policies to Latin America. Although U.S. officials viewed developments through a Cold War prism, the foreign policy of anticommunism probably alone cannot explain why the United States sacrificed all principle in its anti-Jagan campaign. Put another way, the anticommunist convictions of U.S. officials had myriad manifestations and permutations.

An analysis of the U.S. war against Cheddi and Janet Jagan and the PPP must first confront the finding that U.S. officials had little hard evidence to sustain their conviction that PPP members threatened U.S. national security. When, in October 1953, the Churchill government dispatched troops to British Guiana, it alleged that the Jagans, Burnham, and the PPP intended to foment a Communist revolution. The government declined, however, to put those charges in print. It privately conceded that it had no evidence that PPP leaders worked with international Communists based in the Soviet bloc. Moreover, Governor Alfred Savage and his security officers dismissed accusations that PPP leaders had arson and sabotage on their minds. By 1954, the Churchill government had been reduced to claiming that nefarious intentions could be gleaned from the PPP's effort to undermine the position and influence of the Boy Scouts and Girl Guides. Between 1955 and 1964, Governors Savage, Renison, Grey, and Luyt consistently rejected U.S. claims that Jagan and the PPP secretly worked with Communists. The governors based those conclusions on their investigations of British Guiana's political milieu and the intelligence they continued to receive from security officers. The governors investigated reports of Soviet meddling and Cuban arms transfers and always found them baseless. Career servants in the Foreign Office and the Macmillan and Wilson governments listened to protests that the United States could not abide a Jagan government. British officials decided that it was in the national interest of the United Kingdom to appease the United States. But British officials never accepted the U.S. characterization of Jagan and his supporters as international Communists.

Other foreigners repeatedly advised U.S. officials that they misjudged the political culture of British Guiana. Business executives representing British sugar companies and Canadian aluminum enterprises testified that they trusted Jagan to respect their investments. They correctly feared that their business prospects would suffer under a Burnham regime. Both Cold War allies and nonaligned states also told U.S. officials that they held exaggerated fears about Jagan. Canada, Ghana, India, Israel, and Trinidad and Tobago either vouched for Jagan or lamented the direction of U.S. policy. Like the United Kingdom, these nations judged racial relations, not political radicalism, to be the central issue in British Guiana. In the Cold War era, Israel's

Golda Meir commanded as much respect among U.S. officials and the U.S. public as any foreign leader. Meir recommended keeping Jagan in the Western camp with U.S. economic aid.

Cheddi Jagan gave every indication of wanting to associate with the United States. Between 1959 and 1963, he repeatedly requested a substantial U.S. economic aid package for his country. Jagan's fateful trip to Washington D.C. in October 1961 to meet President John Kennedy can be compared to Fidel Castro's journey to Washington in April 1959. The young Cuban revolutionary surprised Eisenhower administration officials by not asking for economic aid. He apparently wanted to demonstrate to his public that he would be the first Cuban leader not dependent on U.S. goodwill. Jagan, on the other hand, was astute enough to understand that the economic aid program he envisioned would magnify the U.S. presence in his country. After his unsuccessful audience with President Kennedy, Jagan continued to seek U.S. cooperation, most notably in his lengthy, impassioned letter of April 1963 to Kennedy. Jagan also responded to the proportional representation schemes with counterproposals that would preserve majority rule and safeguard the political rights of British Guiana's black minority. Jagan had a personal history of racial tolerance and sensitivity. He attended Howard University and denounced the racial discrimination that African Americans suffered. The PPP that Jagan founded was a multiracial political party. Jagan, an Indian and a Hindu, celebrated his fiftieth wedding anniversary with a white, Jewish woman from Chicago.

Neither Jagan's actions, words, nor personal story moved U.S. officials. Secretary of State Dean Rusk once compared Jagan to Adolf Hitler. U.S. officials could not make such odious comparisons based on reports they received from intelligence analysts based in Washington or diplomats stationed in Georgetown. The Special National Intelligence Estimate for British Guiana of March 1961 set the boundaries for the intelligence community's reporting on Jagan and the PPP. The analysts pointed to Jagan's association with acknowledged Communists. But they also noted that they could find no evidence that international Communists tried to exploit British Guiana. They further predicted that a Guyana under Jagan would develop ties with the Soviet bloc and Castro's Cuba but would also want economic aid from the United States and the United Kingdom. Subsequent intelligence estimates reiterated those basic findings. Perhaps the evidence definitively tying Jagan and his supporters to an international conspiracy went up in flames when the CIA allegedly burned its records on British Guiana. Maybe, one day, the CIA will open its archives and let the public read the damning evidence that one of the agency's spies collected in British Guiana. But the declassified intelligence record currently does not sustain charges that Jagan intended to take his country into the Soviet camp.

The U.S. representatives in Georgetown, such as Consuls Maddox, Woods, and Melby, similarly presented nuanced analyses of Jagan's political intentions. Like the United Kingdom's royal governors, U.S. diplomats focused on the colony's distressing racial confrontations in their political reporting. To be sure, Consul Everett Melby carried out the Kennedy administration's aggressive policy toward Jagan. But his reporting reflected his deep personal unease with the violence of 1962–63. And Melby always recommended reaching a settlement with Prime Minister Jagan. Because neither intelligence analysts nor foreign service officers produced direct evidence, the presidential administrations resorted to introducing circumstantial evidence to support their case against the Jagans and the PPP. In July 1963, for example, Secretary Rusk informed U.S. embassies throughout the world that Janet Jagan had flown from Vienna to Rio de Janiero to attend a conference on a ticket purchased by unnamed, suspect sources. In Rusk's mind, airfare constituted proof of a Communist conspiracy.

Although only presidential aide Arthur Schlesinger Jr. persistently raised questions about the U.S. campaign against the Jagans, high-ranking officials privately conceded the obvious about the nature of the allegations leveled against the couple. Attorney General Robert Kennedy used revealing language, when he recalled that his brother the president "was convinced that Jagan was probably a Communist."[1] In 1964, National Security Adviser McGeorge Bundy admitted in a telephone conversation with Under Secretary of State George Ball that "we don't rate him [Jagan] a Communist; we just think he's hopelessly imprisoned. If we knew how to spring him we would." Bundy's stunning confession revealed that Jagan provoked U.S. officials with his words and associations, not his deeds. Like President Jacobo Arbenz Guzmán of Guatemala, Jagan had passed the "duck test" on communism. He and his wife had traveled to Eastern Europe and attended conferences organized by Communists. The party organ, *Thunder*, took a radical point of view on international events. On national television in the United States, Jagan had declined to condemn the Soviet Union. Jagan labeled himself a "Communist," although he had a unique, complex, even baffling definition of communism. As Raymond T. Smith, the astute analyst of British Guiana at midcentury, observed, Jagan seemed to want to accept some principles of communist philosophy without worrying too much about the implications of their application in the real world of the Soviet-American confrontation.[2]

Prime Minister Jagan could have possibly justified his views to U.S. officials if he had lived outside of the Western Hemisphere, the traditional U.S. sphere of influence. During the Cold War, the United States argued that its credibility in international affairs depended on preserving a secure and stable hemisphere. Secretary Rusk once advised Argentine diplomats that the Soviet Union might be tempted to attack West Berlin if it perceived weakness "in our own backyard." The United States adamantly opposed any Latin American nation establishing political or commercial ties with the Soviet bloc.[3] Caribbean leaders, like Eric Williams of Trinidad and Tobago, warned Jagan that he had to heed U.S. foreign policy concerns. Jagan could be characterized as being either naïve, stubborn, or foolish for ignoring such warnings. But Jagan's apparent defiance of U.S. power can also be explained by his attachment to a global outlook. He did not perceive himself solely as a citizen of the Western Hemisphere. As a subject of the British Empire, he tried to emulate the United Kingdom's policy of conducting diplomatic and commercial relations with the Soviet bloc, the People's Republic of China, and Communist Cuba. Jagan, an Indian, admired "the Indian way," the principles of the Congress Party, and Prime Minister Jawaharal Nehru's success at winning economic assistance from both the United States and the Soviet Union. As a student of international affairs, he understood that the United States supported Israel, a country that espoused socialist ideals.

Jagan misperceived not only Guyana's role in the global balance of power but also the U.S. loathing of Castro's Cuba. Since 1959, an article of faith of U.S. policymakers has been that the young Fidel Castro deceived the world. The Cuban had cloaked his Communist revolutionary aspirations within the language of reformist nationalism. U.S. officials vowed not to be fooled again. Jagan and his wife visited Cuba and spoke favorably of the Cuban Revolution. He struck a deal to sell rice to Cuba and secured a promise of Cuban economic aid. Jagan's Cuban policy promoted British Guiana's national interest, providing a vital market to Indian rice growers. U.S. officials, however, judged Jagan's Cuban policy as compelling evidence that the Jagans and the PPP lied about their revolutionary intentions; they aimed to create a "second Cuba" on the South American continent. U.S. policymakers responded to the perceived threat in British Guiana in the way they responded in Cuba. The CIA, working with the AFL-CIO, incited strikes and riots that led to arson, sabotage, terrorism, and murder in the British colony. During the war against Castro's Cuba, U.S. officials discussed creating pretexts for invading the island, including sinking a boatload of Cuban refugees, shooting Cuban exiles in Florida, or bombing the U.S. military base at Guantánamo Bay.[4] A similar mindset informed official proposals of how the United States could encourage Cheddi Jagan to become a terrorist.

As did Cuba, British Guiana became entwined in U.S. domestic politics. During the 1960 presidential campaign, John Kennedy had denounced the Eisenhower-Nixon foreign policy team for "losing" Cuba to communism. In part, Kennedy repaid the Republicans for claiming that the Democrats had "lost" China in the late 1940s. The Bay of Pigs debacle and the Cuban Missile Crisis represented Kennedy's greatest failure and triumph in international affairs. As revealed in his verbal assault on Prime Minister Harold Macmillan at Birch Grove in June 1963, Kennedy was determined to keep British Guiana from joining Cuba as a subject of debate in the 1964 presidential campaign. Partisans from the political right and left reinforced Kennedy's political judgment. Conservative Democrats, like Senator Thomas Dodd, and right-wing newspapers, like the *Dallas Morning News*, deplored Jagan. Liberal Democrats, such as union leaders and African Americans, either denounced Jagan or spoke favorably of Forbes Burnham. No prominent interest group, like an Indian benevolent or friendship society, defended Jagan in the United States; between 1953 and 1969, the United States had, because of historic immigration restrictions, a minuscule population of citizens from South Asia.

Explanations for the U.S. intervention in British Guiana readily fall within the traditional categories—national security, balance of power, credibility, domestic politics, interest-group pressures—that historians of international relations offer when analyzing the motives of a powerful democratic nation. What seems certain is that another conventional interpretation—economic imperatives—does not explain the U.S. war against Jagan and the PPP. When scholars study the Cold War interventions in Guatemala, Cuba, Brazil, and Chile they ask whether the United States acted to protect the respective U.S. investments in bananas, sugar, telephone companies, and copper. The United States has customarily defended the free-trade and investment principles that are central to the international capitalist system. But the United

States had a minimal economic presence in impoverished British Guiana, and no U.S. businessman ever raised the issue of the political direction of the colony with U.S. officials. In fact, international capitalists preferred Jagan and the PPP over Burnham and the PNC.

Some scholars have urged historians of U.S. foreign relations to include race and gender in their explanatory models in order to gain a "deeper understanding of the cultural assumptions from which foreign policies spring." Issues of race and gender informed the U.S. approach to British Guiana and its leaders, albeit in distinctive ways. Historian Emily Rosenberg has argued that white policymakers attach similar symbolic characteristics to women, nonwhite people, and tropical countries. They are "emotional, irrational, irresponsible, unbusinesslike, unstable, and childlike." Women and nonwhites of the tropics are "naturally dependent" people.[5] U.S. and United Kingdom officials focused on one woman in British Guiana—Janet Rosenberg Jagan. Their depiction of the nurse from Chicago went, however, against stereotypes. She was the "dynamic Janet," intelligent and practical but also domineering and ruthless. Janet Jagan was "the brain behind" her husband and the "organizational wheelhouse" of the PPP. Secretaries of state anxiously inquired about the state of the Jagans' marriage, hoping that Cheddi Jagan would pursue moderation once free of his radical, "dominating" wife. Diplomats further snickered that Janet Jagan was sexually aggressive and promiscuous. They reacted in horror, however, to stories that she had sexual relations with nonwhites, including with "splendid, virile" Cuban revolutionaries. Men kept "falling under the spell" of Janet Jagan. Only when the Cheddi Jagan had been ousted from power in late 1964 did diplomats stop fearing Janet Jagan. In 1965, U.S. Consul Delmar Carlson reported that she looked "dumpy." Unadulterated sexism obviously fueled many of the male characterizations of Janet Jagan. Carlson excused, for example, Peter D'Aguiar's alleged extramarital affairs. But when U.S. and United Kingdom officials called Janet Jagan smart and organized, they attached positive attributes to the leading white politician in British Guiana and a native of the United States.

By implication, Cheddi Jagan and his countrymen lacked the drive and insight of whites. Governor Ralph Grey referred to the Guyanese as "children." Indians seemed especially dependent to U.S. officials. In his study of U.S. relations with India from 1947 to 1964, the Nehru years, Andrew J. Rotter has argued that U.S. officials perceived Indians as failing to meet

Western standards of manliness. Nehru's India angered and frustrated the United States because it declared neutrality in the Cold War and built a strong relationship with the Soviet Union. In Rotter's view, U.S. officials decided that India pursued a deviant foreign policy less because of geopolitical realities and more because of the shortcomings of its effeminate male leaders. Indian men were not Cold Warriors because they were passive, emotional, and lacked heterosexual energy.[6] U.S. officials did indeed refer to the Indians of Guyana as being "timid" and "docile." Unlike "aggressive" blacks, they allegedly lacked the physical stamina to be police officers.

U.S. officials found Cheddi Jagan similarly wanting. Left unspoken in the endless reports about his wife's sexual exploits was the question of why Jagan permitted her to betray him. U.S. officials also repeated the British observation that Jagan appeared "scrawny" after his 1964 political defeat. Eisenhower, Kennedy, and Johnson administration officials notably referred to Jagan as "Cheddi" in memorandums and dispatches. By comparison, after 1957 British officials wrote about "Dr. Jagan," honoring the degree in dentistry that Jagan had earned at prestigious Northwestern University. In 1997, a few months after her husband's death, Janet Jagan gave her interpretation of why her husband's international and domestic opponents treated him like a "boy" and why she had been portrayed as "a sort of Svengali" who manipulated him. As she related to a correspondent from the *New York Times*, "When Cheddi was first elected to Parliament 50 years ago, he broke all the traditions. He had no social background whatsoever and was what they called a coolie boy. So of course they said I wrote all his speeches because I was white, when in reality he was a brilliant intellectual and an ardent reader."[7]

The U.S. embrace of Forbes Burnham and his black followers also bears examination. The United States has a tragic history of black slavery and racial discrimination against African Americans. U.S. foreign policymakers transferred this domestic racism to international affairs. As outlined by Michael H. Hunt in his influential study, *Ideology and U.S. Foreign Policy* (1987), U.S. diplomats developed a "hierarchy of race." White Anglo-Saxons stood at the top and the despised minorities in the United States, Amerindians and blacks, fell to the bottom. U.S. officials attached positive and negative characteristics to Latin Americans and East Asians and placed them in the middle of the hierarchy of race.[8] The United States focused on British Guiana, however, during the period of the U.S. civil rights movement. U.S. leaders, especially the Kennedy and Johnson administrations, pushed for simple justice for African Americans for principled reasons and because civil rights legislation would help the United States appeal to people of color throughout the world. Kennedy and Johnson officials reacted positively to the educated, well-spoken, lawyerly Burnham. For his part, Burnham proved adept at manipulating his hosts, constantly denouncing communism and praising President Johnson for his commitment to civil rights.[9] Burnham profited from having the support of groups and individuals associated with the civil rights movement, such as union leaders and prominent black Democrats like Representative Adam Clayton Powell Jr. Senator Dodd, the leading congressional opponent of Jagan and a friend of Burnham, also fervently opposed discrimination against African Americans.[10] Burnham probably also seemed more familiar to U.S. citizens because he was the "leader of the African Christians," as one State Department officer put it. In contrast, interest groups representing Hindus and Muslims wielded no discernible influence in the United States from 1953 to 1969.[11]

Whether the misunderstandings and stereotypes that surround issues of gender, ethnicity, race, and religion can principally explain international relations remains a subject of scholarly debate.[12] The argument presented here emphasizes that three presidential administrations persuaded themselves that, in the context of the Cold War, the Jagans and their PPP posed unacceptable threats to U.S. vital interests. What probably can be concluded is that cultural blinders kept U.S. officials from empathizing with Cheddi Jagan and identifying Burnham's essential nature. U.S. officials never dwelled on Cheddi Jagan's remarkable achievements in surmounting poverty and discrimination. Jagan had a personal story, which included triumphing at U.S. universities, that usually appealed to U.S. citizens. On the other hand, the legitimate enthusiasm for black progress at home and abroad may have blinded U.S. officials in Washington to Forbes Burnham's intentions. Burnham's ostensible conversion to anticommunism obviously enhanced his appeal. Nonetheless, policymakers had ample warnings from intelligence analysts, U.S. diplomats in Georgetown, and British officials that Burnham was an unprincipled demagogue whose rule would prove disastrous for Guyana.

Presidential aide Arthur M. Schlesinger Jr. agrees that the United States deluded itself about Burnham and misjudged Cheddi Jagan. Schlesinger remains the only U.S. official to write or speak openly about British Guiana. Schlesinger's denunciation of U.S. policy has, however, created an intellectual dilemma for him. President John F. Kennedy designed the policy that drove Jagan from power. The president's rejection of Jagan does not fit into the laudatory profile of Kennedy in Schlesinger's influential memoir, *A Thousand Days* (1965). Schlesinger has absolved Kennedy of fault for the disasters that befell Guyana by implicitly raising the "bureaucratic politics" argument. The CIA seized on British Guiana, deciding that "this was some great menace, and they got the bit between the teeth." Covert intervention in the colony gave the CIA a "great chance to show their stuff." As Schlesinger presents it, the CIA acted like a "rogue elephant," trampling on the policies of governmental superiors.[13]

Political scientists properly point out that presidents are not omnipotent and that foreign policies are not always the purposeful acts of unified national governments. Powerful bureaucracies, like the CIA and the Department of Defense, may attempt to impose their will on foreign policy, intimidating the president or the Department of State. Other scholars caution, however, that intramural fights may be "struggles over tactics rather than strategy, pace rather than direction."[14] During the Cold War, elected officials, agencies, and departments shared the core anticommunist values outlined in the containment doctrine, domino theory, and NSC 68. Although Kennedy encountered willful subordinates during his presidency, Schlesinger's suggestion that the CIA exceeded its authority in British Guiana cannot be sustained. In his confidential correspondence with Prime Minister Macmillan and his June 1963 meeting with him at Birch Grove, Kennedy demanded that the United Kingdom replace Jagan. The president cited the CIA-aided riots of 1962 and general strike of 1963 as proof that Jagan could not govern the colony. To be sure, in early 1964 McGeorge Bundy briefed President Johnson that CIA operatives, "the professionals," were "hardnosed" in insisting that the Colonial Office immediately evict Jagan and resume direct rule. Bundy presented this information to Johnson, however, as a tactical issue. He and Secretary Rusk agreed that Jagan must go "by hook or by crook."

One last historiographic issue—the role of nonstate actors in international relations—deserves highlighting. The CIA used the good offices of the AFL-CIO to provide cover for its agents and as a conduit for funneling money and propaganda into British Guiana. But U.S. unions went beyond serving as an instrument of U.S. foreign policy. With its "International Affairs Department" that mirrored the geographical and regional divisions of the State Department, the AFL-CIO organized itself to conduct foreign policy.

The AFL-CIO financed these international operations with money from U.S. government sources. Until the end of the 1950s, the Eisenhower administration gave scant attention to British Guiana. From the beginning of the decade, union executives like Jay Lovestone and Serafino Romualdi charged that the Jagans and the PPP opposed the free-trade union movement and favored Communist unions. They made British Guiana an issue of public debate. Once the Democrats took power in 1961, union leaders had direct access to the executive branch and repeatedly advised the Kennedy and Johnson administrations to attack the Jagans. Union leaders also took the lead in showcasing Forbes Burnham throughout the United States.

Although scholarly concerns are important to address, the significant issue to reflect on is the consequence of the U.S. intervention in British Guiana. In Arthur Schlesinger Jr.'s words, a "great injustice was done to Cheddi Jagan."[15] The injustices included destroying a popularly elected government, undermining democratic electoral procedures, wrecking the economy of a poor nation, and inciting racial warfare. Forbes Burnham, the vicious racist embraced by the United States, made Guyana a dangerous, brutal place and a daily nightmare for the majority Indian population. Guyana remains a devastated country with a racially polarized population. In contemporary terms, Guyana might be dubbed "collateral damage," the sad but inevitable consequence that ensues in the fog of war. The United States fought the good war resisting Soviet tyranny and imperial designs but, at times, miscalculated and went too far in its Cold War zeal; Guyana's destruction must be measured against Eastern Europe's liberation. The problem with such rationalizations is that U.S. policymakers repeatedly and summarily rejected sober analyses about British Guiana's political life provided by sources friendly to U.S. interests. In their war against the Jagans, three presidential administrations sacrificed the ideals and values they claimed to uphold in the battle against international Communism. The U.S. intervention in British Guiana is a Cold War story of imperialism, gender bias, political expediency, and racism.

notes

In addition to the abbreviations used in the text, the following
abbreviations appear in the notes.

BPP	*British Parliamentary Papers*
CAB	Cabinet Office
CO	Colonial Office
DDEL	Dwight D. Eisenhower Library, Abilene, Kans.
DO	Dominions Office
DSR	Department of State Records
FAOHC	*U.S. Foreign Affairs Oral History Collection*, CD-ROM
FCO	Foreign and Commonwealth Office
FO	Foreign Office
FRUS	*Foreign Relations of the United States*
GMLA	George Meany Labor Archives, Silver Spring, Md.
IAD	International Affairs Department
IADCF	International Affairs Department: Country File
JCL	Jimmy Carter Library, Atlanta, Ga.
JFKL	John F. Kennedy Library, Boston, Mass.
LBJL	Lyndon Baines Johnson Library, Austin, Tex.
NA	National Archives
NSAM	National Security Action Memorandum
NSF	National Security File
NSFCO	National Security File: Country File
OH	Oral History
OSANSA	Office of Special Assistant for National Security Affairs
PM	Prime Minister
POF	President's Office File
POFCO	President's Office File: Country File

POL   Political Affairs
POL BR GU Political Affairs: British Guiana
PREM   Prime Minister's Office Records
PRO   Public Records Office, Kew, Richmond, Surrey, U.K.
RG   Record Group
WHCF   White House Central File

INTRODUCTION

1   U.S. Department of State, *Background Note: Guyana*, 1–6; U.S. Central Intelligence Agency, *World Factbook 2002: Guyana*, 2–8.

2   The website addresses are <http://www.state.gov/r/pa/ei/bgn/1984pf.htm> and <http://www.cia.gov/cia/publications/factbok/print/gy.html>.

3   U.S. Department of State, *Background Note: Guyana*, 2–6; U.S. Central Intelligence Agency, *World Factbook 2002: Guyana*, 3–5.

4   *New York Times*, 30 October 1994, 10.

5   Spinner, *Political and Social History of Guyana*, 89–130; Singh, *Guyana*, 29–42.

6   Morris, *CIA and American Labor*, 78–79, 152–56; Radosh, *American Labor*, 393–405.

7   Agee, *Inside the Company*, 293–94, 406; Smith, *Portrait of a Cold Warrior*, 357–58.

8   *New York Times*, 22 February 1967, 1, 17; *Sunday Times*, 16 April 1967, 1, 3 and 23 April 1967, 3.

9   Fraser, *Ambivalent Anti-Colonialism*, 123–202.

10 *FRUS, 1961–1963*, 12:ix–x, 513–613.

11 Rabe, *Most Dangerous Area*, 79–98. See also Fraser, " 'New Frontier' of Empire," 583–609.

12 Daniels, "Great Injustice to Cheddi Jagan," 203–24; Sillery, "Salvaging Democracy," 3.

13 Leonard, "Central America and the United States," 1–30.

14 *FRUS, 1952–1954, Guatemala*, iii–v.

15 For the historical literature on U.S. relations with Latin America since 1961, see Beisner, *American Foreign Relations*, 2:1505–62. See also Kornbluh, *Pinochet File*.

16 Eisenhower Library to author, 7 March 2003 (letter in author's possession).

17 Rabe, "John F. Kennedy and Latin America," 542–43.

18 David S. Patterson of Historical Office of State Department to author, 30 May 2001 (letter in author's possession).

19 Schlesinger to Kennedy, 8 March 1962, *FRUS, 1961–1963*, 12:548.

20 Kennedy to Macmillan, 10 September 1963, CAB 21/5523, PRO.

21 Paragraph 8 of Special National Intelligence Estimate 87.2–62, "The Situation and Prospects in British Guiana," 11 April 1962, *FRUS, 1961–1963*, 12:566. This same document can be found in folder 87.2 British Guiana, box 9, NSF: National Intelligence Estimates, LBJL.

22 B. Brentnol Blackman, assistant secretary (Education) of Caribbean Congress of

Labour, to Meany, 29 April 1963, British Guiana (1) folder, box 17, RG 18-001, IADCF, Series 4: Latin America and the Caribbean, GMLA.

23 Kennedy, "Imperial History," 345; Rabe, "Marching Ahead," 297–308.

24 Marks, "World According to Washington," 265–82.

25 Clifford, "Bureaucratic Politics," 161–68.

26 McCormick, "State of American Diplomatic History," 119–41.

27 Hunt, *Ideology and U.S. Foreign Policy*, 46–91; Rosenberg, "Gender," 116–24; Rosenberg, "Turning to Culture," 497–514; Williams and Chrisman, *Colonial Discourse*, 1–20.

28 Fukuyama, *End of History*. For a discussion of Cold War "triumphalism," see Gaddis, *We Now Know*, 294–95, and Leffler, "Cold War," 523–24.

CHAPTER ONE

1 Churchill to Colonial Secretary Oliver Lyttleton, 27 May 1953, PM Minute 302/53, PREM 11/827, PRO.

2 Adamson, *Sugar without Slaves*, 15–18; Newman, *British Guiana*, 3–9; Singh, *Guyana*, 2–3; Spinner, *Political and Social History of Guyana*, 1–2; Smith *British Guiana*, 1–10.

3 Spinner, *Political and Social History of Guyana*, 3–6; Costa, *Crowns of Glory*, 5–37.

4 Costa, *Crowns of Glory*, 39–85.

5 Ibid., 39–85, 207–50.

6 Adamson, *Sugar without Slaves*, 31. See also Moore, *Race, Power and Social Segmentation*, 51–76; Singh, *Guyana*, 7–8.

7 Smith, *British Guiana*, 134–44; Moore, *Race, Power and Social Segmentation*, 93–135; Moore, "Colonial Images," 127–41.

8 Northrup, "Migration," 88–100; Heuman, "British West Indies," 470–93; Hollett, *Passage from India*; Spinner, *Political and Social History of Guyana*, 6–9.

9 Northrup, "Migration," 98; Northrup, *Indentured Labor*, 59–70; Laurence, *Question of Labour*, 78–103, 532–33; Elizabeth Rabe, "From India to the Sugar Fields," 25–36.

10 Governor John Scott to Earl Kimberly, 8 July 1871, CO 111/386, PRO. The author thanks Elizabeth R. Rabe for providing this citation.

11 Adamson, *Sugar without Slaves*, 263.

12 Ibid., 112–13, 145; Laurence, *Question of Labour*, 131–66, 197–228; "Report of Commission Appointed to Inquire into Treatment of Immigrants in British Guiana," June 1871, in *Irish University Press Series of BPP: Emigration*, 24, part 1:262, 266, 302; Appendices to the Report on Treatment of Immigrants in British Guiana, June 1871, ibid., 24, part 2:444, 452, 457; Peter Rushworth to Earl of Kimberly, 5 July 1873, CO 111/398, PRO.

13 Magistrate George William Des Voeux to Earl Granville, 25 December 1869, *Irish University Press Series of BPP: Emigration*, 24, part 1:173–86.

14 Luckhoo quoted in Daniels, "Great Injustice to Cheddi Jagan," 93. See also New-

man, *British Guiana*, 48–51; Elizabeth Rabe, "From India to the Sugar Fields," 37–59; Seecharan, *"Tiger in the Stars,"* 355; Heuman, "British West Indies," 485; Laurence, *Question of Labour*, 384–431; Singh, *Guyana*, 8–10; Smith, *British Guiana*, 141.

15 Adamson, *Sugar without Slaves*, 13–14; Heuman, "British West Indies," 490; Singh, *Guyana*, 6–7; Spinner, *Political and Social History of Guyana*, 9–10.

16 Johnson, "British Caribbean," 615; Smith, *British Guiana*, 8; Spinner, *Social and Political History of Guyana*, 9–12.

17 Jagan, *West on Trial*, 62; Fraser, *Ambivalent Anti-Colonialism*, 37–48; David, *Economic Development of Guyana*, xvii–xviii.

18 Fraser, *Ambivalent Anti-Colonialism*, 16–17, 62–76.

19 Naipaul, *Middle Passage*, 132. See also Swan, *British Guiana*, 133.

20 Hintzen, *Costs of Regime Survival*, 33–34; Singh, *Guyana*, 19; Rich, *Race and Empire*, 155–60; Spinner, *Political and Social History of Guyana*, 28–29.

21 Jagan, *West on Trial*, 11–23, 43–56.

22 U.S. Consul Everett Melby to State Department on Jagan testimony, 8 July 1962, 741D.00/7–862, DSR, NA; Governor Patrick Renison to Colonial Office on talks between Renison, Undersecretary of State John Profumo, and Jagan, 4 May 1958, CO 1031/2412, PRO; transcript of Jagan interview on *Meet the Press*, 15 October 1961, folders 9/63 to 11/22/63, box 15A, NSFCO: British Guiana, JFKL; Newman, *British Guiana*, 83–84; Spinner, *Political and Social History of Guyana*, 17–22.

23 An insightful account of Janet Rosenberg Jagan's life is presented in Wasserman, *Thunder in Guyana*.

24 Jagan, *West on Trial*, 54–56.

25 Sires, "British Guiana," 562; Spinner, *Political and Social History of Guyana*, 22–31.

26 Jagan, *West on Trial*, 69–100; Sires, "British Guiana," 560.

27 Newman, *British Guiana*, 31–76; Smith, *British Guiana*, 1–10, 134–43.

28 Despres, *Cultural Pluralism*, 14–16, 30, 279; Halperin, "Racism and Communism," 100–106; Moore, "Colonial Images," 156–58; Seecharan, *"Tiger in the Stars,"* 368. For a twenty-first century variation on the cultural pluralism theme, see Chua, *World on Fire*, 6–12, 112–15.

29 Daniels, "Great Injustice to Cheddi Jagan," 22–23, 143–48.

30 Smith, *British Guiana*, 134–43, 198–206; International Bank, *Economic Development of British Guiana*, 10–15. See also Landis, "Racial Polarization," 255–67; Rodney, *History of the Guyanese Working People*, 174–89; Moore, *Race, Power, and Social Segmentation*, 213–23.

31 Colonial Office, *Report of the Commission of Inquiry into Disturbances*, 7.

32 Goldsworthy, *Colonial Issues*, 9, 15; Goldsworthy, "Keeping Change Within Bounds," 81.

33 Colonial Office, *British Guiana: Report of the Constitutional Commission, 1950–1951*; Spinner, *Political and Social History of Guyana*, 33–35.

34 Jagan, *West on Trial*, 100.

35 Minute by Mayle, 28 June 1951, CO 1031/128, Mayle to Charles Campbell Woolley,

10 November 1951, CO 1031/776, notes by Mayle on visit to British Guiana, 12 March 1952, CO 1031/776, PRO.

36　Churchill to President Eisenhower, 8 August 1954, *FRUS, 1952–1954*, 6:1050–52. See also Goldsworthy, "Keeping Change Within Bounds," 82–85.

37　Lyttleton, *Memoirs*, 352–55.

38　Churchill to Lyttleton, 5 May 1953, PM Minute 130/53, PREM 11/827, PRO.

39　James S. Lay, Executive Secretary of NSC, to NSC, "Security of Strategically Important Industrial Operations in Foreign Countries," 1 October 1953, NSC 163/1 Industrial Operations Foreign Countries folder, box 7, OSANSA, NSC series, Policy Papers subseries, DDEL; Lay to NSC, "Source of U.S. Aluminum Supply in Time of War," 16 October 1953, *FRUS, 1952–1954*, 1:1021–27; minutes of 167th meeting of NSC, ibid., 1036–38.

40　Consul Eugene H. Johnson to State Department, 19 April 1950, 741D.00/4–1950, Vice Consul T. E. Burke to State Department, 9 December 1950, 741D.00/12–950, Vice Consul Wesley Jorgensen to State Department, 19 November 1952, 841D.2569/11–1952, DSR, NA.

41　Eisenhower to Churchill, 22 July 1954, *FRUS, 1952–1954*, 6:1045–48; Churchill to Eisenhower, 8 August 1954, ibid., 1050–52. See also Churchill to Eisenhower, 5 April 1953, *FRUS, 1952–1954*, 9:2042–44; Lyttleton, *Memoirs*, 355.

42　A copy and analyses of NSC 68 can be found in May, *American Cold War Strategy*.

43　Bowie and Immerman, *Waging Peace*, 149–221; Rabe, *Eisenhower and Latin America*, 42–63.

44　MacShane, *International Labour*, 79–96; Morgan, *Covert Life*, 145, 198–99, 214–15.

45　Zieger, *CIO*, 253–93; MacShane, *International Labour*, 97–118; Battista, "Unions and Cold War Foreign Policy," 443.

46　Morgan, *Covert Life*, 338–40; MacShane, *International Labour*, 139–43; Romualdi, *Presidents and Peons*, 420; Zieger and Gall, *American Workers*, 220.

47　Romualdi to Lovestone, 25 March 1953, folder 2, box 9, Romualdi, "Free British Guiana Labor Fights Takeover by Cheddi Jagan Regime," *Inter-American Labor Bulletin*, December 1961, folder 5, box 11, Romualdi Papers, Kheel Center, Cornell University; Romualdi, *Presidents and Peons*, 345–52.

48　Alexander to Romualdi, 3 May 1953, Alexander file, 1953, box 3/1, RG 18–009 IAD, Staff Files: Serafino Romualdi Files, 1945–1961, GMLA; Alexander to Lovestone, 9 June 1953, Alexander (3–4) 1953 folder, box 3, RG 18–003, IAD: Jay Lovestone Files, 1939–1974, GMLA. Lovestone underscored Alexander's advice to contact the State Department.

49　Jagan, *West on Trial*, 120.

50　Spinner, *Political and Social History of Guyana*, 36–43; Singh, *Guyana*, 22–25.

51　Churchill to Lyttleton and Lyttleton to Churchill, both 5 May 1953, PM Minute 130/53, PREM 11/827, PRO.

52　Minute by P. V. Rogers on meeting with Campbell, 26 June 1953, CO 1031/119, letter of H. L. Steele, attorney for Sandbach, Parker, and Co., to directors of Demerara Company, Liverpool, 10 September 1953, CO 1031/118, PRO.

53   Vernon to Mayle and subsequent CO minutes, 13 July 1953, CO 1031/119, Colonial Office to Lyttleton, 1 October 1953, CO 1031/119, PRO.

54   Savage to Colonial Office, 5 May 1953, CO 1031/128, Savage to Colonial Office, 13 September 1953, CO 1031/119, Savage to Colonial Office, 19 September 1953, CO 1031/119, PRO; Savage to Colonial Office, 6 October 1953, minutes of Cabinet meeting, 6 October 1953, PREM 11/827, PRO.

55   H. Hopkinson to Colonial Office on meeting with Savage, 18 October 1954, PREM 11/827, PRO.

56   "Analysis of Security Situation in British Guiana," by Rose, 16 July 1953, CO 1031/119, PRO.

57   Churchill to Lyttleton, 27 September 1953, PM Minute 302/53, PREM 11/827, PRO; Colonial Office to Lyttleton, 1 October 1953, CO 1031/119, PRO.

58   Lyttleton, *Memoirs*, 427–28; Savage to Colonial Office, 7 November 1954, CO 1031/1435, PRO.

59   Fraser, *Ambivalent Anti-Colonialism*, 130; Johnson, "British Caribbean," 618.

60   Comments of T. W. Garvey of Foreign Office on "White Paper," 19 October 1953, FO 371/103121, PRO; Colonial Office, *British Guiana: Suspension of the Constitution*.

61   Minutes of Cabinet meeting, 29 October 1953, PREM 11/827, PRO; Margaret Joy Tibbetts, second secretary in London embassy, to State Department, 26 October 1953, 741D.00/10–2653, DSR, NA; Sires, "British Guiana," 568.

62   Hinden, "Case of British Guiana," 18–22; Goldsworthy, *Colonial Issues*, 234–37; Howe, *Anticolonialism in British Politics*, 135–37, 207–10; Spinner, *Political and Social History of Guyana*, 49–59.

63   Spinner, *Political and Social History of Guyana*, 53; Despres, *Cultural Pluralism*, 222–27.

64   Lyttleton, *Memoirs*, 429.

65   Maddox to State Department, 13 October 1953, 741D.00/10–1353, DSR, NA; Jagan, *West on Trial*, 138–39.

66   Fraser, *Ambivalent Anti-Colonialism*, 129; Spinner, *Political and Social History of Guyana*, 44, 53.

67   Mayle to Savage, 8 July 1953, CO 1031/118, PRO; minutes of Cabinet discussion, 2 October 1953, PREM 11/827, PRO.

68   Maddox to State Department, 27 May 1953, 741D.00/5–2753, DSR, NA; *Time*, 1 June 1953, 34.

69   Maddox to State Department, 16 July 1953, 741D.00/7–1653, DSR, NA; Fraser, *Ambivalent Anti-Colonialism*, 127–28.

70   Maddox to State Department, 4 May 1953, 741.00/5–453, Maddox to State Department, 16 July 1953, 741D.00/7–1653, DSR, NA.

71   Maddox to State Department, 20 August 1953, 741D.00/8–2053, Maddox to State Department, 5 October 1953, 741D.00/10–553, DSR, NA.

72   Memorandum of conversation between G. Hayden Raynor of Bureau of North American Affairs and James Penfield of London embassy, 5 October 1953, 741D.00/10–553, DSR, NA.

73 Minutes of 165th meeting of NSC, 8 October 1953, 165th meeting folder, box 4, NSC Series, Ann Whitman File, DDEL.

74 Dulles circular to American Republics, 6 October 1953, 741D.00/10–653, DSR, NA; Second Progress Report on NSC 144/1, 20 November 1953, *FRUS, 1952–1954*, 4:29–30, 37–38.

75 Smith to embassy in New Delhi, 16 October 1953, 741D.00/10–1653, DSR, NA.

76 Ibid.; Raynor of Bureau of North American Affairs to Livingston Merchant of European Division, 15 May 1953, 741D.00/5–1553, DSR, NA.

77 Immerman, *CIA in Guatemala*, 102.

CHAPTER TWO

1 Colonial Office, "Paper on Constitutional Crisis in British Guiana," 11 February 1955, CO 1031/1422, PRO.

2 Cabinet meeting minutes, 15 September 1954, Henry Brooke of Treasury to prime minister, 20 September 1954, PREM 11/827, PRO.

3 Savage to Colonial Office, 25 May 1954, CO 1031/1435, PRO.

4 Cabinet meeting minutes, 22 June 1955, PREM 11/827, PRO.

5 Philip Rogers to Thomas Lloyd, Colonial Office, 15 July 1955, CO 1031/1432, PRO.

6 Cabinet meeting minutes, 29 October 1953, PREM 11/827, PRO.

7 Savage to Colonial Office, 13 December 1953, CO 1031/790, Savage to Colonial Office, 7 November 1954, CO 1031/1435, PRO.

8 Tinker, *Banyan Tree*, 68; Jagan, *West on Trial*, 150–60; Wasserman, *Thunder in Guyana*.

9 Colonial officer Derek Lakeman in Georgetown to Colonial Office, 1 September 1955, note on discussion between Governor Renison and Sir Thomas Lloyd, 7 October 1955, W. G. Ash, chief information officer, United Kingdom Information Office, to W. T. A. Cox of Colonial Office Information Department, 11 September 1956, CO 1031/1432, memorandum of conversation between Lennox-Boyd and Patrick Gordon-Walker, n.d. [October 1955], CO 1031/1433, minute by Philip Rogers, Colonial Office, 25 January 1957, CO 1031/1426, PRO.

10 Note on discussion between Renison and Lloyd, 7 October 1955, CO 1031/1432, PRO; for data on unemployment see Consul A. John Cope to State Department, 14 July 1958, 841D.061/7–1458, DSR, NA.

11 Mayle to Rogers on Governor Savage's request, 2 February 1954, CO 1031/1329, Colonial Office to Renison on Five-Year Plan, 27 December 1955, Renison to Colonial Office, 4 January 1956, CO 1031/1568, Renison to Rogers, 3 January 1956, Renison to Rogers, 3 July 1956, CO 1031/1432, PRO.

12 Memorandum of discussion between Mayle and George Woodcock of TUC, 1 July 1954, minutes of meeting between TUC officials and Colonial Office, 3 January 1957, CO 1031/1449, Mayle to John Gutch in Georgetown on Janet Jagan and Ishmael, 19 June 1954, N. D. Watson of Colonial Office's Development and Welfare

Office to Lloyd, 16 December 1954, Woodcock of TUC to Mayle on Dalgleish mission, 23 December 1954, CO 859/773, PRO.

13   Spinner, *Political and Social History of Guyana*, 56–58; Colonial Office, *Report of the British Guiana Constitutional Commission, 1954*.

14   Spinner, *Political and Social History of Guyana*, 56–58; Jagan, *West on Trial*, 160–62.

15   Consul Douglas Jenkins Jr. to State Department, 6 March 1956, 741D.00/3–656, DSR, NA.

16   Burnham, *Destiny to Mould*, 3–8. See also Swan, *British Guiana*, 133–34; Despres, *Cultural Pluralism*, 210–16; Hintzen, *Costs of Regime Survival*, 48; Singh, *Guyana*, 1, 26–29; Spinner, *Political and Social History of Guyana*, 61–64; Naipaul, *Middle Passage*, 133.

17   Wallace, "British Guiana," 543. See also Newman, *British Guiana*, 85–86.

18   Second Progress Report on NSC 144/1, 20 November 1953, *FRUS, 1952–1954*, 4:29, 30, 37–38.

19   Progress Report on NSC 5432/1, 19 January 1955, *FRUS, 1955–1957*, 6:97; NSC 5613/1, 25 September 1956, ibid., 123; Outline of Plan of Operations for Latin America Prepared by Operations Coordinating Board, 18 April 1957, ibid., 157; Fraser, *Ambivalent Anti-Colonialism*, 143–44.

20   Maddox to State Department, 15 April 1954, 741D.00/4–1554, Maddox to State Department, 8 June 1955, 741D.00/6–855, Jenkins to State Department, 20 April 1956, 741.00D/4–2056, DSR, NA.

21   Memorandum by William B. Connett Jr., Office of Middle American Affairs, to Robert Woodward, Office of American Republic Affairs, 27 January 1954, 741D.00/1–2754, Maddox to State Department, 5 April 1954, 741D.00/4–554, Maddox to State Department, 26 May 1955, 741D.00/5–2655, Cope to State Department, 22 October 1956, 741D.00/10–2256, Second Secretary Peter Rutter, embassy in London, to State Department, 18 November 1954, 741D.00/11–1854, DSR, NA.

22   W. H. Braine, United Kingdom embassy in Washington, to A. Greenhough, Ministry of Labor, 18 February 1955, CO 859/773, PRO; Jenkins to State Department, 6 June 1956, 741D.00/6–656, DSR, NA; Fraser, *Ambivalent Anti-Colonialism*, 142.

23   Mayle to Savage, 16 May 1955, CO 859/773, Renison to Colonial Office, 6 October 1956, CO 859/774, PRO.

24   J. M. Campbell of Booker Brothers to editor, *International Free Trade Unions News*, 28 January 1954, Lovestone to Campbell, 2 March 1954, Campbell to Lovestone, 25 March 1954, Lovestone to Campbell, 31 March 1954, folder 24 "British Guiana, 1954," box 10, RG 18–003, IAD: Jay Lovestone Files, GMLA.

25   Alexander to Romualdi, 6 July 1954, Alexander 1954 file, box 3, RG 18–009, IAD, Staff Files: Serafino Romualdi's Files, GMLA; Alexander interviews with Dalgleish, Burnham, and Mrs. Richard Ishmael, 4–6 February 1956, folder 15, box 3, RG 18–003, IAD: Jay Lovestone Files, GMLA; Alexander report, 14 February 1956, folder 3, box 9, Romualdi Papers, Kheel Center, Cornell University.

26   Report by Romualdi, "Free Labor's Ten-Year Struggle to Preserve Independence," March 1962, folder 11, British West Indies, 1961–1965, box 69, RG 1–38, Office of

the President: George Meany Files, GMLA; Jenkins to State Department, 6 June 1956, 741D.oo/6–656, Cope to State Department, 29 July 1957, 841D.062/7–2957, memorandum of conversation among Warrick Elrod, Bureau of North American Affairs, Rupert Tello of TUC of British Guiana, and Harry Pollak of AFL-CIO, 14 April 1959, 841D.062/4–1459, DSR, NA; Pollak quoted in *American Federationist*, July 1957, in CO 859/1150, PRO.

27   Goldsworthy, *Colonial Issues*, 35; Goldsworthy, "Keeping Change Within Bounds," 81–108; Lewis, "Dissolution of the British Empire," 343–53; Warner, "Anglo-American Special Relationship," 486–87; Fisher, *Harold Macmillan*, 229–47; Shepherd, *Iain Macleod*, 151–258.

28   Lennox-Boyd to Cabinet, 17 April 1956, PREM 11/1727, PRO; Renison to Colonial Office, 18 December 1957, Colonial Office to Renison, 19 February 1957, CO 1031/1426, PRO.

29   Spinner, *Political and Social History of Guyana*, 71–72; monthly intelligence reports can be found in CO 1031/3712, PRO.

30   E. W. A. Scarlett of Colonial Office to Renison, 19 February 1957, CO 1031/2482, Philip Rogers, Colonial Office, to Renison, 19 February 1957, CO 1031/1426, PRO; Jagan, *West on Trial*, 183–84.

31   Cope to State Department, 22 October 1956, 741D.oo/10–2256, Cope to State Department, 25 February 1957, 741D.oo/2–2557, Cope to State Department, 5 April 1957, 741D.oo/4–557, DSR, NA.

32   Minute by Scarlett, Colonial Office, on Renison visit to Washington, CO 1031/2204, PRO; Marselis C. Parsons Jr., Bureau of North American Affairs, to C. Burke Elbrick, European Affairs, 16 July 1957, 741D.oo/7–1657, memorandum of conversation between Elbrick and Renison, 26 July 1957, 741D.oo/7–2657, DSR, NA.

33   Renison to Colonial Office, 16 August 1957, PREM 11/1727, PRO; Spinner, *Political and Social History of Guyana*, 72–73.

34   Foreign Office circular on 1957 election, 26 August 1957, CAB 21/2880, PRO.

35   Macmillan to Colonial Secretary, 14 August 1957, PM Personal Minute 413/57, PREM 11/1727, PRO.

36   John Wesley Jones, European Division, to Murphy on meeting with Caccia, 16 August 1957, 741D.oo/8–1657, Herter to Georgetown on conversation between Murphy and Caccia, 16 August 1957, 741D.oo/8–1657, Fisher Howe, executive secretary of state, to Major John Eisenhower on 1957 election, 16 August 1957, 741D.oo/8–1657, DSR, NA.

37   Fraser, *Ambivalent Anti-Colonialism*, 174.

38   Herter to Georgetown on conversation between Murphy and Caccia, 16 August 1957, 741D.oo/8–1657, DSR, NA.

39   William N. Dale, Bureau of North American Affairs, to Jones, European Division, 10 December 1957, 741D.oo/12–1057, Cope to State Department, 9 July 1958, 741D.oo/7–958, memorandum of conversation between Dale and Congressman Adam Clayton Powell, 24 April 1959, 741D.oo/4–2459, DSR, NA.

40   Fraser, *Ambivalent Anti-Colonialism*, 175; Hope, *Post-War Planning Experience*,

2–7; Cope to State Department on British Guiana's vital statistics, 2 June 1958, 841D.401/6–258, DSR, NA.

41 Cope to State Department on Jagan trip to London, 10 September 1958, 741D.00/9–1058, DSR, NA; Fraser, *Ambivalent Anti-Colonialism*, 176; Jagan, *West on Trial*, 191–95; memorandum of conversation between Jagan and Development Loan Fund officials, 17 August 1959, 741D.5MSP/8–1759, memorandum of conversation between Jagan and officers, led by Milton Rewinkel, in Bureau of North American Affairs, 18 August 1959, 741D.5MSP/8–1859, DSR, NA.

42 Cope to State Department, 9 July 1958, 741D.00/7–958, DSR, NA; monthly intelligence reports by Special Branch, 15 March 1960 and 12 April 1960, CO 1031/3712, PRO.

43 Senate Committee on Foreign Relations, *Study Mission in the Caribbean Area*, 16–21.

44 Woods to State Department, 10 February 1959, 841D.00TA/2–1059, DSR, NA.

45 Deputy Under Secretary of State Loy Henderson to Georgetown on loan applications, 15 December 1959, 841D.10/12–1559, DSR, NA.

46 Fraser, *Ambivalent Anti-Colonialism*, 181–83; Assistant Secretary of State for European Affairs Foy D. Kohler to Murphy, 26 May 1959, 741D.00/5–2659, DSR, NA; "Special National Intelligence Estimate on Threats to the Stability of the U.S. Military Facilities in the Caribbean Area and in Brazil," 10 March 1959, *FRUS, 1958–1960*, 5:366. On briefing books on Macmillan-Eisenhower meetings see boxes 74, 76, 78, and 80 in Confidential File: Subject Series, DDEL.

47 Woods to State Department, 26 August 1959, 841D.10/8–2659, Consul General Robert McGregor, Jamaica, to State Department on conversation with Jagan, 27 November 1959, 841D.00/11–2759, DSR, NA.

48 Colonial Undersecretary of State John Profumo to Colonial Secretary Lennox-Boyd on conversation with Jagan, 19 April 1958, CO 1031/2412, PRO.

49 Jagan, *West on Trial*, 150–51.

50 Jenkins to State Department on Renison radio address, 3 August 1956, 741D.00/8–356, DSR, NA; Spinner, *Political and Social History of Guyana*, 75–76.

51 Macleod to Macmillan, 7 March 1960, PREM 11/3666, PRO.

52 Spinner, *Political and Social History of Guyana*, 75–78; Smith, *British Guiana*, 8; Jagan, *West on Trial*, 202–4.

53 Ambassador John Hay Whitney, London, to State Department, 28 March 1960, 741D.00/3–2860, DSR, NA.

54 Macmillan, *Pointing the Way*, 163–64.

55 Memorandum of conversation between Dulles and Ambassador Heinz Krekeler, 11 February 1957, *FRUS, 1955–1957*, 4:523–24; 417th meeting of NSC, 18 August 1959, *FRUS, 1958–1960*, 7, Part 2:243–53; memorandum of conversation between Eisenhower and Ambassador to Portugal C. Burke Elbrick, 9 November 1960, ibid., 645–46.

56 Herter to Presidential Aide General Andrew Goodpaster, 8 December 1960, Herter-December 1960 (2) folder, box 13, Dulles-Herter series, Ann Whitman file, DDEL; Macmillan to Eisenhower, 9 December 1960, *FRUS, 1958–1960*, 7, Part 2:875–76.

57   NSC 6002/1, "Statement of U.S. Policy toward the West Indies," 21 March 1960, *FRUS, 1958–1960*, 5:433–43.

58   Rabe, *Eisenhower and Latin America*, 117–33, 162–73.

59   Foreign Office note on Jagan trip, 31 March 1960, AK1633/7, FO 371/148310, PRO; Woods to State Department on Jagan trip, 10 May 1960, 741D.00/5–1060, DSR, NA.

60   United Kingdom embassy in Havana to Foreign Office, 14 April 1960, AK1633/3, FO 371/148310, PRO; Szulc, *Fidel*, 541.

61   Ambassador Whitney, London, to State Department, 29 August 1960, 841D.10/8–2960, Herter to London, Moscow, Havana, and Georgetown, 7 September 1960, 841D.10/9–760, Woods to State Department, 10 May 1960, 741D.00/5–1060, DSR, NA.

62   Herter to London embassy, 7 September 1960, 841D.10/9–760, DSR, NA. See also Fraser, *Ambivalent Anti-Colonialism*, 183.

63   Ambassador H. Stanley Fordham, Havana, to Foreign Office, "Annual Review of 1959," 20 January 1960, AK1011/1, FO 371/148178, Foreign Officer Henry Hankey memorandum on relations with the United States and Cuba, 7 March 1960, AK1015/18, FO 371/148180, Hankey to Macmillan on Cuba, 10 June 1960, AK1015/38, FO 371/148181, embassy in Moscow to Foreign Office on Cuba, 28 November 1960, AK10338/14, FO 371/148211, embassy in Havana to Foreign Office, 23 November 1960, AK10338/15, FO 371/148211, PRO.

64   Macmillan quoted in Ashton, *Kennedy, Macmillan, and the Cold War*, 71.

65   Governor Grey to Angus M. MacKintosh of Colonial Office, 13 February 1961, Colonial Secretary Macleod to Grey, 20 July 1961, Grey to Nicholas B. J. Huijsman of Colonial Office, 1 December 1961, CO 1031/3907, PRO; Spinner, *Political and Social History of Guyana*, 74–75.

66   Embassy in Caracas to Foreign Office, 15 September 1960, V1635/3, FO 371/148695, PRO.

67   Ambassador Whitney to State Department on discussions with Colonial Office, 9 October 1960, 841D.10/9–760, DSR, NA.

68   Melby to State Department, 8 September 1960, 841D.10/9–860, Melby to State Department, 13 September 1960, 841D.10/9–1360, DSR, NA.

69   Grey to Colonial Office, "British Guiana in 1961," 13 June 1961, A10110/5, FO 371/155720, PRO.

70   Melby to State Department, 31 August 1960, 741D.00/8–3160, Under Secretary of State C. Douglas Dillon to embassy in London, 16 September 1960, 741D.00/9–1660, memorandum of conversation between Rockwood Foster of Bureau of North American Affairs and Richard Decorum of *British Guiana Evening Post*, 19 September 1960, 741D.00/9–1960, Melby to State Department, 7 October 1960, 741D.00/10–760, DSR, NA.

71   Memorandum of conversation about Peter D'Aguiar between officials in Bureau of North American Affairs and Albert R. Erda of Mt. Vernon, N.Y., 28 December 1960, 741D.00/12–2860, DSR, NA.

72 Hunt, *Undercover*, 98–99; Gleijeses, *Shattered Hope*, 288.

73 Memorandum of conversation between F. N. Spotts, Bureau of North American Affairs, and H. M. E. Cholmondeley, Department of Education of British Guiana, 11 January 1961, 741D.00/1–1161, Melby to State, 20 September 1960, 741D.00/9–3060, DSR, NA.

74 Memorandum of conversation between President Kennedy and Prime Minister Macmillan, 30 June 1963, *FRUS, 1961–1963*, 12:607–9. See also Rabe, *Most Dangerous Area*, 17–22.

CHAPTER THREE

1 Shepherd, *Iain Macleod*, 239.

2 U.S. Consulate, Georgetown, to State Department, 18 December 1961, 841D.00/12–1861, Consul Melby to State Department, 8 March 1962, 841D.06/3–862, DSR, NA; David, *Economic Development of Guyana*, 4–5, 240–41; International Bank, *Economic Development of British Guiana*, 10.

3 U.S. Consulate, Georgetown, to State Department, 18 December 1961, 841D.00/12–1861, DSR, NA; Colonial Attaché J. D. Hennings, Washington, to Governor Grey, 29 November 1960, AU16330/2, FO 371/148627, PRO; Jagan quoted in Grey to Colonial Office, 4 November 1960, CO 1031/4304, PRO.

4 Foreign Office minute by Hutchinson, 30 November 1961, A10110/121, FO 371/155726, PRO.

5 Reports on educational policy, CO 1031/1303, PRO; Melby to State Department, 31 May 1961, 741D.00/5–3161, DSR, NA; Daniels, "Great Injustice to Cheddi Jagan," 163.

6 Memorandum of conversation between Grey and State Department officers Rockwood Foster and Melby, 16 February 1961, *FRUS, 1961–1963*, 12:513; Grey to Colonial Office, "British Guiana in 1961," 13 June 1961, A10110/5, FO 371/155720, PRO.

7 Commonwealth Secretary Sandys to Macmillan, 11 January 1962, PREM 11/3666, PRO.

8 Grey to Colonial Office, "British Guiana in 1961," 13 June 1961, A10110/5, FO 371/155720, PRO; Grey to Nicholas Huijsman of Colonial Office, 30 January 1962, CO 1031/3647, PRO.

9 Intelligence Committee report, 9 May 1961, CO 1031/3713, PRO.

10 Grey to Angus M. MacKintosh of Colonial Office, 13 February 1961, CO 1031/3907, PRO.

11 Grey to Melby, 27 February 1962, CO 1031/3906, Grey to Colonial Office, 29 November 1963, CO 1031/4991, PRO.

12 Ambassador Bruce, London, to State Department on conversation with Fraser, 17 August 1961, 5/19/61–8/23/61 folder, box 14A, NSFCO: British Guiana, JFKL.

13 Memorandum of conversation between Grey and Schlesinger, 28 April 1961, British Guiana 4/28/61–10/30/61 folder, box WH-3A, Schlesinger White House Files, Schlesinger Papers, JFKL; Jones, London, to State Department on conver-

sations with Colonial Office, 9 August 1961, 5/19/61–8/23/61 folder, box 14A, NSFCO: British Guiana, JFKL; Jones, London, to State Department on conversation with Colonial Office officials about Burnham, 26 August 1961, 741D.00/8–2661, DSR, NA.

14 Spinner, *Political and Social History of Guyana*, 78–82; Naipaul, *Middle Passage*, 124–42; Daniels, "Great Injustice to Cheddi Jagan," 115; Grey to Colonial Office, "British Guiana in 1961," 13 June 1961, A10110/5, FO 371/155720, PRO.

15 Foreign Office minutes by Henry Hankey, 5 December 1961, A10110/124, and December 1961, A10110/135, FO 371/155726, PRO.

16 Melby to State Department, 25 August 1961, 8/24/61–9/6/61 folder, box 14A, NSFCO: British Guiana, JFKL; speech of 5 November 1961 in Burnham, *A Destiny to Mould*, 14–23.

17 Rabe, *Most Dangerous Area*, 13–22, 63–71.

18 Schlesinger, *Thousand Days*, 773.

19 Guthman and Shulman, *Robert Kennedy*, 295.

20 Johnson quoted in memorandum of conversation between U.S. and Colonial Office officials, 17 March 1962, *FRUS, 1961–1963*, 12:558–64; Rusk to embassy of United Kingdom, 11 August 1961, ibid., 519–20; memorandum of conversation between Kennedy and Villeda Morales, 30 November 1962, ibid., 331–33.

21 Special National Intelligence Estimate, "Prospects for British Guiana," 21 March 1961, ibid., 514–17.

22 Memorandum of conversation between Rusk, Home, Bruce, and Caccia, 6 April 1961, 741D.00/4–661, DSR, NA; memorandum of conversation between Rusk and Home, 6 April 1961, PREM 11/3666, PRO; Sillery, "Salvaging Democracy," 68–72.

23 Record of actions of NSC meeting, 5 May 1961, *FRUS, 1961–1963*, 12:517–18; Helms, *Look Over My Shoulder*, 196–209; Thomas, *Very Best Men*, 316.

24 Memorandum of conversation between Berle and D'Aguiar, 26 May 1961, 741D.00/5–2661, DSR, NA.

25 William Burdett to consulate in Georgetown, 7 August 1961, 741D.00/8–761, memorandum of conversation between Johnson and Dr. Sweet, 28 August 1961, 741D.00/8–2861, DSR, NA.

26 Jagan, *West on Trial*, 206–7; Rabe, *Most Dangerous Area*, 69, 114; Helms, *Look Over My Shoulder*, 397.

27 Kennedy to Bundy, 7 August 1961, President's Doodles File, JFKL; Department of State to Rusk in Paris, 5 August 1961, *FRUS, 1961–1963*, 12:519; Rusk to Home, 11 August 1961, ibid., 519–20.

28 Home to Rusk, 18 August 1961, ibid., 521–22.

29 Rusk to Home, 26 August 1961, ibid., 522–23.

30 W. L. Gorrell Barnes of Colonial Office to Sir Roger Stevens of Foreign Office, 30 August 1961, A10110/22, FO 371/155721, Grey to Ambler Thomas of Colonial Office, 26 September 1961, A10110/63, FO 371/155723, PRO.

31 Melby to State Department on interview with Jagan, 23 August 1961, 5/19/61–8/23/61 folder, box 14A, NSFCO: British Guiana, JFKL; Schlesinger to Kennedy,

28 August 1961, *FRUS, 1961–1963*, 12:523–24; Stevenson to Rusk, 26 February 1962, ibid., 545–46.

32 Rusk to U.S. embassy in Ottawa, 12 August 1961, U.S. embassy in Ottawa to Rusk, 24 August 1961, 5/19/61–8/23/61 folder, box 14A, NSFCO: British Guiana, JFKL; U.K. embassy in Ottawa to Commonwealth Relations Office, 20 October 1961, A10110/80, FO 371/155722, PRO.

33 Dodd to President Kennedy, 5 September 1961, folder 739, box 24, Dodd Papers, University of Connecticut Libraries; notes on meeting with Mr. Donhi of Senator Dodd's office by Dennis A. Fitzgerald of International Cooperation Agency, 23 August 1961, 7–8/61 folder, box 31, Fitzgerald Papers, DDEL; memorandum of conversation between Melby and Senator Dodd, 6 September 1961, 741D.00/9–661, DSR, NA; David Martin, assistant to Senator Dodd, to Schlesinger, 30 October 1962, British Guiana folder, box W-3, Schlesinger Papers, JFKL; memorandum by Burdett of briefing for congressional leaders, 16 April 1962, British Guiana folder, box 391, NSF: Ralph Dungan Files, JFKL.

34 Louis Martin of Democratic National Committee to Dungan, 31 October 1961, British Guiana 4/28/61–10/30/61 folder, box WH-3A, White House Files, Schlesinger Papers, JFKL; Help Guiana Committee to Richard Goodwin, 13 May 1961, British Guiana folder, box 3, Goodwin Papers, JFKL.

35 Memorandum by Ben Segal of AFL-CIO, "Trade Union Situation in British Guiana," 23 October 1961, British Guiana 4/28/61–10/30/61 folder, box WH 3-A, White House Files, Schlesinger Papers, JFKL; Report on McCabe fact-finding tour of British Guiana, 24 October 1961 to 12 November 1961, folder 21-Caribbean 1961, box 17, RG 18–001, IADCF, 1945–1971, Series 4: Latin America and the Caribbean, GMLA.

36 Schlesinger to Rusk, 19 October 1961, 10/13/61–10/20/61 folder, box 14A, NSFCO: British Guiana, JFKL; Department of State to Certain Posts, "US Program for British Guiana," 4 October 1961, *FRUS, 1961–1963*, 12:533–34; Schlesinger to President Kennedy, 12 January 1962, ibid., 540–41.

37 Department of State to embassy in United Kingdom, 5 September 1961, ibid., 530.

38 W. F. Dawson of Colonial Office to David Crichton of Foreign Office, 5 September 1961, A10110/25, FO 371/155721, PRO; Foreign Office minute by Hankey on September 1961 Anglo-American meeting on British Guiana, 2 November 1961, A10110/96, FO 371/155724, PRO; Bruce to State Department, 13 September 1961, 9/7/61–9/28/61 folder, box 14A, NSFCO: British Guiana, JFKL; Ashton, *Kennedy, Macmillan, and the Cold War*, 68.

39 Memorandum of conversation between Rusk and Jagan, 23 October 1961, Jagan Briefing Book folder, box 15, NSFCO: British Guiana, JFKL.

40 Memorandum of conversation between Kennedy and Jagan, 25 October 1961, *FRUS, 1961–1963*, 12:536–38; Melby to State Department, 14 October 1961, 10/13/61–10/20/61 folder, box 14A, NSFCO: British Guiana, JFKL.

41 Grey to Colonial Secretary Maudling, 6 November 1961, A10110/103, FO 371/155725, PRO.

42 Schlesinger, *Thousand Days*, 774–78; telephone conversation between Schlesinger and Under Secretary of State George Ball, 18 October 1961, telephone conversation between Ball and Deputy Under Secretary of State U. Alexis Johnson, 18 October 1961, British Guiana folder, box 2, Ball Papers, JFKL.

43 Transcript of *Meet the Press* interview, 15 October 1961, Jagan Briefing Book folder, box 15, NSFCO: British Guiana, JFKL; Colonial Office Attaché Hennings (Washington) to Grey, 19 October 1961, A10110/95, FO 371/155724, embassy in Ottawa to Foreign Office, 20 October 1961, A10110/80, FO 371/155723, PRO.

44 Goodwin to Kennedy, 25 October 1961, British Guiana folder, box 3, Goodwin Papers, JFKL.

45 *New York Times*, 17 February 1962, 1–2, 20 February 1962, 7; Wallace, "British Guiana," 517; Grey to Colonial Office, 18 February 1962, A10110/41, FO 371/ 161948, PRO; Melby to State Department, 23 February 1962, 741.00D/2–2362, DSR, NA.

46 E. M. West of Colonial Office to Foreign Office, 5 March 1962, A11010/58/G, FO 371/161948, PRO; memorandum of conversation between Schlesinger, Macleod, and Maulding, 27 February 1962, *FRUS, 1961–1963*, 12:549; Melby to State Department on statement of Jock Campbell of Booker Brothers, 14 June 1962, 841D.00/ 6–1462, DSR, NA.

47 Melby to State Department, 22 February 1962, 841D.062/2–2262, consulate in Georgetown to State Department, 27 February 1962, 741D.00/2–2762, DSR, NA; Colonial Office, *Report of the Commission of Inquiry into Disturbances*.

48 Melby to State Department, 1 March 1962, 741D.00/3–162, DSR, NA. See also Newman, *British Guiana*, 91–95.

49 Colonial Office, *Report of the Commission of Inquiry into Disturbances*; Foreign Office circular on report of Commission of Inquiry, 3 October 1962, A11010/230, FO 371/161957, PRO; Melby to State Department on report of Commission of Inquiry, 5 October 1962, 741D.00/10–562, DSR, NA; Spinner, *Political and Social History of Guyana*, 93–99.

50 Melby to State Department, 1 March 1962, 3/62–5/62 folder, box 15, NSFCO: British Guiana, JFKL.

51 Note on Home and Rusk meeting in Bermuda, 21 December 1961, PREM 11/3666, PRO; memorandum of conversation between Burdett and Dennis Greenhill of British embassy, 8 January 1962, 741D.00/1–862, Melby to State Department, 13 January 1962, 741D.00/1–1362, DSR, NA.

52 Rusk (Burdett) to consulate in Georgetown, 7 November 1961, 741D.13/11–761, Ambassador Bruce, London, to State Department, 15 December 1961, 741D.00/12– 1561, Jones, London, to State Department, 3 February 1962, 741D.00/2–362, Melby to State Department, 7 November 1961, 741D.13/11–761, DSR, NA.

53 Kennedy to Hamilton, 12 January 1962, *FRUS, 1961–1963*, 12:542; Hamilton OH, 26–27, JFKL.

54 Melby to State Department, 22 February 1962, 841D.10/2–2262, DSR, NA; State Department to Melby, 22 February 1962, 11/61–2/62 folder, box 15, NSFCO: British Guiana, JFKL.

55 Schlesinger to Ambassador Bruce on conversation with Maulding, 1 March 1961, *FRUS, 1961–1963*, 12:550–51.

56 Grey to Colonial Office, 20 February 1962, CO 1031/4283, PRO; Melby to State Department, 19 February 1962, 841D.061/2–1962, DSR, NA.

57 *New York Times*, 30 October 1994, 10.

58 Agee, *Inside the Company*, 293–94, 406; Smith, *Portrait of a Cold Warrior*, 353–58.

59 Agee, *Inside the Company*, 176; Blum, *CIA*, 118; Goulden, *Jerry Wurf*, 102–3; Lens, "Labor and the CIA," 25–29; Sillery, "Salvaging Democracy," 143, 145; *New York Times*, 22 February 1967, 1, 17; *Sunday Times* (London), 16 April 1967, 1, 3, 23 April 1967, 3.

60 Schlesinger testimony in *Nation* in "Tale of Two Books," 763–64; *New York Times*, 30 October 1994, 10.

61 Fraser OH, 9, JFKL.

62 State Department to embassy in London on Kennedy conversation with Ormsby-Gore, 20 February 1962, 11/61–2/62 folder, box 15, NSFCO: British Guiana, JFKL; Ormsby-Gore to Foreign Office, 29 February 1962, A10110/27, FO 371/161947, PRO.

63 Hennings, Washington, to Ambler Thomas of Colonial Office on conversation with William Burdett of State Department, 22 February 1962, A10110/126, FO 371/161952, PRO.

64 Rusk to Home, 19 February 1962, *FRUS, 1961–1963*, 12:544–45; Tyler to Rusk, 18 February 1962, ibid., 542–44. Some of the excised portions of Tyler's memorandum can be found in 11/61–2/62 folder, box 15, NSFCO: British Guiana, JFKL.

65 NSAM No. 135, 8 March 1962, *FRUS, 1961–1963*, 12:551–52.

66 Macmillan quoted in Ashton, *Kennedy, Macmillan, and the Cold War*, 69.

67 Home to Rusk, 26 February 1962, *FRUS, 1961–1963*, 12:546–48.

68 Memorandum of conversation among Schlesinger, Macleod, and Maulding, 27 February 1962, ibid., 549.

69 Grey to Huijsman of Colonial Office, 31 March 1962, CO 1031/3647, PRO; Hennings to Thomas of Colonial Office, 22 February 1962, A10110/126, FO 371/161952, Hennings to Thomas, 28 February 1962, A10110/51, FO 371/161948, PRO.

70 Rusk to Kennedy, 7 March 1962, 3/62–5/62 folder, box 15, NSFCO: British Guiana, JFKL.

71 Fraser to Home on conversation with Kennedy, 22 March 1962, PREM 11/3666, PRO; Fraser OH, 9–11, JFKL.

72 Fraser to Home on conversation with Kennedy, 22 March 1962, PREM 11/3666, PRO. Both Macmillan and his aide, Philip de Zulueta, read Fraser's report. Zulueta to Fraser, 26 March 1962, PREM 11/3666, PRO.

73 Macmillan to Brook, 3 May 1962, PM Minute 112/62, PREM 11/3666, Macmillan to Kennedy, 25 May 1962, PREM 11/3666, PRO; Macmillan to Kennedy, 30 May 1962, A11010/208/G, FO 371/1611956, PRO.

74 Macmillan, *Pointing the Way*, 335–36, 352–53; Dallek, *Unfinished Life*, 415; Fisher,

Harold Macmillan, 257–64, 289–90; Horne, *Macmillan*, 2:290; Ashton, *Kennedy, Macmillan, and the Cold War*, 20–21.

75 Ashton, *Kennedy, Macmillan, and the Cold War*, 4–16, 223–26; Kandiah and Staerck, " 'Reliable Allies,' " 135–70.

76 Foreign Office minute by Hankey, 20 February 1962, A10110/51, FO 371/161948, PRO; Zulueta to Macmillan, 15 May 1962, PREM 11/3666, PRO.

77 E. M. West of Colonial Office to Foreign Office, 5 March 1962, A10110/58/G, FO 371/161948, PRO; Melby to State Department on memorandum of conversation between Grey and Burdett, 27 March 1962, 741D.00/3–2762, DSR, NA; memorandum by Burdett on congressional briefing on British Guiana, 16 April 1962, British Guiana folder, box 391, NSF: Ralph Dungan Files, JFKL.

78 Edmunds minute on Colonial Office discussions with U.S. officials, 11 May 1962, FO 371/161953, PRO; Rich, *Race and Empire*, 188.

79 Rusk to Kennedy, 12 July 1962, *FRUS, 1961–1963*, 12:575–76; memorandum for Special Group (memorandum not declassified), 13 June 1962, ibid., 571; Schlesinger to Kennedy, 21 June 1962, ibid., 572–73; Bundy to Kennedy, 13 July 1962, ibid., 577; Schlesinger to Kennedy, 19 July 1962, ibid., 578; Bundy to Helms, 6 August 1962, ibid., 581.

80 Lord Harlech (William David Ormsby-Gore) OH, 46–47, JFKL.

81 Naftali, Zelikow, and May, *John F. Kennedy*, 1:440–43.

82 Melby to State Department on memorandum of conversation between Burdett and Burnham, 28 March 1962, 3/62–5/62 folder, box 15, NSFCO: British Guiana, JFKL.

83 Memorandum of conversation between Schlesinger, State Department officers, and Burnham, 3 May 1962, 741D.00/5–362, Burdett to embassy in London on Burnham visit, 7 May 1962, 741D.00/5–762, memorandum of conversation between Deputy Under Secretary of State Johnson and Burnham, 14 September 1962, 741D.00/9–1462, DSR, NA; Sillery, "Salvaging Democracy," 164.

84 Grey to R. W. Piper of Foreign Office, 11 September 1962, A11010/223, and 12 September 1962, A11010/224, FO 371/161957, PRO.

85 The analysis of Burnham is excised in the published version of the National Intelligence Estimate, "The Situation and Prospects in British Guiana," 11 April 1962, *FRUS, 1961–1963*, 12:564–69. The uncensored version can be found in 87.2 British Guiana folder, box 9, NSF: Intelligence Estimates, LBJL.

86 Grey to R. W. Piper of Foreign Office, 11 September 1962, A11010/223, FO 371/161957, PRO; McLellan to Richard Ishmael, 24 October, 26 October, and 29 November 1962, in British Guiana, 1962 folder (15), box 16, RG 18–001, IADCF, 1945–1971, Series 4: Latin America and the Caribbean, GMLA; William Doherty Jr. of AFL-CIO to Vice President Johnson, 21 June 1962, in State Department to Johnson, 26 June 1962, 741D.00/6–2662, DSR, NA.

87 Rabe, *Most Dangerous Area*, 69–70.

88 Wallace J. Legge, Inter-American Representative of Postal, Telephone, and Tele-

graph International, to William Doherty Jr., 30 April 1962, American Institute of Free Labor Development folder, box 16, RG 18–007, IAD: International Labor Organization Activities, GMLA; Romualdi to J. Peter Grace of W. R. Grace and Co., 19 July 1963, folder 8, box 2, Romualdi Papers, Kheel Center, Cornell University.

89 Melby to State Department containing memorandum of conversation between Burdett and Antony Tasker, chairman of Booker Brothers, 26 March 1962, 741D.00/3–2662, memorandum of conversation between State Department officer Willis Armstrong, James Campbell of Demerara Bauxite, and Thomas Covel of Aluminum Limited, 31 October 1962, 841D.0511/10–3162, DSR, NA.

90 Memorandum of conversation between Home and Meir, 28 September 1962, A1109/36, FO 371/162016, PRO; Melby to State Department on conversation with Ambassador Oron, 6 September 1962, 841D.0084A/9–662, Burdett to U.S. embassy in Tel Aviv, 29 August 1962, 841D.0084A/8–2962, DSR, NA.

91 Horne, *Harold Macmillan*, 2:48, 243, 395.

92 Fisher, *Harold Macmillan*, 293.

93 Sandys to prime minister, 10 September 1962, Zulueta to J. T. A. Howard-Drake of Colonial Office with instructions for Ormsby-Gore, 12 September 1962, A10110/222/G, FO 371/161957, PRO; Fraser, " 'New Frontier' of Empire," 602–4.

94 Colonial Office, *Report of the British Guiana Independence Conference*; Commonwealth circular on Independence Conference, 25 October 1962, A10110/241, FO 371/161959, PRO; Jagan, *West on Trial*, 267–87.

95 Colonial Office briefing on British Guiana for prime minister's meeting with Kennedy, 7 December 1962, A10110/261, FO 371/161959, PRO.

CHAPTER FOUR

1 Memorandum of conversation between Burdett of State Department and Hennings of United Kingdom embassy, 14 February 1963, POL BR GU, DSR, NA.

2 Sir Hilton Poynton to Duncan Sandys, n.d. [April 1963], Colonial Office to Governor Grey, 18 April 1963, CO 1031/4744, PRO.

3 United Kingdom mission at United Nations circular, 22 March 1963, UN1515/45, FO 371/172595, PRO; Rusk to consulate in Georgetown on Burnham appearance at United Nations, 12 March 1963, POL 3 BR GU, DSR, NA.

4 Shepherd, *Iain Macleod*, 239; Ashton, *Kennedy, Macmillan, and the Cold War*, 24.

5 Grey to Sandys, 4 March 1963, Grey to Ambler Thomas of Colonial Office, 24 April 1964, CO 1031/4402, PRO.

6 Colonial Office minutes attached to Grey to Thomas, 24 April 1964, CO 1031/4402, PRO.

7 Grey to Colonial Office, 7 February 1963, Grey to Jagan, 17 February 1963, Grey to Colonial Office on *Mitshurinsk*, 21 July 1963, CO 1031/4991, PRO.

8 Desmond A. Murphy, Georgetown, to Colonial Office, 21 January 1963, CO 1031/4998, PRO.

9   Grey to Poynton, 17 April 1963, A11024/14, FO 371/167738, PRO; Grey to Melby, 17 April 1963, 5/16/63–6/63 folder, box 15, NSFCO: British Guiana, JFKL.

10 Jagan to Kennedy, 16 April 1963, *FRUS, 1961–1963*, 12:595–603.

11 Minutes by Patricia Hutchinson and A. D. Parsons of Foreign Office, 26 April 1962, A11024/14, FO 371/167738, PRO.

12 William H. Brubeck of State Department to Bundy on Jagan letter, 18 May 1963, box 112A, POF: Security File: British Guiana Security File, 1961–1963, JFKL; Kennedy to Jagan, 3 June 1963, 5/16/63–6/63 folder, box 15, NSFCO: British Guiana, JFKL.

13 Ormsby-Gore to Foreign Office on Kennedy inquiry, 15 March and 8 April 1963, Foreign Office to embassy in Washington, 27 March 1963, A11010/14, FO 371/167689, PRO.

14 Memorandum by Sandys for Overseas Policy Committee, 25 May 1963, CO 1031/4402, minute by Poynton, 25 March 1963, CO 1031/4744, PRO.

15 Melby to State Department, 14 March 1963, *FRUS, 1961–1963*, 12:584–94.

16 J. E. Killick in United Kingdom embassy, Washington, to Richard Slater of Foreign Office on conversation with State Department on Harold Wilson, 20 March 1963, A10110/17, FO 371/167689, PRO; Benjamin Read, executive secretary of State Department, to Bundy on Labor Party, 28 July 1963, 7/63–8/63 file, box 15, NSFCO: British Guiana, JFKL.

17 Memorandum of conversation (participants and contents excised), 20 March 1963, *FRUS, 1961–1963*, 12:594.

18 Minute by Poynton, 25 March 1963, CO 1031/4744, PRO.

19 Macmillan quoted in Sillery, "Salvaging Democracy," 201–2; *Sunday Times* (London), 23 April 1967, 4.

20 Memorandum of conversation between Robin Piper of Colonial Office and officials of TUC, 10 April 1963, Grey to Colonial Office on conversations with trade union officials, 4 June 1963, CO 1031/5006, PRO; *Sunday Times* (London), 16 April 1967, 1, 3; Daniels, "Great Injustice to Cheddi Jagan," 210.

21 Jagan, *West on Trial*, 230–40; Daniels, "Great Injustice to Cheddi Jagan," 204–11. Daniels participated in the strike.

22 Speech of 14 April 1963 in Burnham, *Destiny to Mould*, 36–42. See also Landis, "Racial Polarization," 264–65; Spinner, *Political and Social History of Guyana*, 100–102; David, *Economic Development of Guyana*, 4–5; Collins, "Civil Service of British Guiana," 3–15.

23 Hintzen, *Costs of Regime Survival*, 54.

24 B. Brentnol Blackman, assistant secretary (Education) of Caribbean Congress of Labour, to Meany, 29 April 1963, British Guiana folder 1, box 17, RG 18–001, IADCO, 1945–1971: British Guiana, Series 4: Latin America and the Caribbean, GMLA.

25 McCabe to Andrew McLellan on rations, 1 May and 3 May 1963, British Guiana folder 1, box 17, RG 18–001, IADCO, 1945–1971: British Guiana, Series 4: Latin America and the Caribbean, GMLA; Lens, "Lovestone Diplomacy," 12; Daniels, "Great Injustice to Cheddi Jagan," 204–5.

26 Agee, *Inside the Company*, 293–94; Blum, *CIA*, 118–22; Lens, "Labor and the CIA," 25–29; Radosh, *American Labor*, 393–405; *New York Times*, 22 February 1967, 17; *Sunday Times* (London), 16 April 1967, 1, 3.

27 Bulletin of May 1963 of Public Service International, British Guiana folder 1, box 17, 18–001, IADCF, 1945–1971, Series 4: Latin America and the Caribbean, GMLA.

28 Ibid.

29 Gene Meakins to McLellan, 11 March 1964, British Guiana folder 1, box 17, RG 18–001, IADCF, 1945–1971, Series 4: Latin America and the Caribbean, GMLA.

30 McCabe to Lee with attached report, 11 April 1963, Public Services International folder 7, box 23, RG 18–007, IAD: International Labor Organization Activities, GMLA; memorandum of conversation between McCabe and Joseph Mintzes of State Department, 9 April 1963, POL BR GU, DSR, NA.

31 Meakins to McLellan, 28 August 1964, British Guiana folder 3, box 17, RG 18–001, IADCF, 1945–1971, Series 4: Latin America and the Caribbean, GMLA.

32 McLellan to Bertie Nichols of Transport Worker's Union of British Guiana, 29 July 1963, British Guiana folder 1, box 17, RG 18–001, IADCF, 1945–1971, Series 4: Latin America and the Caribbean, GMLA.

33 Colonial Office to E. Wakefield containing Kennedy to Macmillan, 4 June 1963, CO 1031/4402, PRO.

34 Grey to Colonial Office on Venezuelan oil, 19 May 1963, AV1162/3, FO 371/168522, Grey to Colonial Office on Cuban oil, 20 June 1963, AV1162/6, FO 371/168522, PRO; Sillery, "Salvaging Democracy," 203–4; Ashton, *Kennedy, Macmillan, and the Cold War*, 71.

35 Rabe, "After the Missiles of October," 713–24; memorandum for record by Desmond Fitzgerald of CIA on meeting at the White House on covert policy toward Cuba, 19 June 1963, *FRUS, 1961–1963*, 13:837–38.

36 Rusk to U.S. embassies, 11 July 1963, POL 1 BR GU, DSR, NA.

37 A. D. Parsons of Foreign Office to embassy in Rio de Janeiro, 14 March 1963, R. A. Burroughs in embassy in Rio de Janeiro to Foreign Office, 5 April 1963, FO 371/167703, PRO.

38 Romano, "No Diplomatic Immunity," 546–79; Borstelmann, " 'Hedging Our Bets,' " 435–63; Dudziak, *Cold War Civil Rights*, 152–202.

39 Borstelmann, " 'Hedging Our Bets,' " 455–61; Noer, "New Frontiers and Old Priorities," 253–83.

40 State Department to embassy in United Kingdom, 21 June 1963, *FRUS, 1961–1963*, 12:605–6.

41 Memorandum for record, with attachment, of meeting with president by Richard Helms of CIA, 21 June 1963, ibid., 604–5; Department of State to embassy in United Kingdom, 21 June 1963, ibid., 605–6.

42 Colonial Office brief for Macmillan on talks with Kennedy, June 1963, "Joint Assessment by U.S. and British Officials," 27 June 1963, CO 1031/4402, PRO; Sillery, "Salvaging Democracy," 205–7.

43 Memorandum of conversation at Birch Grove, England, 30 June 1963, *FRUS, 1961–1963*, 12:607–9.

44 Macmillan, *At the End of the Day*, 471–72.

45 Colonial Office minute by Nicholas Huijsman of meeting with Sandys, 2 July 1963, Macmillan letter to Kennedy, 18 July 1963, contained in Kennedy to Macmillan, 10 September 1963, CO 1031/4402, PRO.

46 Macmillan quoted in Ashton, *Kennedy, Macmillan, and the Cold War*, 15.

47 Kennedy to Macmillan, 10 September 1963, CO 1031/4402, PRO.

48 Macmillan to Kennedy, 28 September 1963, CO 1031/4402, PRO.

49 Summary of meetings, "British Guiana: Anglo-US Consultations on Future Cooperation," 16 October 1963, CO 1031/4403, PRO.

50 Rusk to embassy in Santiago, 13 July 1963, POL BR GU, DSR, NA.

51 News conference, 20 August 1963, *Public Papers of the President: John F. Kennedy, 1963*, 633.

52 Ralph Dungan to Bundy transmitting USIS plan for British Guiana, 3 October 1963, 9/63–11/22/63 folder, box 15A, NSFCO: British Guiana, JFKL; Donald Wilson, Deputy Director of USIA, to Dungan, 16 October 1963, folder 8/62–12/64, box 391, Dungan Files, JFKL.

53 Meakins to McLellan, 2 October 1963, McLellan to Meakins, 4 October 1963, British Guiana folder 2, box 17, 18–001, IADCF, 1945–1971, Series 4: Latin America and the Caribbean, GMLA.

54 Colonial Office minute on Campbell call on Sandys, 24 July 1963, CO 1031/4411, PRO; Brereton, *History of Modern Trinidad*, 223–49. See also Ryan, *Race and Nationalism*.

55 Grey's interview, 13 September 1963, Ormsby-Gore to Home on conversation with Bundy, 17 September 1963, CO 1031/4404, PRO.

56 Melby to State Department, 5 September 1963, *FRUS, 1961–1963*, 12:610–11; State Department to Melby, 7 September 1963, ibid., 613.

57 Minute by Sir Hilton Poynton of conversation with Jagan, 27 September 1963, CO 1031/4402, PRO; Jagan, *West on Trial*, 278.

58 Minute of meeting between Sandys and Rusk, 19 December 1963, CO 1031/4411, PRO.

59 Colonial Office, *Report of the British Guiana Constitutional Conference, 1963*.

60 Melby to State Department on conversation with Ishmael, 21 November 1963, POL 14 BR GU, DSR, NA.

61 Consulate in Georgetown to State Department on local reaction to London Conference, 1 November 1963, 9/63–11/22/63 folder, box 15A, NSFCO: British Guiana, JFKL; Singh, *Guyana*, 34; Spinner, *Political and Social History of Guyana*, 103–4.

62 Jagan, *West on Trial*, 278–80.

63 Record of conversation between Home and Rusk, 26 November 1963, A11010/216, FO 371/167690, PRO; minute of meeting between Sandys and Rusk, 19 December

1963, CO 1031/4411, PRO; State Department memorandum of conversation between Rusk and Sandys, 19 February 1963, 12/63–7/64 folder, box 55, NSFCO: British Guiana, LBJL.

64   Rusk to consulate in Georgetown, 8 November 1963, POL 14 BR GU, DSR, NA.

65   Colonial Office account of 15 November 1963 debate in Commons on British Guiana, CO 1031/4405, PRO.

66   Melby to State Department on conversation with Grey, 22 November 1963, POL 15 BR GU, DSR, NA; Melby to State Department, 17 February 1964, Richard Eriscson, first secretary in London embassy to State Department on conversation with Campbell, 21 November 1963, POL 19 BR GU, DSR, NA; Grey to Ambler Thomas of Colonial Office, 14 January 1964, CO 1031/4403, PRO.

67   Rabe, *Most Dangerous Area*, 95–98.

68   Briefing prepared by William Tyler of European Division for Rusk for conversation with Prime Minister Douglas-Home, 12 December 1963, British Guiana Special File, box 5, NSF: Intelligence File, LBJL.

69   Memorandum by Bundy of conversation between president and prime minister, 13 February 1964, PM Home visit folder, box 213, NSFCO: United Kingdom, LBJL.

70   Luyt to Colonial Office, 21 April 1964, CO 1031/4406, Luyt to Colonial Office on Cuban ships, 24 March and 13 May 1964, CO 1031/4991, PRO; Luyt to Piper, 23 April 1964, AK1062/9, FO 371/174036, Slater minute on conversation with Luyt, 17 September 1964, A19110/211, FO 371/173352, PRO.

71   Carlson to State Department, 10 August 1964, POL 2 BR GU, DSR, NA; Carlson to State Department on D'Aguiar, 23 September 1964, POL 12–1 BR GU, DSR, NA; memorandum by Gordon Chase of conversation between Carlson and Bundy on Burnham, 14 September 1964, British Guiana Special File, box 5, NSF: Intelligence File, LBJL.

72   Wallace, "British Guiana," 514, 532–40; Spinner, *Political and Social History of Guyana*, 105–6; Daniels, "Great Injustice to Cheddi Jagan," 234–39; Wasserman, *Thunder in Guyana*.

73   Carlson to State Department, 8 February 1965, POL 23 BR GU, DSR, NA; Luyt to Colonial Secretary Greenwood, 12 March 1965, CO 1031/4408, PRO; Wallace, "British Guiana," 540.

74   Burnham quoted in Tinker, *Banyan Tree*, 72.

75   Carlson to State Department, 13 April 1964, POL 23 BR GU, DSR, NA.

76   Luyt to Colonial Office, 1 June 1964, CO 1031/5025, Poynton to Sandys on arresting political leaders, 29 May 1964, CO 1031/4411, PRO.

77   Jagan did not hold the United States responsible for the 1964 violence. *West on Trial*, 305–12.

78   Rusk to President Johnson, with background memorandum on Macmillan to Kennedy of 18 July 1963, 6 February 1964, PM Home visit folder, box 213, NSFCO: United Kingdom, LBJL.

79   Burdett to Bundy, 10 December and 12 December 1963, British Guiana Special File, box 5, NSF: Intelligence File, LBJL.

80 Bundy to Johnson, 11 February 1964, 11/63–2/64 folder (1), box 1, NSF: Memorandums to President, LBJL.

81 General Maxwell Taylor to Secretary of Defense, 15 February 1964, British Guiana Special File, box 5, NSF: Intelligence File, LBJL.

82 CIA to NSC, 27 June and 23 July 1964, Cables, 12/63–7/64, folder, box 55, NSFCO: British Guiana, LBJL; State Department Division of Intelligence and Research to acting secretary of state, 12 May 1964, Memos, 12/63–7/64, folder, box 55, NSFCO: British Guiana, LBJL; Meakins to McLellan on minutes of PPP meetings, 4 February 1964, folder 3, box 17, RG 18–001, IADCF, Series 4: Latin America and the Caribbean, GMLA.

83 Report on British Guiana on McCabe activities, 21 to 26 March 1964, folder 3, box 17, RG 18–001, IADCF, Series 4: Latin America and the Caribbean, GMLA.

84 Meakins to McLellan, 28 August and 23 September 1964, McLellan to R. K. Singh of British Guiana, 3 March 1964, folder 3, box 17, RG 18–001, IADCF, Series 4: Latin America and the Caribbean, GMLA.

85 State Department circular on British Guiana, 29 November 1963, Memos, 12/63–7/64, folder, box 55, NSFCO: British Guiana, LBJL.

86 Memorandum of telephone conversation between Bundy and Ball, 2 March 1964, box 1, Ball Papers, LBJL.

87 Rusk to Georgetown on visit of Canadian Minister Paul Martin, 5 December 1963, Cables, 12/63–7/64, folder, box 55, NSFCO: British Guiana, LBJL.

88 Helms to Bundy, 26 November 1963, British Guiana Special File, box 5, NSF: Intelligence File, LBJL; "British Guiana Survey," March 1964, Survey folder, box 56, NSFCO: British Guiana, LBJL.

89 Memorandum of conversation between Jai Narine Singh and William B. Cobb of State Department, 26 June 1964, POL 19 BR GU, DSR, NA; minute of Colonial Office meeting with Sandys on new political parties in British Guiana, 25 February 1964, CO 1031/4411, PRO.

90 CIA to Bundy, 26 August 1964, British Guiana Special File, box 5, NSF: Intelligence File, LBJL; Gordon Chase to Bundy, 7 December 1964, Cables, 12/64–10/65, folder, box 55, NSFCO: British Guiana, LBJL.

91 Minute by Richard Slater of Foreign Office on Anglo-American meeting on British Guiana, 20 July 1964, A19110/175G, FO 371/173553, PRO; U.N. Ambassador Stevenson to State Department on meeting with PNC mayor of Georgetown, 18 March 1964, Cables, 12/63–7/1964, folder, box 55, NSFCO: British Guiana, LBJL.

92 Meakins to McLellan, 20 March and 23 September 1964, McLellan to Meakins, 8 October 1964, British Guiana folder 3, box 17, RG 18–001, IADCF, Series 4: Latin America and the Caribbean, GMLA.

93 Under Secretary Ball to Georgetown, 10 November 1964, Carlson to State Department, 12 November 1964, Cables, 8/64–11/64, folder, box 55, NSFCO: British Guiana, LBJL; Carlson to State Department, 5 November 1964, POL BR GU, DSR, NA.

94 Chase to Bundy on CIA/State Department meeting on British Guiana, 9 September 1964, British Guiana Special File, box 5, NSF: Intelligence File, LBJL.

95   Intelligence memorandum on British Guiana by CIA, 4 December 1964, Memorandums, 12/64–10/65 folder, box 55, NSFCO: British Guiana, LBJL.

96   Senate Select Committee, *Covert Action in Chile*, 14–19, 57–58; Bundy to President Johnson, transmitting 1 May 1964 memorandum from Assistant Secretary of State Thomas Mann to Rusk, 13 May 1964, "Presidential Election in Chile," 5/64 (4) folder, box 1, NSF: Memorandums to President, LBJL.

97   Luyt to Piper of Colonial Office on relations between Hindus and Muslims, 14 September 1965, CO 1031/4854, PRO.

98   Embassy in Trinidad to State Department on conversation with Indian High Commissioner Nair, 7 May 1964, POL 15–1 BR GU, DSR, NA; Carlson to State Department, 25 May 1964, POL 19 BR GU, DSR, NA; CIA to State Department on meeting between Jagan and Consul Carlson, 28 June 1964, British Guiana Special File, box 5, NSF: Intelligence File, LBJL.

99   Memorandum of conversation by Chase of meeting between Bundy, Helms, and State Department officers, 2 July 1964, British Guiana Special File, box 5, NSF: Intelligence File, LBJL.

100 U.S. embassy in Jamaica to State Department on meeting between Caribbean heads of state, 22 January 1964, POL 19 BR GU, DSR, NA; memorandum of conversation between Assistant Secretary Mann and Ambassador Ellis Clarke of Trinidad, 29 June 1964, POL BR GU, DSR,, NA.

101 Under Secretary Ball to U.S. embassy in Trinidad, 13 May 1964, Cables, 12/63–7/64, folder, box 55, NSFCO: British Guiana, LBJL.

102 Sandys to Rusk, 30 July 1964, A19110/189G, FO 371/173352, PRO; Bundy handwritten rejection of proposal by Sandys on memorandum, and Chase to Bundy, 31 July 1964, British Guiana Special File, box 5, NSF: Intelligence File, LBJL.

103 Ambassador Bruce to State Department, 21 April 1964, POL 19 BR GU, DSR, NA; account of remarks by Robert Edwards, 21 July 1964, British Guiana Special File, box 5, NSF: Intelligence File, LBJL; Wilson's remarks, 17 June 1964, CO 1031/4406, PRO; Howe, *Anticolonialism in British Politics*, 223–29.

104 Hatch, "Volcano in Guiana," 630; Hatch, "Plan for Guiana," 754.

105 Memorandum of conversation between Gordon Walker and William Tyler, 19 February 1964, POL 15, BR GU, DSR, NA; memorandum of conversation between Mayhew and M. Gordon Knox, 8 April 1964, POL-Political Affairs, BR GU, DSR, NA; Bruce to State Department, 21 April 1964, POL 19 BR GU, DSR, NA.

106 Memorandum of conversation between Ben Segal of AFL-CIO and Joseph Mintzes of State Department, 13 April 1964, POL 19 BR GU, DSR, NA; Gordon Chase of NSC to Bundy, 14 September 1964, British Guiana Special File, box 5, NSF: Intelligence File, LBJL; CIA paper on Labor Party and British Guiana, 13 August 1964, CIA (1) folder, box 8, NSF: Agency File, LBJL.

107 Bruce to State Department, 20 October 1964, Chase to Bundy, 20 October 1964, Memorandums, 8/64–11/64, folder, box 55, NSFCO: British Guiana, LBJL.

108 Greenwood to Gordon Walker, 23 October 1964, Walker to Greenwood, 26 October 1964, CO 1031/4407, PRO.

109 Rusk to President Johnson, 24 October 1964, Rusk to Johnson on his conversation with Walker, 27 October 1964, "Gordon Walker Talks with President" folder, box 213, NSFCO: United Kingdom, LBJL; memorandum of conversation between Johnson and Walker, 27 October 1964, *FRUS, 1964–1968*, 12:469–72.

110 Memorandum of conversation between Wilson and Jagan, 29 October 1964, PREM 13/137, PRO; Jagan, *West on Trial*, 322.

111 Minute by Greenwood of meeting with prime minister and foreign secretary, 9 November 1964, CO 1031/4407, PRO; memorandum of conversation between Wilson and Greenwood, 9 November 1964, memorandum of conversation among Wilson, Walker, and Greenwood, 25 November 1964, PREM 13/137, PRO.

112 Memorandum of conversation between Wilson and Ball, 30 November 1964, PREM 13/137, PRO; memorandum of conversation between Walker and Rusk, 7 December 1964, A19110/278, FO 371/173553, PRO.

113 Luyt to Greenwood, 12 March 1965, CO 1031/4408, PRO.

114 Agee, *Inside the Company*, 406.

115 Singh, *Guyana*, 40.

116 Carlson to State Department, 23 November 1964, POL 23–8 BR GU, DSR, NA; Spinner, *Political and Social History of Guyana*, 113–15.

CHAPTER FIVE

1 Note on Cabinet meeting, 18 December 1964, PREM 13/137, PRO; Interim Development Plan, 13 January 1965, CO 1031/4686, PRO.

2 Interim Development Plan, 13 January 1965, CO 1031/4686, PRO; memorandum of conversation between John Rennie of Foreign Office and Jack Vaughan of State Department, 19 March 1965, A1127/23, FO 371/179180, PRO; Singh, *Guyana*, 120.

3 Memorandum of conversation between Tyler and Michael N. F. Stewart of United Kingdom embassy, 8 January 1965, POL 2 BR GU, DSR, NA; "Record of Anglo-US Consultations after Election of 1964," 17–18 December 1964, A10110/13G, FO 371/179144, PRO.

4 Minute by Rennie, 7 January 1965, A1127/9, FO 371/179180, PRO; J. E. Killick, United Kingdom Embassy, to Slater of American Department of Foreign Office, 14 June 1965, A10110/69, FO 371/179144, PRO.

5 CIA Office of National Estimates, "Prospects for British Guiana," Special Memorandum No. 3–65, 25 January 1965, Cables, 12/64–10/65, folder, box 55, NSFCO: British Guiana, LBJL.

6 State Department to Georgetown on meeting with British officials, 4 January 1965, Cables, 12/64–10/65 folder, box 55, NSFCO: British Guiana, LBJL; memorandum of conversation between Tyler and King, 27 January 1965, POL 19 BR GU, DSR, NA.

7 Killick to Foreign Office on Carlson, 30 July 1965, A10110/94, FO 371/179144, PRO; Carlson to State Department, 11 April 1965, Cables, 12/64–10/65, folder, box 55, NSFCO: British Guiana, LBJL; Carlson to State Department, "Annual Report," 17 September 1965, POL 2 BR GU, DSR, NA.

8   Bundy to Presidential Aide Jack Valenti, 7 April 1965, Cables, 12/64–10/65, folder, box 55, NSFCO: British Guiana, LBJL.

9   Carlson to State Department, "Annual Report," 17 September 1965, POL 2 BR GU, DSR, NA; Premdas, "Guyana," 136.

10 Spinner, *Political and Social History of Guyana*, 121; Singh, *Guyana*, 40.

11 Singh, *Guyana*, 49; Spinner, *Political and Social History of Guyana*, 119–20; Jagan, *West on Trial*, 325–39.

12 United Kingdom embassy in Havana to Foreign Office, 31 December 1964, AK1041/1, D. R. Ashe in Havana to Foreign Office, 30 March 1965, AK1041/3, FO 371/179456, PRO.

13 Stevenson to State Department, 22 January 1965, POL 7 BR GU, DSR, NA; Carlson to State Department, 9 December 1965, POL 12 BR GU, DSR, NA; J. Harold Shullaw, Bureau of North American Affairs, to Walter J. Stoessel, European Division, on Jagan visa, 5 October 1965, Cables, 12/64–10/65 folder, box 55, NSFCO: British Guiana, LBJL.

14 Milton Gregg, Canadian High Commissioner, Georgetown, to Canadian Ministry of Foreign Affairs, 25 January 1965, CO 1031/4408, meeting of Commonwealth Prime Ministers, 22 June 1965, CO 1031/4409, PRO.

15 Hilton Poynton to Governor Luyt, 5 January 1965, Gordon Walker to Greenwood, 5 January 1965, note on meeting between Wilson and Greenwood, 7 January 1965, PREM 13/137, PRO.

16 Luyt to Colonial Office on Burnham, 24 January 1965, Colonial Office to Luyt on Greenwood trip, 18 February 1965, Greenwood speech to Commonwealth writers, 25 February 1965, CO 1031/4408, PRO.

17 Greenwood to prime minister, 22 March 1965, CAB 21/5523, PRO; minute by Greenwood on visit to British Guiana, 23 March 1965, CO 1031/4408, PRO.

18 Minutes of cabinet meeting on British Guiana, 29 March 1965, CAB 130/228, PRO.

19 Greenwood minute of telephone conversation with Wilson, 28 March 1965, CO 1031/5041, PRO; Wilson notation of 5 May 1965 on dispatch, Colonial Office to Luyt, 5 April 1965, PREM 13/137, PRO.

20 Wilson, *Personal Record*, 191.

21 Minute by Greenwood on visit to British Guiana, 23 March 1965, CO 1031/4408, PRO; memorandum of conversation between Willis C. Armstrong of U.S. embassy in London and Sandys, 14 February 1965, POL 15–1 BR GU, DSR, NA.

22 Carlson to State Department on conversation with Greenwood, 15 February 1965, Cables, 12/64–10/65, folder, box 55, NSFCO: British Guiana, LBJL.

23 Luyt to Colonial Office, 17 April 1965, CO 1031/4408, PRO.

24 Spinner, *Political and Social History of Guyana*, 117–18; Jagan, *West on Trial*, 333.

25 Jagan, *West on Trial*, 336–37; Wilson to Jagan, 13 November 1965, PREM 13/136, PRO.

26 Spinner, *Political and Social History of Guyana*, 120–21.

27 Helms to Bundy, 14 July 1965, Chase to Bundy, 14 July 1965, CIA report on con-

versation with Burnham, 27 August 1965, Cables, 12/64–10/65, folder, box 55, NSFCO: British Guiana, LBJL.

28 Minutes of Cabinet meeting with Governor Luyt, 8 November 1965, CAB 130/248, PRO.

29 Memorandum of conversation between Greenwood and Rusk, 18 October 1965, PREM 13/734, PRO; memorandum of conversation between Rusk and Greenwood, POL 16 BR GU, DSR, NA.

30 Chase to Bundy, 13 October 1965, Chase to Bundy, 18 October 1965, memorandum of conversation between Bundy and Greenwood, 18 October 1965, Cables, 12/64–10/65, folder, box 55, NSFCO: British Guiana, LBJL.

31 Chase to Bundy on consultations with Carlson, 5 October 1965, CIA Office of National Estimates, "British Guiana Moves Toward Independence," Special Memo 25–65, 29 October 1965, both in Cables, 12/64–10/65, folder, box 55, NSFCO: British Guiana, LBJL; Helms to Bundy, "British Guiana," 10 December 1965, Cables, 12/65–1/68, folder, box 56, NSFCO: British Guiana, LBJL.

32 Burnham to Rusk, 12 February 1966, POL 16 BR GU, DSR, NA.

33 Goulden, *Jerry Wurf*, 102–3; Lens, "Labor and the CIA," 25–29; *New York Times*, 22 February 1967, 1, 17.

34 McCabe to "Brothers," 18 September 1964, folder 7, box 23, RG 18–007, IAD: International Labor Organization Activities, GMLA.

35 Meakins to McLellan, 24 July 1964, folder 3, box 17, RG 18–001, IADCF, 1945–1971, Series 4: Latin America and the Caribbean, GMLA.

36 Doherty to Joseph Beirne, secretary-treasurer of American Institute of Free Labor Development, 12 September 1969, folder 6, box 17, RG 18–007, IAD: International Labor Organization Activities, GMLA.

37 Report, "Guyana: The Independence Celebrations," 5 July 1966, DO 200/235, PRO.

38 Luyt to Colonial Office, 25 May 1966, CO 1031/5071, PRO.

39 Colonial Office to Commonwealth Office, "Background Paper on British Guiana," 30 March 1966, CO 1031/5071, PRO.

40 Jagan, *West on Trial*, 344.

41 National Intelligence Estimate 87.2–67, "Guyana," 7 December 1967, folder 87.2, box 9, NSF: National Intelligence Estimates, LBJL; Spinner, *Political and Social History of Guyana*, 122.

42 High Commissioner to Foreign and Commonwealth Office, 10 April 1969, FCO 63/136; CIA Intelligence Memorandum, "Recent Economic Performance in Guyana and Prospects for 1968," December 1967, Memorandums, 5/66–11/68, folder, box 56, NSFCO: British Guiana, LBJL.

43 Singh, *Guyana*, 40; Spinner, *Political and Social History of Guyana*, 122.

44 CIA Special Report, "Guyana After Independence, 15 July 1966," CIA, "Report on Guyana's PPP: Problems and Prospects," 10 February 1967, Memorandums, 5/66–11/68, folder, box 56, NSFCO: British Guiana, LBJL; Carlson to State Department, 12 June 1967, POL 14 Guyana, DSR, NA.

45 Crosthwait to Dennis Cleary of Commonwealth Office on June 1966 note of Martin K. Ewans of Commonwealth Office, 2 August 1966, DO 200/235, PRO.

46 Ewans's note on Guyana, June 1966, Crosthwait to Cleary on Ewans note, 2 August 1966, Johnston minute on Ewans's note, 6 July 1966, DO 200/235, PRO; note by A. Michael Palliser on conversation with Rostow, 30 July 1966, PREM 13/2698, PRO.

47 Briefing for Prime Minister Wilson on visit of Forbes Burnham, June 1968, FCO 23/256, PRO.

48 CIA Special Report, "Guyana After Independence," 15 July 1966, Thomas H. Karamessines, Deputy Director of Plans of CIA, to Rostow on Burnham's plans for next election, 12 June 1968, Memorandums, 5/66–11/68, folder, box 56, NSFCO: British Guiana, LBJL.

49 Carlson to State Department, 12 June 1967, POL 14 Guyana, DSR, NA; Carlson to State Department, 12 September 1967, POL Guyana-USSR, DSR, NA; Carlson to State Department, 21 November 1967, POL 14 Guyana, DSR, NA; Kattenberg OH, *FAOHC*.

50 Rostow to Johnson, 20 July 1966, Memorandums, 5/66–11/68, folder, box 56, NSFCO: British Guiana, LBJL; Carlson to Assistant Secretary of State for Latin American Affairs Lincoln Gordon on Burnham visit, 4 August 1966, POL 7 BR GU, DSR, NA.

51 Cobb OH, *FAOHC*. See also speech of 8 April 1968 in Burnham, *Destiny to Mould*, 268–71.

52 Carlson to State Department, 11 May 1967, POL 2 Guyana, DSR, NA.

53 Fitzgibbons to Sayre, 15 December 1966, POL 12 BR GU, DSR, NA.

54 Karamessines to Rostow on Burnham's plans, 12 June 1968, Memorandums, 5/66–11/68, folder, box 56, NSFCO: British Guiana, LBJL.

55 Singh, *Guyana*, 40–41; Spinner, *Political and Social History of Guyana*, 123–25; Ridgwell, *Forgotten Tribes of Guyana*, 187–90.

56 *Sunday Times* (London), 16 April 1967, 1, 3, and 23 April 1967, 3.

57 Spinner, *Political and Social History of Guyana*, 125–27; U.S. embassy, London, to State Department on investigations of electoral fraud, 16 December and 19 December 1968, POL 14 Guyana, DSR, NA.

58 Hughes to Rusk, 21 November 1967, POL 14 Guyana, DSR, NA.

59 Kattenberg OH, *FAOHC*. See also U.S. embassy, Stockholm, to State Department on absentee voting, 19 January 1968, POL 14 Guyana, DSR, NA; Spinner, *Political and Social History of Guyana*, 123.

60 Rusk to Johnson, 20 January 1968, POL 7 Guyana, DSR, NA; Rusk to U.S. embassy, Georgetown, on Johnson meeting with Burnham, 23 January 1968, Cables, 5/66–11/68, folder, box 56, NSFCO: British Guiana, LBJL; memorandum by William Bowdler of NSC on Johnson conversation with Burnham, 26 July 1968, Memorandums, 5/66–11/68, folder, box 56, NSFCO: British Guiana, LBJL.

61 Hill to Carlson, 20 June 1968, Carlson to Hill, 29 June 1968, POL 14 Guyana, DSR, NA; Rusk (Oliver) to Carlson, 17 October 1968, POL 15–2 Guyana, DSR, NA.

62 Hughes to Rusk, 13 December 1968, POL 14 Guyana, DSR, NA.

63 Rostow to Johnson on PL 480 loan, 11 July 1968, Gaud to Johnson, 18 November 1968, Rostow to Johnson, 23 November 1968, Memorandums, 5/66–11/68 folder, box 56, NSFCO: British Guiana, LBJL.

64 Spinner, *Political and Social History of Guyana*, 125–27; Singh, *Guyana*, 40–42; Ridgwell, *Forgotten Tribes of Guyana*, 200–220.

65 State Department to U.S. embassy in Georgetown with attached 23 December 1968 message from State Department to Rostow, 26 December 1968, Carlson to State Department, 31 December 1968, POL 14 Guyana, DSR, NA; Rostow to Johnson, 24 December 1968, folder 1/1/68–1/20/69, box 21, NSF: Head of State Correspondence File, LBJL.

66 Memorandum of conversation between Hill and D'Aguiar in State Department to U.S. embassy, Georgetown, 16 January 1969, POL 7 Guyana, DSR, NA; Spinner, *Political and Social History of Guyana*, 128.

67 Premdas, "Guyana," 140; Singh, *Guyana*, 44.

68 Singh, *Guyana*, 42–44, 62; Spinner, *Political and Social History of Guyana*, 145–46, 191–93.

69 High Commissioner Kenneth G. Ritchie to Foreign Secretary Sir Alec Douglas-Home, 1 October 1970, FCO 63/457, PRO.

70 Singh, *Guyana*, 76–81, 87; Spinner, *Social and Political History of Guyana*, 162; Jeffrey and Baber, *Guyana*, 137; Ridgwell, *Forgotten Tribes of Guyana*, 31–34.

71 Conway, "Caribbean Diaspora," 343–50; Watson and Craig, *Guyana at the Crossroads*, 22; Premdas, "Guyana," 146; Spinner, *Political and Social History of Guyana*, 170.

72 Spinner, *Political and Social History of Guyana*, 156–57; Singh, *Guyana*, 60; Watson and Craig, *Guyana at the Crossroads*, 25.

73 Jeffrey and Baber, *Guyana*, 129–36; Hope, *Post-War Planning Experience*, 16–24; Premdas, "Guyana," 141, 154; Singh, *Guyana*, 47. See also 24 August 1969 speech by Burnham presenting his vision of a "cooperative socialist republic" in Burnham, *Destiny to Mould*, 152–60.

74 Burke OH, *FAOHC*.

75 Singh, *Guyana*, 105–15; Jeffrey and Baber, *Guyana*, 149–54.

76 Singh, *Guyana*, 114; Spinner, *Political and Social History of Guyana*, 165, 183–85; Ridgwell, *Forgotten Tribes of Guyana*, 36–38.

77 High Commissioner W. S. Bates to Foreign Secretary Douglas-Home, 31 December 1970, FCO 631/715, PRO.

78 Singh, *Guyana*, 82–86; Burke OH, *FAOHC*.

79 John A. Sankey, High Commissioner's Office, to Foreign and Commonwealth Office, 11 April 1970, FCO 63/457, PRO; Sankey to Foreign and Commonwealth Office, 18 June 1971, FCO 63/720, PRO; Premdas, "Guyana," 138–39; Singh, *Guyana*, 120–23, 134–36.

80 Bates to Foreign and Commonwealth Office, 29 August 1972, FCO 63/955, PRO; Manley, *Guyana Emergent*, 14.

81 Burke OH and Ambassador Clint A. Lauderdale OH, *FAOHC*.

82 Manley, *Guyana Emergent*, 64–71; Gleijeses, *Conflicting Missions*, 368–69; Maingot, "Grenada and the Caribbean," 132–38; Singh, *Guyana*, 48.

83 *New York Times*, 25 May 1976, 2, 24 May 1976, 1, 14.

84 Lauderdale OH, *FAOHC*. See also Jeffrey and Baber, *Guyana*, 35–37; Spinner, *Political and Social History of Guyana*, 159, 168; Hintzen, *Costs of Regime Survival*, 68.

85 Carlson to State Department, 28 August 1969, POL 12 GU, DSR, NA; Sillery, "Salvaging Democracy," 250–52.

86 Singh, *Guyana*, 49–54.

87 Minute by D. G. Allen, Caribbean Department of Foreign and Commonwealth Office, on report, "Annual Review of Guyana for 1970," 1 January 1971, FCO 63/714, PRO.

88 Kissinger, *Years of Renewal*, 726, 914; Gleijeses, *Conflicting Missions*, 368–69; Singh, *Guyana*, 130.

89 Ptolemy A. Reid, Deputy Prime Minister of Guyana, to Vice President Walter Mondale, 9 September 1977, folder CO 63: Guyana, box CO-29, WHCF: Subject File, JCL; Singh, *Guyana*, 122–23.

90 Lauderdale OH, *FAOHC*.

91 Spinner, *Political and Social History of Guyana*, 194–99, 204, 211.

92 World Bank, *Guyana*, xi–xvi; Watson and Craig, *Guyana at the Crossroads*, 9–17, 68, 75; Pastor, "George Bush and Latin America," 361–87.

93 Jones OH, *FAOHC*; Council of Freely Elected Heads of Government, *Observing Guyana's Electoral Process*, 40–41.

94 Jagan quoted in Watson and Craig, *Guyana at the Crossroads*, 72; and Jones OH, *FAOHC*.

95 Jones OH, *FAOHC*.

96 Schlesinger, *Thousand Days*, 779; "Tale of Two Books," 763–64; *New York Times*, 30 October 1994, 10.

CONCLUSION

1 Guthman and Shulman, *Robert Kennedy*, 294.

2 Smith, *British Guiana*, 205. See also Newman, *British Guiana*, 83–84.

3 Memorandum of conversation between Rusk and Argentine diplomats, 18 January 1962, *FRUS, 1961–1963*, 12:292–94; Rabe, *Most Dangerous Area*, 59–60. For a discussion of "credibility" in U.S. diplomacy, see McMahon, "Credibility and World Power," 455–71.

4 Rabe, "After the Missiles of October," 721; Giglio and Rabe, *Debating the Kennedy Presidency*, 37.

5 Rosenberg, "Gender," 116–24. See also Ashton, *Kennedy, Macmillan, and the Cold War*, 6–9; Keith, "Imperial Mind," 19–29.

6 Rotter, "Gender Relations," 518–42; Rotter, *Comrades at Odds*.

7 *New York Times*, 14 December 1997, 1, 6.

8 Hunt, *Ideology and U.S. Foreign Policy*, 46–91.

9   Sillery, "Salvaging Democracy," iii. For a discussion of the ability of local elites in the Western Hemisphere to manipulate the United States, see Leonard, "Central America and the United States," 1–30; Longley, *Sparrow and the Hawk*.

10   Dodd to Attorney General Kennedy, 31 March 1961, folder 742, box 24, and Dodd to President Kennedy, 28 June 1962, folder 1042, box 32, Dodd Papers.

11   For a discussion of the role of religion in international relations see essays by Andrew J. Rotter, Robert Dean, Robert Buzzanco, and Patricia R. Hill in "Roundtable," 593–640.

12   For a concise critique of this "new diplomatic history" see Brands, "Review of *Comrades at Odds*," 1595–96. See also Buzzanco, "Where's the Beef," 623–32; Ashton, *Kennedy, Macmillan, and the Cold War*, 226.

13   "Tale of Two Books," 763–64; *New York Times*, 30 October 1994, 10. For a discussion of the CIA's alleged tendency to act like a "rogue elephant," see Senate Select Committee, *Alleged Assassination Plots*.

14   Clifford, "Bureaucratic Politics," 161–68.

15   "Tale of Two Books," 763–64.

BIBLIOGraPHY

PRIMARY SOURCES

Private Papers

AFL-CIO. International Affairs Department: Country Files. Record Group 18–001.
   George Meany Memorial Labor Archives. Silver Spring, Md.
——. International Affairs Department: International Labor Organization Activities.
   Record Group 18–007. George Meany Memorial Labor Archives. Silver Spring, Md.
——. International Affairs Department: Jay Lovestone Files, 1939–1974. Record Group
   18–003. George Meany Memorial Labor Archives, Silver Spring, Md.
——. International Affairs Department: Staff Files: Serafino Romualdi's Files, 1944–
   1961. Record Group 18–009. George Meany Memorial Labor Archives. Silver
   Spring, Md.
——. Office of the President: George Meany Files, 1940–1980. Record Group 1–38.
   George Meany Memorial Labor Archives. Silver Spring, Md.
Ball, George W. John F. Kennedy Library. Boston, Mass.
——. Telephone Notes File. Lyndon Baines Johnson Library. Austin, Tex.
Dodd, Thomas J. Archives and Special Collections Department. Thomas J. Dodd
   Research Center. University of Connecticut Libraries. Storrs, Conn.
Fitzgerald, Dennis A. Dwight D. Eisenhower Library. Abilene, Kans.
Goodwin, Richard N. John F. Kennedy Library. Boston, Mass.
Lovestone, Jay. Kheel Center. Cornell University. Ithaca, N.Y.
Romualdi, Serafino. Kheel Center. Cornell University. Ithaca, N.Y.
Schlesinger, Arthur M., Jr. John F. Kennedy Library. Boston, Mass.

Unpublished Government Documents and Records

National Security File. John F. Kennedy Library. Boston, Mass.
——. Lyndon Baines Johnson Library. Austin, Tex.
President's Office File. John F. Kennedy Library. Boston, Mass.

United Kingdom. Cabinet Office Records. Public Record Office. Kew, Richmond, Surrey.

———. Colonial Office Records. Public Record Office. Kew, Richmond, Surrey.

———. Dominions Office Records. Public Record Office. Kew, Richmond, Surrey.

———. Foreign and Commonwealth Records. Public Record Office. Kew, Richmond, Surrey.

———. Foreign Office Records. Public Record Office. Kew, Richmond, Surrey.

———. Prime Minister's Office Records. Public Record Office. Kew, Richmond, Surrey.

U.S. Department of State. Decimal Files, 1950–1963. Record Group 59. National Archives. College Park, Md.

———. Subject-Numeric Files, 1963–1969. Record Group 59. National Archives. College Park, Md.

White House Central File. Jimmy Carter Library. Atlanta, Ga.

———. John F. Kennedy Library. Boston, Mass.

White House Office of the Special Assistant for National Security Affairs. Dwight D. Eisenhower Library. Abilene, Kans.

Whitman, Ann, File. Dwight D. Eisenhower Library. Abilene, Kans.

Oral Histories

Armstrong, Oscar Vance. *The U.S. Foreign Affairs Oral History Collection*. CD-ROM. Association for Diplomatic Studies and Training. Arlington, Va.

Burke, John R. *The U.S. Foreign Affairs Oral History Collection*. CD-ROM. Association for Diplomatic Studies and Training. Arlington, Va.

Cobb, William B., Jr. *The U.S. Foreign Affairs Oral History Collection*. CD-ROM. Association for Diplomatic Studies and Training. Arlington, Va.

Fraser, Hugh. John F. Kennedy Library. Boston, Mass.

Hamilton, Fowler. John F. Kennedy Library. Boston, Mass.

Harlech, Lord (William David Ormsby Gore). John F. Kennedy Library. Boston, Mass.

Jones, George F. *The U.S. Foreign Affairs Oral History Collection*. CD-ROM. Association for Diplomatic Studies and Training. Arlington, Va.

Kattenberg, Paul M. *The U.S. Foreign Affairs Oral History Collection*. CD-ROM. Association for Diplomatic Studies and Training. Arlington, Va.

Lauderdale, Clint A. *The U.S. Foreign Affairs Oral History Collection*. CD-ROM. Association for Diplomatic Studies and Training. Arlington, Va.

Published Government and International Organization Documents and Records

The Council of Freely Elected Heads of Government. *Observing Guyana's Electoral Process, 1990–1992*. Foreword by Jimmy Carter. Atlanta: Carter Center for Emory University, 1993.

Emigration, 1860–1871. Vol. 24 of *Irish University Press Series of British Parliamentary Papers*. Shannon: Irish University Press, 1971.

International Bank for Reconstruction and Development. *The Economic Development of British Guiana: Report of Mission Organized by the International Bank for Reconstruction and Development*. Baltimore: Johns Hopkins University Press, 1953.

United Kingdom. Colonial Office. *British Guiana: Report of the Commonwealth Team of Observers on the Election, December 1964*. Document No. 359. London: Her Majesty's Stationery Office, 1965.

——. *British Guiana: Suspension of the Constitution*. Command Document No. 8980. London: Her Majesty's Stationery Office, 1953.

——. *Report of the British Guiana Constitutional Commission, 1950–1951*. Document No. 280. London: His Majesty's Stationery Office, 1951.

——. *Report of the British Guiana Constitutional Commission, 1954*. Command Document No. 9274. London: Her Majesty's Stationery Office, 1954.

——. *Report of the British Guiana Constitutional Conference, 1963*. Command Document No. 2203. London: Her Majesty's Stationery Office, 1963.

——. *Report of the British Guiana Independence Conference, 1962*. Command Document No. 1870. London: Her Majesty's Stationery Office, 1962.

——. *Report of the Commission of Inquiry into Disturbances in British Guiana in February 1962*. Document No. 354. London: Her Majesty's Stationery Office, 1962.

U.S. Central Intelligence Agency. *World Factbook 2002: Guyana*. Washington, D.C.: Government Printing Office, 2002.

U.S. Congress. Senate. Committee on Foreign Relations. *Study Mission in the Caribbean Area, December 1957: Report of Senator George D. Aiken*. 85th Cong., 2d sess. Washington, D.C.: Government Printing Office, 1958.

——. Select Committee to Study Governmental Operations with Respect to Intelligence Activities. *Alleged Assassination Plots Involving Foreign Leaders*. Senate Report No. 465. 94th Cong., 1st sess. Washington, D.C.: Government Printing Office, 1975.

——. *Covert Action in Chile, 1963–1973: Staff Report*. 94th Cong., 1st sess. Washington, D.C.: Government Printing Office, 1975.

U.S. Department of State. *Background Note: Guyana*. Washington, D.C.: Government Printing Office, 2001.

——. *Foreign Relations of the United States, 1952–1968*. Washington, D.C.: Government Printing Office, 1983–2003.

U.S. General Services Administration. *Public Papers of the President: John F. Kennedy, 1961–1963*. 3 vols. Washington, D.C.: Government Printing Office, 1962–1964.

World Bank. *Guyana: From Economic Recovery to Sustained Growth*. Washington, D.C.: International Bank for Reconstruction and Development/World Bank, 1993.

Autobiographies, Memoirs, Published Papers

Agee, Philip. *Inside the Company: CIA Diary*. New York: Stonehill Publishing, 1972.

Burnham, Forbes. *A Destiny to Mould: Selected Discourses by the Prime Minister of Guyana*. Compiled by C. A. Nascimento and R. A. Burrowes. London: Longman Caribbean, 1970.

Guthman, Edwin O., and Jeffrey Shulman, eds. *Robert Kennedy in His Own Words: The Unpublished Recollections of the Kennedy Years*. New York: Bantam Books, 1988.

Helms, Richard. *A Look Over My Shoulder: A Life in the Central Intelligence Agency*. New York: Random House, 2003.

Hunt, E. Howard. *Undercover: Memoirs of an American Secret Agent*. New York: Berkeley Publishing, 1974.

Jagan, Cheddi. *The West on Trial: The Fight for Guyana's Freedom*. New York: International Publishers, 1972.

Kissinger, Henry A. *Years of Renewal*. New York: Simon and Schuster, 1999.

Lyttleton, Oliver (Viscount Chandos). *The Memoirs of Lord Chandos*. London: Bodley Head, 1962.

Macmillan, Harold. *At the End of the Day, 1961–1963*. New York: Harper and Row, 1973.

——. *Pointing the Way, 1959–1961*. New York: Harper and Row, 1972.

Naftali, Timothy, Philip Zelikow, and Ernest May, eds. *John F. Kennedy: The Great Crises*. 3 vols. New York: W. W. Norton, 2001.

Naipaul, V. S. *The Middle Passage: The Caribbean Revisited*. New York: Vintage Books, 2002.

Romualdi, Serafino. *Presidents and Peons: Recollections of a Labor Ambassador in Latin America*. New York: Funk and Wagnalls, 1967.

Schlesinger, Arthur M., Jr. *A Thousand Days: John F. Kennedy in the White House*. Boston: Houghton Mifflin, 1965.

Smith, Joseph Burkholder. *Portrait of a Cold Warrior*. New York: G. P. Putnam's Sons, 1976.

Wilson, Harold. *A Personal Record: The Labour Government, 1964–1970*. Boston: Little, Brown, 1971.

Newspapers and Magazines

New York Times
Sunday Times (London)
Time

SECONDARY SOURCES

Books

Adamson, Alan H. *Sugar without Slaves: The Political Economy of British Guiana, 1838–1904*. New Haven, Conn.: Yale University Press, 1972.

Ashton, Nigel J. *Kennedy, Macmillan, and the Cold War: The Irony of Interdependence*. Houndmills, Basingstoke, Hampshire: Palgrave Macmillan, 2002.

Beisner, Robert L., ed. *American Foreign Relations since 1600: A Guide to the Literature*. 2nd ed. 2 vols. Santa Barbara, Calif.: ABC-CLIO, 2003.

Blum, William. *The CIA: A Forgotten History: U.S. Global Interventions since World War 2.* London: Zed Books, 1986.

Bowie, Robert R., and Richard H. Immerman. *Waging Peace: How Eisenhower Shaped an Enduring Cold War Strategy.* New York: Oxford University Press, 1998.

Brereton, Bridget. *A History of Modern Trinidad, 1783–1962.* London: Heinemann Educational Books, 1981.

Chua, Amy. *World on Fire: How Exporting Free Market Democracy Breeds Ethnic Hatred and Global Instability.* New York: Doubleday, 2003.

Costa, Emilia Viotti da. *Crowns of Glory, Tears of Blood: The Demerara Slave Rebellion of 1823.* New York: Oxford University Press, 1994.

Dallek, Robert. *An Unfinished Life: John F. Kennedy, 1961–1963.* Boston: Little, Brown, 2003.

David, Wilfred L. *The Economic Development of Guyana, 1953–1964.* London: Oxford University Press, 1969.

Despres, Leo A. *Cultural Pluralism and Nationalist Politics in British Guiana.* Chicago: Rand, McNally, 1967.

Dudziak, Mary L. *Cold War Civil Rights: Race and the Image of American Democracy.* Princeton, N.J.: Princeton University Press, 2000.

Edwardes, Michael. *Nehru: A Political Biography.* Baltimore: Penguin Books, 1971.

Fisher, Nigel. *Harold Macmillan: A Biography.* New York: St. Martin's Press, 1982.

———. *Iain Macleod.* London: Andre Deutsch, 1973.

Fraser, Cary. *Ambivalent Anti-Colonialism: The United States and the Genesis of West Indian Independence, 1940–1964.* Westport, Conn.: Greenwood Press, 1994.

Fukuyama, Francis. *The End of History and the Last Man.* New York: Free Press, 1992.

Gaddis, John Lewis. *We Now Know: Rethinking Cold War History.* New York: Oxford University Press, 1997.

Giglio, James N., and Stephen G. Rabe. *Debating the Kennedy Presidency.* Lanham, Md.: Rowman and Littlefield, 2003.

Gleijeses, Piero. *Conflicting Missions: Havana, Washington, and Africa, 1959–1976.* Chapel Hill: University of North Carolina Press, 2002.

———. *Shattered Hope: The Guatemalan Revolution and the United States, 1944–1954.* Princeton, N.J.: Princeton University Press, 1991.

Goldsworthy, David. *Colonial Issues in British Politics, 1945–1961: From "Colonial Development" to "Wind of Change."* Oxford: Clarendon Press, 1971.

Goulden, Joseph C. *Jerry Wurf: Labor's Last Angry Man.* New York: Atheneum, 1982.

Hintzen, Percy C. *The Costs of Regime Survival: Racial Mobilization, Elite Domination, and Control of the State in Guyana and Trinidad.* Cambridge: Cambridge University Press, 1989.

Hollett, David. *Passage from India to El Dorado: Guyana and the Great Migration.* Cranbury, N.J: Fairleigh Dickinson University Press, 1999.

Hope, Kempe R. *The Post-War Planning Experience in Guyana.* Tempe: Latin American Studies Center of Arizona State University, 1978.

Horne, Alistair. *Harold Macmillan.* Vol. 2, *1957–1986.* New York: Viking, 1989.

Howe, Stephen. *Anticolonialism in British Politics: The Left and the End of Empire, 1918–1964*. Oxford: Clarendon Press, 1993.

Hunt, Michael H. *Ideology and U.S. Foreign Policy*. New Haven, Conn.: Yale University Press, 1987.

Immerman, Richard H. *The CIA in Guatemala: The Foreign Policy of Intervention*. Austin: University of Texas Press, 1982.

Jeffrey, Henry B., and Colin Baber. *Guyana: Politics, Economics, and Society*. Boulder, Colo.: Lynne Rienner Publishers, 1986.

Kornbluh, Peter. *The Pinochet File: A Declassified Dossier on Atrocity and Accountability*. New York: New Press, 2003.

Laurence, K. O. *A Question of Labour: Indentured Immigration into Trinidad and British Guiana, 1875–1917*. New York: St. Martin's Press, 1994.

Lewis, William Roger, ed. *The Oxford History of the British Empire*. 5 vols. Oxford and New York: Oxford University Press, 1999.

Longley, Kyle. *The Sparrow and the Hawk: Costa Rica and the United States during the Rise of José Figueres*. Tuscaloosa: University of Alabama Press, 1997.

MacShane, Denis. *International Labour and the Origins of the Cold War*. New York: Oxford University Press, 1992.

Manley, Robert H. *Guyana Emergent: The Post-Independence Struggle for Nondependent Development*. Boston: G. K. Hall, 1979.

May, Ernest R., ed. *American Cold War Strategy: Interpreting NSC 68*. Boston: Bedford Books, 1993.

Moore, Brian L. *Race, Power, and Social Segmentation in Colonial Society: Guyana after Slavery, 1838–1891*. New York: Gordon and Breach Science Publishers, 1987.

Morgan, Ted. *A Covert Life: Jay Lovestone, Communist, Anti-Communist, and Spymaster*. New York: Random House, 1999.

Morris, George. *CIA and American Labor: The Subversion of the AFL-CIO's Foreign Policy*. New York: International Publishers, 1967.

Newman, Peter. *British Guiana: Problems of Cohesion in an Immigrant Society*. London: Oxford University Press, 1964.

Northrup, David. *Indentured Labor in the Age of Imperialism, 1834–1922*. Cambridge: Cambridge University Press, 1995.

Plummer, Brenda Gayle. *Window on Freedom: Race, Civil Rights, and Foreign Affairs, 1945–1988*. Chapel Hill: University of North Carolina Press, 2003.

Rabe, Stephen G. *Eisenhower and Latin America: The Foreign Policy of Anticommunism*. Chapel Hill: University of North Carolina Press, 1988.

———. *The Most Dangerous Area in the World: John F. Kennedy Confronts Communist Revolution in Latin America*. Chapel Hill: University of North Carolina Press, 1999.

Radosh, Ronald. *American Labor and United States Foreign Policy*. New York: Random House, 1969.

Rich, Paul B. *Race and Empire in British Politics*. Cambridge: Cambridge University Press, 1986.

Ridgwell, W. M. *The Forgotten Tribes of Guyana*. London: Tom Stacey, 1972.

Rodney, Walter. *A History of the Guyanese Working People, 1881–1905*. Baltimore: Johns Hopkins University Press, 1981.

Rotter, Andrew J. *Comrades at Odds: The United States and India, 1947–1964*. Ithaca, N.Y.: Cornell University Press, 2000.

Ryan, Selwyn. *Race and Nationalism in Trinidad and Tobago: A Study of Decolonization in a Multiracial Society*. Toronto: University of Toronto Press, 1972.

Seecharan, Clem. *"Tiger in the Stars": The Anatomy of Indian Achievement in British Guiana, 1919–1929*. London: Macmillan Education, 1997.

Shepherd, Robert. *Iain Macleod*. London: Hutchinson, 1994.

Singh, Chaitram. *Guyana: Politics in a Plantation Society*. New York: Praeger, 1988.

Smith, Raymond T. *British Guiana*. Westport, Conn.: Greenwood Press, 1980.

Spinner, Thomas J., Jr. *A Political and Social History of Guyana, 1945–1983*. Boulder, Colo.: Westview Press, 1984.

Swan, Michael. *British Guiana: The Land of Six Peoples*. London: Her Majesty's Stationery Office, 1957.

Szulc, Tad. *Fidel: A Critical Portrait*. New York: William Morrow, 1986.

Thomas, Evan. *The Very Best Men: Four Who Dared: The Early Years of the CIA*. New York: Simon and Schuster, 1995.

Tinker, Hugh. *The Banyan Tree: Overseas Emigrants from India, Pakistan, and Bangladesh*. Oxford: Oxford University Press, 1977.

Von Eschen, Penny M. *Race against Empire: Black Americans and Anticolonialism, 1937–1957*. Ithaca, N.Y.: Cornell University Press, 1997.

Watson, Dennis, and Christine Craig, eds. *Guyana at the Crossroads*. North-South Center, University of Miami. New Brunswick, N.J.: Transaction Publishers, 1992.

Williams, Patrick, and Laura Chrisman, eds. *Colonial Discourse and Post-Colonial Theory: A Reader*. New York: Columbia University Press, 1994.

Wise, David, and Thomas B. Ross. *The Invisible Government*. New York: Random House, 1964.

Zieger, Robert H. *The CIO, 1935–1955*. Chapel Hill: University of North Carolina Press, 1995.

Zieger, Robert H., and Gilbert J. Gall. *American Workers, American Unions*. 3rd ed. Baltimore: Johns Hopkins University Press, 2002.

Articles

Battista, Andrew. "Unions and Cold War Foreign Policy in the 1980s: The National Labor Committee, the AFL-CIO, and Central America." *Diplomatic History* 26 (Summer 2002): 419–51.

Borstelmann, Thomas. " 'Hedging Our Bets and Buying Time': John Kennedy and Racial Relations in the American South and Southern Africa." *Diplomatic History* 24 (Summer 2000): 435–63.

Brands, H. W. Review of *Comrades at Odds*, by Andrew J. Rotter. *Journal of American History* 88 (March 2002): 1595–96.

Buzzanco, Robert. "Where's the Beef? Culture without Power in the Study of U.S. Foreign Relations." *Diplomatic History* 24 (Fall 2000): 623–32.

Clifford, J. Garry. "Bureaucratic Politics." *Journal of American History* 77 (June 1990): 161–68.

Collins, B. A. N. "The Civil Service of British Guiana in the General Strike of 1963." *Caribbean Quarterly* 10 (June 1964): 3–15.

Conway, Dennis. "The Caribbean Diaspora." In *Understanding the Contemporary Caribbean*, edited by Richard S. Hillman and Thomas J. D'Agostino, 333–53. Boulder, Colo.: Lynne Rienner, 2003.

Fraser, Cary. "The 'New Frontier' of Empire in the Caribbean: The Transfer of Power in British Guiana, 1961–1964." *International History Review* 23 (September 2000): 583–610.

Goldsworthy, David. "Keeping Change Within Bounds: Aspects of Colonial Policy during the Churchill and Eden Government, 1951–1957." *Journal of Imperial and Commonwealth History* 81, 1 (1990): 81–108.

Halperin, Ernst. "Racism and Communism in British Guiana." *Journal of Inter-American Studies* 7 (January 1965):95–134.

Hatch, John. "A Plan for Guiana." *New Statesman* 67 (15 May 1964): 754.

——. "Volcano in Guiana." *New Statesman* 67 (24 April 1964): 630.

Heuman, Gad. "The British West Indies." In *The Nineteenth Century*. Vol. 3 of *The Oxford History of the British Empire*, edited by William Roger Lewis and Andrew Porter, 470–93. Oxford and New York: Oxford University Press, 1999.

Hinden, Rita. "The Case of British Guiana." *Encounter* 2 (January 1954): 18–22

Johnson, Howard. "The British Caribbean from Demobilization to Constitutional Decolonization." In *The Twentieth Century*. Vol. 4 of *The Oxford History of the British Empire*, edited by William Roger Lewis and Judith M. Brown, 597–622. Oxford and New York: Oxford University Press, 1999.

Kandiah, Michael David, and Gillian Staerck. " 'Reliable Allies': Anglo-American Relations." In *British Foreign Policy, 1955–1964: Contracting Options*, edited by Wolfram Kaiser and Gillian Staerck, 135–70. Houndmills, Basingstoke, Hampshire: Macmillan, 2000.

Kennedy, Dane. "Imperial History and Post-Colonial Theory." *Journal of Imperial and Commonwealth History* 24 (September 1996): 345–63.

Landis, Joseph B. "Racial Polarization and Political Conflict in Guyana." In *Ethnicity and Nation-Building: Comparative, International, and Historical Perspectives*, edited by Wendell Bell and Walter E. Freeman, 255–67. Beverly Hills, Calif.: Sage Publications, 1974.

Leffler, Melvyn P. "The Cold War: What Do 'We Now Know'?" *American Historical Review* 104 (April 1999): 501–24.

Lens, Sidney. "Labor and the CIA." *Progressive*, April 1977, 25–29.

——. "Lovestone Diplomacy." *Nation*, 5 July 1965, 10–16, 27–28.

Leonard, Thomas M. "Central America and the United States: Overlooked Foreign Policy Objectives." *Americas*, July 1993, 1–30.

Lewis, William Roger. "The Dissolution of the British Empire." In *The Twentieth Century*. Vol. 4 of *The Oxford History of the British Empire*, edited by William Roger Lewis and Judith M. Brown, 329–56. Oxford and New York: Oxford University Press, 1999.

Maingot, Anthony P. "Grenada and the Caribbean: Mutual Linkages and Influences." In *Grenada and Soviet/Cuban Policy: Internal Crisis and U.S./OECS Intervention*, edited by Jiri Valenta and Herbert J. Ellison, 130–47. Boulder, Colo.: Westview Press, 1986.

Marks, Sally. "The World According to Washington." *Diplomatic History* 11 (Summer 1987): 265–82.

McCormick, Thomas J. "The State of American Diplomatic History." In *The State of American History*, edited by Herbert J. Bass, 119–41. Chicago: Quadrangle, 1970.

McMahon, Robert J. "Credibility and World Power: Exploring the Psychological in Postwar American Diplomacy." *Diplomatic History* 15 (Fall 1991): 455–71.

Meisler, Stanley. "Meddling in Latin America: Dubious Role of AFL-CIO." *Nation*, 10 February 1964, 133–38.

Moore, Robert J. "Colonial Images of Blacks and Indians in Nineteenth-Century Guyana." In *The Colonial Caribbean in Transition: Essays on Postemancipation Social and Cultural History*, edited by Bridget Brereton and Kevin A. Yelvington, 126–58. Gainesville: University of Florida Press, 1999.

Naipaul, V. S. "A Handful of Dust: Return to Guiana." *New York Review of Books*, 11 April 1991, 15–20.

Noer, Thomas J. "New Frontiers and Old Priorities in Africa." In *Kennedy's Quest for Victory: American Foreign Policy, 1961–1963*, edited by Thomas G. Paterson, 253–83. New York: Oxford University Press, 1989.

Northrup, David. "Migration from Africa, Asia, and the South Pacific." In *The Nineteenth Century*. Vol. 3 of *The Oxford History of the British Empire*, edited by William Roger Lewis and Andrew Porter, 88–100. Oxford and New York: Oxford University Press, 1999.

Pastor, Robert A. "George Bush and Latin America: The Pragmatic Style and the Regionalist Option." In *Eagle in a New World: American Grand Strategy in the Post-Cold War Era*, edited by Kenneth A. Oye, Robert J. Lieber, and Donald Rothchild, 361–87. New York: HarperCollins, 1992.

Premdas, Ralph D. "Guyana: Socialist Reconstruction or Political Opportunism?" *Journal of Inter-American Studies* 20 (May 1978): 133–78.

Rabe, Stephen G. "After the Missiles of October: John F. Kennedy and Cuba, November 1962 to November 1963." *Presidential Studies Quarterly* 30 (December 2000): 714–26.

——. "John F. Kennedy and Latin America: The 'Thorough, Reliable, and Accurate Record' (Almost)." *Diplomatic History* 23 (Summer 1999): 539–52.

——. "Marching Ahead (Slowly): The Historiography of Inter-American Relations." *Diplomatic History* 13 (Summer 1989): 297–316.

Romano, Renee. "No Diplomatic Immunity: African Diplomats, the State Department, and Civil Rights, 1961–1964." *Journal of American History* 87 (September 2000): 546–79.

Rosenberg, Emily S. "Gender." *Journal of American History* 77 (June 1990): 116–24.

———. "Turning to Culture." In *Close Encounters of Empire: Writing the Cultural History of U.S.-Latin American Relations*, edited by Gilbert M. Joseph, Catherine C. Legrand, and Ricardo D. Salvatore, 497–514. Durham, N.C.: Duke University Press, 1998.

Rotter, Andrew J. "Gender Relations, Foreign Relations: The United States and South Asia, 1947–1964." *Journal of American History* 81 (September 1994): 518–42.

Rotter, Andrew J., Robert Dean, Robert Buzzanco, and Patricia R. Hill. "Roundtable: Culture, Religion, and International Relations." *Diplomatic History* 24 (Fall 2000): 593–640.

Sires, Ronald V. "British Guiana: Suspension of the Constitution." *Western Political Quarterly* 7 (December 1954): 554–69.

"Tale of Two Books." *Nation*, 4 June 1990, 763–64.

Wallace, Elisabeth. "British Guiana: Causes of the Present Discontents." *International Journal* 19 (Autumn 1964): 513–44.

Warner, Geoffrey. "The Anglo-American Special Relationship." *Diplomatic History* 13 (Fall 1989): 479–99.

Dissertations and Theses

Daniels, Gordon Oliver. "A Great Injustice to Cheddi Jagan: The Kennedy Administration and British Guiana, 1961–1963." Ph.D. diss., University of Mississippi, 2000.

Keith, LeeAnna Y. "The Imperial Mind and U.S. Intervention in the Dominican Republic, 1961–1966." Ph.D. diss., University of Connecticut, 1999.

Rabe, Elizabeth R. "From India to the Sugar Fields: The Lives of Indian Indentured Laborers in British Guiana, 1854–1884." Honors thesis, Hamilton College, 2004.

Sillery, Jane L. "Salvaging Democracy? The United States and Britain in British Guiana, 1961–1964." Ph.D. diss., Queen's College, Oxford University, 1996.

Documentary Film

Wasserman, Suzanne. *Thunder in Guyana*. New York: Women Make Movies Distributor, 2003.

InDex

Stephen G. Rabe, *U.S. Intervention in British Guiana: A Cold War Story* (2005).

Christopher Endy, *Cold War Holidays: American Tourism in France* (2004).

Salim Yaqub, *Containing Arab Nationalism: The Eisenhower Doctrine and the Middle East* (2003).

Francis J. Gavin, *Gold, Dollars, and Power: The Politics of International Monetary Relations, 1958–1971* (2003).

William Glenn Gray, *Germany's Cold War: The Global Campaign to Isolate East Germany, 1949–1969* (2003).

Matthew J. Ouimet, *The Rise and Fall of the Brezhnev Doctrine in Soviet Foreign Policy* (2003).

Pierre Asselin, *A Bitter Peace: Washington, Hanoi, and the Making of the Paris Agreement* (2002).

Jeffrey Glen Giauque, *Grand Designs and Visions of Unity: The Atlantic Powers and the Reorganization of Western Europe, 1955–1963* (2002).

Chen Jian, *Mao's China and the Cold War* (2001).

M. E. Sarotte, *Dealing with the Devil: East Germany, Détente, and Ostpolitik, 1969–1973* (2001).

Mark Philip Bradley, *Imagining Vietnam and America: The Making of Postcolonial Vietnam, 1919–1950* (2000).

Michael E. Latham, *Modernization as Ideology: American Social Science and "Nation Building" in the Kennedy Era* (2000).

Qiang Zhai, *China and the Vietnam Wars, 1950–1975* (2000).

William I. Hitchcock, *France Restored: Cold War Diplomacy and the Quest for Leadership in Europe, 1944–1954* (1998).